# JOSÉ ORTEGA Y GASSET

BORN IN Madrid in 1883, José Ortega y Gasset was one of the intellectual leaders of the Spanish Republican government. After the establishment of the Republic, Ortega became a member of Parliament. He also held for many years the chair of metaphysics at the University of Madrid and was editor of the influential journal of opinion, *Revista de Occidente*. After the Spanish Civil War, Ortega became an exile from Spain, living for a time in Buenos Aires, later settling in Lisbon. In recent years he visited Spain to lecture in Madrid. Books by Ortega include his most widely read work *The Revolt of the Masses, Man and Crisis,* originally published in Spanish under the title of *En Torno A Galileo, Man and People, Meditations on Quixote, History as a System,* and *What is Philosophy?* Señor Ortega died in 1955.

"Ortega y Gasset, after Nietzsche, is perhaps the greatest 'European' writer."

—Albert Camus

### by JOSÉ ORTEGA Y GASSET

**THE REVOLT OF THE MASSES**
**MAN AND PEOPLE**
**MAN AND CRISIS**
**WHAT IS PHILOSOPHY?**
**MEDITATIONS ON QUIXOTE**
**HISTORY AS A SYSTEM**

JOSE ORTEGA Y GASSET

# MAN AND
# PEOPLE

**AUTHORIZED TRANSLATION FROM THE SPANISH
BY WILLARD R. TRASK**

**The Norton Library**

W · W · NORTON & COMPANY · INC · New York

# Contents

# Contents

# Publisher's Note

BEGINNING with the short Prologue which, in 1940, he prefixed to his *Ideas and Beliefs* (*Ideas y creencias*), and on many later occasions, Ortega announced the forthcoming appearance of a new book containing his sociological doctrine, under the title *Man and People*. Both before and after that date he expounded his idea of "usages" as constituting the social. In Buenos Aires he gave two courses, of six and four lectures respectively; in Madrid, a course of twelve lectures; two courses in Germany, at Munich and Hamburg, and another in Switzerland, each comprising four lectures. The texts of all these provide different expositions of his thought on the principles of a new sociology.

Ortega himself prepared the present volume, adhering, in general, to the text that he had prepared for his course at the Instituto de Humanidades in Madrid, and adding further discussions of certain questions. Ortega contemplated a second part or sequel to this volume which would discuss the state, law, society, nation, and inter-nation, but death overtook him before its completion. In *Man and People* the basic questions of principle—not of application—are treated in a way which places the urgent problem today raised by sociological themes on a plane not reached, in this respect, by any other philosophy.

# Man and People

# 1

# Being In One's Self and Being Beside One's Self

My subject is this: Today people constantly talk of laws and law, the state, the nation and internationalism, public opinion and public power, good policy and bad, pacifism and jingoism, "my country" and humanity, social justice and social injustice, collectivism and capitalism, socialization and liberalism, the individual and the collectivity, and so on and so on. And they not only talk, in the press, at their clubs, cafés, and taverns; they also argue. And they not only argue; they also fight for the things that these words designate. And once started fighting, they kill each other—by hundreds, by thousands, by millions. It would be ingenuous to suppose that, in what I have just said, I refer to any specific nation. It would be ingenuous, because the supposition would be equivalent to believing that these ferocious performances are confined to particular parts of our planet; when, on the contrary, they are a universal phenomenon, which is progressively spreading and by which very few of the European and American peoples will succeed in remaining unaffected. Doubtless the cruel conflict will be more mortal among some than among others and it may be that one or another will possess the inspired serenity necessary to reduce the havoc to a minimum. Because certainly conflict is not inevitable; but no less certainly it is very difficult to avoid. Very difficult indeed, because to avoid it will require the collaboration of many factors that differ both qualitatively and in importance—splendid virtues, together with humble precautions.

One of these precautions—humble, I repeat, but obligatory if a country is to pass unscathed through these terrible times—is somehow to contrive that a sufficient number of persons in it shall be thoroughly aware of the degree to which these ideas (let us call them ideas)—all these ideas about which there is all this talk and fighting and arguing and slaughter—are grotesquely confused and superlatively vague.

Everybody talks, talks, talks about these questions, but what is said about them lacks the minimum of clarity without which talking becomes a harmful operation. Because talking always has certain consequences. And since talking about these subjects has become general—for years, people have practically talked about nothing else, and allowed no one to talk about anything else—the consequences of all this chatter are, obviously, very serious.

One of the greatest misfortunes of our time is the acute incongruity between the importance that all these questions have at present and the crudeness and confusion of the concepts of them which these words represent.

Observe that all these ideas—law, code of laws, state, internationalism, collectivity, authority, freedom, social justice, and so on—even when they do not explicitly express it, always imply, as their essential ingredient, the idea of the social, of society. If this idea is not clear, all these words do not mean what they pretend to and are mere empty show. Now, whether we admit it or not, in the incorruptible depths of our being we are all of us conscious that on these subjects we have only random, vague, silly, or muddled notions. Because, unfortunately, crudeness and confusion in regard to these matters exists not only among the masses but also among scholars—to the point where it is impossible to refer the uninitiated to any book or article where he can really correct and refine his sociological concepts.

I shall never forget the surprise mingled with shame and shock which I felt when, many years ago, conscious of my ignorance on this subject, I hurried, full of illusion, all the sails of hope spread wide, to books on sociology . . . and found something incredible—namely, that books on sociology have nothing clear to say about what the social is, about what society is. Even worse: not only do they fail to give us a precise notion of what the social is, of what society is; but, reading these books, we further discover that their authors—our esteemed sociologists—have not made any serious effort to clarify—even to themselves, let alone to their readers—the elementary phenomena in which the social fact consists. In the very works whose titles seem to announce that their authors intend to treat the subject fundamentally, we soon see that they avoid it—we might almost say, conscientiously. They hurry over these phenomena—which are, I repeat, preliminary and indispensable—as over red-hot coals; and with an occasional exception, never more than partial (Durkheim, for example), we see them rush on, with enviable boldness, to hold forth upon the most terribly concrete themes of human living together.

Obviously, I cannot demonstrate this to you now; I will content myself with making the following simple statistical observations, which seem to me more than sufficient.

*First:* The works in which Auguste Comte founded the science of sociology amount to more than five thousand pages of quite small print. Now, in all those pages we do not find lines enough to make up one page devoted to telling us what Auguste Comte understands by *society*.

*Second:* The book in which this science or pseudo science celebrates its first triumph on the intellectual horizon—Spencer's *Principles of Sociology,* published between 1876 and 1896—has at least 2500 pages. I do not think there are as many as fifty lines in which the author asks himself what are these strange realities, "societies," with which his voluminous book is concerned.

*Lastly:* Some years ago Bergson published his book— a fascinating book, by the way—*The Two Springs of Morality and Religion.* This hydraulic title, which is a landscape in itself, conceals a 350-page treatise on sociology, in which there is not one line in which the author formally tells us what are the "societies" about which he speculates. Indeed, we emerge from reading it as from a jungle—covered with ants and surrounded by frantic swarms of bees; because all that the author does to enlighten us concerning the strange reality of human societies is to refer us to the anthill and the beehive, to alleged animal societies—about which, of course, we know less than we do about our own.

This is not to say—far from it!—that in these books, as in some others, there are not insights, at times inspired insights, into certain sociological problems. But, for want of clarity in regard to the fundamentals, these happy discoveries remain secret and hermetic, inaccessible to the ordinary reader. To use them, we should have to do what their authors did not do: try to clear up these preliminary and fundamental phenomena; hold ourselves resolutely to defining what the social is, what society is. Because their authors did not do this, like inspired blind men they sometimes manage to touch upon certain realities—I might say, to bump into them—but they do not succeed in seeing them, still less in clarifying them to us. So that our intercourse with these writers proves to be the dialogue between the blind man and the cripple:

"How are you getting on, my good man?" the blind man asks the cripple. And the cripple answers the blind man: "As you see, my friend . . ."

If this sort of thing goes on among the masters of sociological thinking, we can scarcely be surprised if people in the marketplace raise their voices over these questions. When men have nothing clear to say about a matter, instead of keeping quiet, they commonly do the opposite: they "say" in the superlative, that is, they shout. And the shout is the sonorous preliminary to aggression, to combat, to slaughter. *Dove si grida non è vera scienza,* said Leonardo. "Where there is shouting there is no true knowledge."

Thus it is that the ineptitude of sociology, filling people's heads with confused ideas, has finally become one of the plagues of our time. Sociology, in short, is not abreast of the times, and so the times, badly buttressed, fall headlong to destruction.

If this is so, do you not think that one of the best ways of not wholly wasting our time would be to devote ourselves to clarifying, to some extent, what the social is, what society is? You—many of you, at least—know very little or nothing at all about the subject. For my part, I am not sure that I am not in the same case. Why not put together our ignorances? Why not start a stock company, with a good capital of ignorance, and undertake the enterprise without pedantry or with the least possible amount of it, but with a lively desire to see clearly, with intellectual relish (a virtue that has begun to disappear in Europe) —with the delight that is awakened in us by the hope that we shall suddenly be flooded with light?

So, once again, let us set out in search of clear ideas; that is, of truths.

Few are the peoples who in these latter days still enjoy that tranquillity which permits one to choose the truth, to abstract oneself in meditation. Almost all the world is in tumult, is beside itself, and when man is beside himself he loses his most essential attribute: the possibility of meditating, or withdrawing into himself in order to come to terms with himself and define what it is that he believes, what he truly esteems and what he truly detests. Being beside himself bemuses him, blinds him, forces him to act mechanically in a frenetic somnambulism.

Nowhere do we better see that the possibility of meditation is man's essential attribute than at the zoo, before the cages of our cousins the monkeys. The bird and the crustacean are forms of life too remote from our own for us to see, comparing them with ourselves, anything but gross, abstract differences, vague by their very extremeness. But the simian is so like ourselves that he invites us to pursue the comparison, to discover differences that are more concrete and more fertile.

If we can remain still for a time in passive contemplation of the simian scene, one of its characteristics will presently, and as if spontaneously, stand out and come to us like a ray of light. This is that the infernal little beasts are constantly on the alert, perpetually uneasy, looking and listening for all the signals that reach them from their surroundings, forever intent on their environment as if they feared some constant peril from it, to which they must automatically respond by flight or bite, the mechanical discharge of a muscular reflex. The animal, in short, lives in perpetual fear of the world, and at the same time in a perpetual hunger for the things that are in the world and appear in the world, an ungovernable hunger that also discharges itself without any possible restraint or inhibition, just as the animal's fear does. In either case it is the objects and events in its environment which govern the animal's life, which pull and push it about like a marionette. It does not rule its life, it does not live from *itself*, but is always intent on what is happening outside it, on all that is *other* than itself. The word for "other" in Spanish—*otro*—is nothing but the Latin *alter*. To say, then, that the animal lives not from *itself* but from what is *other* than itself, pulled and pushed and tyrannized over by that *other*, is equivalent to saying that the animal is always estranged from itself, beside itself, that its life is essential *alteración* [1]—possession by all that is *other*.

As we contemplate this fate of unremitting disquietude, there comes a moment when we say to ourselves, "What a job!" Whereby, with complete ingenuousness and without realizing it, we set forth the most essential difference between man and animal. Because the expression means that we feel a strange weariness, a gratuitous weariness, occasioned by our simply imagining ourselves forced to live as they do, perpetually harassed by our environment and tensely attentive to it. But, you will ask, does man perchance not find himself in the same situation as the animal, a prisoner of the world, surrounded by things that terrify him, by things that enchant him, and obliged all his life, inexorably, whether he will or no, to concern himself with them? There is no doubt of it. But with this essential difference—that man can, from time to time, suspend his direct concern with things, detach himself from his surroundings, ignore them, and subjecting his faculty of attention to a radical shift—incomprehensible zoologically—turn, so to speak, his back on the world

[1] [Literally, "otheration." The Spanish word has, in addition to the meaning of English "alteration," that of "state of tumult," "being beside oneself." Throughout this chapter, the author plays on the root meanings of this and another equally untranslatable word, *ensimismamiento*, literally, "within-self-ness," in ordinary usage "being absorbed in thought," "meditation," "contemplation." The chapter title in Spanish is *Ensimismamiento y Alteración.—Trans.*]

and take his stand inside himself, attend to his own inwardness or, what is the same thing, concern himself with himself and not with what is *other*, with things.

In words which, merely from having been worn by use, like old coins, are no longer able to convey their meaning to us with any force, we are accustomed to calling this operation thinking, meditation, contemplation. But these expressions hide the most surprising thing in the phenomenon: man's power of virtually and provisionally withdrawing himself from the world and taking his stand inside himself—or, to use a magnificent word which exists only in Spanish, that man can *ensimismarse* ["be inside himself"].

Observe that this marvelous faculty that man possesses of temporarily freeing himself from his slavery to things implies two very different powers: one is his ability to ignore the world for a greater or less time without fatal risk; the other is his having somewhere to take his stand, to be, when he has virtually left the world. Baudelaire expressed this latter difficulty with romantic and mannered dandyism when, asked where he would choose to live, he answered: "Anywhere, as long as it is out of the world!" But the world is the whole of exteriority, the absolute *without*, which can have no other *without* beyond itself. The only possible without to this *without* is, precisely, a *within*, an *intus*, the inwardness of man, his *self*, which is principally made up of ideas.

Because ideas possess the most extraordinary condition of being nowhere in the world, of being outside of all places; although symbolically we situate them in our heads, as Homer's Greeks situated them in the heart or the pre-Homeric Greeks in the diaphragm or the liver. All these symbolic changes of domicile to which we subject ideas always agree in situating them in one of the viscera; that is, in the innermost part of the body, although the *within* of the body is always a merely relative *within*. In this fashion we give a materialized expression—since we can give no other—to our suspicion that ideas are in no place in space, which is pure exteriority; but that, over against the external world, they constitute another world which is not in the world: our inner world.

That is why the animal has always to be attentive to what goes on outside it, to the things around it. Because, even if the dangers and incitements of those things were to diminish, the animal would perforce continue to be governed by them, by the outward, by what is *other* than itself; because it cannot go *within itself*, since it has no *self*, no *chez soi*, where it can withdraw and rest.

The animal is pure *alteración*. It cannot be within itself. Hence when things cease to threaten it or caress it; when they give it a holiday; in short, when what is *other* ceases to move it and manage it, the poor animal has virtually to stop existing, that is, it goes to sleep. Hence the enormous capacity for somnolence that the animal exhibits, the infra-human torpor which primitive man continues in part; and, on the other hand, the increasing insomnia of civilized man, the almost permanent, sometimes terrible and uncontrollable wakefulness which afflicts men of an intense inner life. Not many years ago my great friend Scheler—one of the most fertile minds of our time, a man whose life was an incessant radiating of ideas—died from inability to sleep.

But of course—and with this we touch for the first time upon something which will be apparent to us again and again at almost every turn and winding of this course, if each time on a deeper level and in virtue of more precise and effectual reasons (those which I now give are neither the one nor the other)—of course these two things, man's power of withdrawing himself from the world and his power of taking his stand within himself are not gifts conferred upon man. I must emphasize this for those of you who are concerned with philosophy: they are not gifts conferred upon man. *Nothing that is substantive has been conferred upon man.* He has to do everything for himself.

Hence, if man enjoys this privilege of temporarily freeing himself from things and the power to enter into himself and there rest, it is because by his effort, his toil, and his ideas he has succeeded in reacting upon things, in transforming them, and creating around himself a margin of security, which is always limited but always or almost always increasing. This specifically human creation is technology. Thanks to it, and in proportion to its progress, man can take his stand within himself. But, vice versa, man is a technician, he is also able to modify his environment in the direction of his convenience, because, seizing every moment of rest that things allowed him, he has used it to retire into himself and form ideas about this world, about these things and his relation to them, to form a plan of attack against his circumstances, in short, to create an inner world for himself. From this inner world he emerges and returns to the outer. But he returns as protagonist, he returns with a *self* which he did not possess before, with his plan of campaign—not to let himself be dominated by things, but to govern them himself, to impose his will and his design upon them, to realize his ideas in that outer world, to mould the planet after the preferences of his inmost being. Far from losing his own self in this return to the world, he carries it thither, projects it energetically and masterfully upon things, in other words, he forces the *other*—the world—little by little to become himself. Man humanizes the world, injects it, impregnates it with his own ideal substance, and it is possible to imagine that one day or another, in the far depths of time, this terrible outer world will become so saturated with man that our descendants will be able to travel through it as today we mentally travel through our own inner selves; it is possible to imagine that the world, without ceasing to be the world, will one day be changed into something like a materialized soul, and, as in Shakespeare's *Tempest,* the winds will blow at the bidding of Ariel, the elf of Ideas.[2]

It seems to me that we can now, if only vaguely and schematically, represent to ourselves what humanity's course has been from this point of view. Let us do so in a brief statement which will at the same time serve us as a summary and a reminder of all that has so far been said.

Man, no less than the animal, finds himself consigned to the world, to the things about him, to his surroundings, his circumstance. At first his existence hardly differs from zoological existence; he too lives governed by his environment, is set among the things of the world as one of them. Yet no sooner do the beings around him give him a moment of repose than man, making a gigantic effort, achieves an instant of concentration—enters into himself, that is—by great efforts keeps his attention fixed upon the ideas that spring up within him, ideas which things have evoked and which have reference to the behavior of things, to what the philosopher will later call "the being of things." For the moment it is only a very crude idea of the world, but one that allows him to sketch a first

[2] I do not say that this is certain—such certainty is the exclusive possession of the *progressivist,* and I am no *progressivist,* as will appear—but I do say that it is possible.

Nor should it be assumed from what I have just said, that I am an idealist. I am *neither a progressivist nor an idealist!* On the contrary, the idea of progress, and idealism—that exquisitely and nobly proportioned name—progress and idealism are two of my *bêtes noires,* because I see in them perhaps the two greatest sins of the last two hundred years, the two greatest forms of irresponsibility. But let us leave this subject, to treat it in due season, and continue quietly along our road.

plan of defense, a preconceived course of conduct. But the things around him neither allow him to devote much time to this concentration, nor even if they allowed it would our primigenial man be capable of prolonging this unusual twist of his attention, this fixation upon the impalpable phantoms of ideas, for more than a few seconds or minutes. This inwardly directed attention, which is being within one's self, is the most antinatural and ultrabiological of phenomena. It took man thousands upon thousands of years to educate his capacity for concentration a little—only a little. What is natural to him is to disperse himself, to divert his thought outward, like the monkey in the jungle and in his cage in the zoo.

Father Chevesta, explorer and missionary, who was the first ethnographer to specialize in the study of the pygmies, probably the oldest known variety of man, and who went into the deepest of tropical jungles to find them— Father Chevesta, who knows nothing of the doctrine I am now expounding and who confines himself to describing what he sees, says in his most recent book, on the dwarfs of the Congo: [3]

"They completely lack the power of concentration. They are always absorbed by external impressions, whose continual change prevents them from withdrawing into themselves, which is the indispensable condition for any learning. To put them on a school bench would be an unbearable torture to these little men. So that the work of the missionary and the teacher becomes extremely difficult."

But even though momentary and crude, this primitive withdrawal into the self tends basically to separate human life from animal life. Because now man, our primigenial man, goes back and again submerges himself in the things of the world, but resisting them, not delivering himself

[3] *Bambuti, die Zwerge des Congo,* 1932.

wholly over to them. He has a plan against them, a project for dealing with them, for manipulating their forms, which produces a minimum transformation of his environment, just enough so that things oppress him a little less and in consequence allow him more frequent and leisurely intervals of withdrawal into himself, of meditation . . . and so on, time after time.

There are, then, three different moments, which are repeated cyclically throughout the course of human history, in forms each time more complex and rich: 1. Man feels himself lost, shipwrecked among things; this is *alteración*. 2. Man, by an energetic effort, withdraws into himself to form ideas about things and possible ways of dominating them; this is being within one's self, *ensimismamiento*, the *vita contemplativa* of the Romans, the *theoretikos bios* of the Greeks, *theory*. 3. Man again submerges himself in the world, to act in it according to a preconceived plan; this is action, *vita activa, praxis*.

Accordingly, *it is impossible to speak of action except in so far as it will be governed by a previous contemplation; and vice versa, contemplation, or being within one's self, is nothing but a projecting of future action.*

Man's destiny, then, is primarily *action*. We do not live to think, but the other way round: we think in order that we may succeed in surviving. This is a point of capital importance, upon which, in my judgment, we must set ourselves in radical opposition to the entire philosophical tradition and make up our minds to deny that *thought*, in any sufficing sense of the word, was given to man once and for all, so that without further ado he finds it at his disposal as a perfect faculty or power, ready to be employed and exercised, as flight was given to the bird and swimming to the fish.

If this pertinacious doctrine were valid, it would follow that as the fish can—from the outset—swim, man could

—from the outset and without further ado—think. Such
a notion deplorably blinds us to perceiving the peculiar
drama, the unique drama, which constitutes the very condition of man. Because if for the present, in order to
understand one another at this moment, we admit the
traditional idea that thought is the characteristic of man
—remember "man, a rational animal"—so that to be a man
would be, as our inspired forefather, Descartes, claimed,
the same as to be *a thinking thing*—it would follow that
man, by being endowed once and for all with *thought*,
by possessing it with the certainty with which a constitutive and inalienable quality is possessed, would be sure
of being man as the fish is in fact sure of being a fish. Now
this is a formidable and a fatal error. Man is never sure
that he will be able to exercise thought—that is, in an
adequate manner; and only if it is adequate is it thought.
Or, in more popular terms: man is never sure that he will
be right, that he will hit the mark. Which means nothing
less than the tremendous fact that, unlike all other en-
tities in the universe, man is not and can never be sure
that he is, in fact, man, as the tiger is sure of being a tiger
and the fish of being a fish.

Far from thought having been bestowed upon man, the
truth is—a truth which I cannot now properly support
by argument but can only state—the truth is that he has
continually been creating thought, making it little by
little, perforce of a discipline, a culture or cultivation; a
millennial, nay, multimillennial effort, without having yet
succeeded—far from it!—in finishing the job. Not only
was thought not given to man from the first, but even at
this point in history he has only succeeded in forming a
small portion and a crude form of what in the simple
and ordinary sense of the word we call thought. And even
the small portion gained, being an acquired and not a
constitutive quality, is always in danger of being lost, and

considerable quantities of it have been lost, many times in fact, in the past; and today we are on the point of losing it again. To such an extent, unlike all the other beings in the universe, is man never surely *man;* on the contrary, being *man* signifies precisely being always on the point of not being man, being a living problem, an absolute and hazardous adventure, or, as I am wont to say: being, in essence, drama! Because there is drama only when we do not know what is going to happen, so that every instant is pure peril and shuddering risk. While the tiger cannot stop being a tiger, cannot be de-tigered, man lives in perpetual danger of being dehumanized. With him, not only is it problematic and contingent whether this or that will happen to him, as it is with the other animals, but at times what happens to man is nothing less than *ceasing to be man.* And this is true not only abstractly and generically but it holds of our own individuality. Each one of us is always in danger of not being the unique and untransferable *self* which he is. The majority of men perpetually betray this *self* which is waiting to be; and to tell the whole truth, our personal individuality is a personage which is never completely realized, a stimulating Utopia, a secret legend, which each of us guards in the depths of his heart. It is thoroughly comprehensible that Pindar summarized his heroic ethics in the well-known imperative: "Become what you are."

The condition of man, then, is essential uncertainty. Hence the cogency of the charmingly mannered *mot* of a fifteenth-century Burgundian gentleman: *"Rien ne m'est sûre que la chose incertaine,"* "I am sure of nought save the uncertain."

No human acquisition is stable. Even what appears to us most completely won and consolidated can disappear in a few generations. This thing we call "civilization"— all these physical and moral comforts, all these conveniences, all these shelters, all these virtues and disciplines which have become habit now, on which we count, and which in effect constitute a repertory or system of securities which man made for himself like a raft in the initial shipwreck which living always is—all these securities are insecure securities which in the twinkling of an eye, at the least carelessness, escape from man's hands and vanish like phantoms. History tells us of innumerable retrogressions, of decadences and degenerations. But nothing tells us that there is no possibility of much more basic retrogressions than any so far known, including the most radical of all: the total disappearance of man as man and his silent return to the animal scale, to complete and definitive *alteración.* The fate of culture, the destiny of man, depends upon our maintaining this dramatic consciousness ever alive in our inmost being, and upon our being well aware, as of a murmuring counterpoint in our entrails, that we can only be sure of insecurity.

No small part of the anguish that is today tormenting the souls of the West derives from the fact that during the past century—and perhaps for the first time in history —man reached the point of believing himself secure. Secure! For the truth is that the one and only person who ever succeeded in feeling and believing himself secure was the pharmaceutical Monsieur Homais, the net result of progressivism! The progressivist idea consists in affirming not only that humanity—an abstract, irresponsible, nonexistent entity invented at the time—that humanity progresses, which is certain, but also that it progresses of necessity. This idea anesthetized the European and the American to that basic feeling of risk which is the substance of man. Because if humanity inevitably progresses, this means that we can abandon all watchfulness, stop worrying, throw off all responsibility, or, as we say in Spain, "snore away" and let humanity bear us inevitably

to perfection and delight. Human history thus loses all
the bone and sinew of drama and is reduced to a peaceful
tourist trip, organized by some transcendent "Cook's."
Traveling thus securely toward its fulfillment, the civilization in which we are embarked would be like the Phaea-
cian ship in Homer which sailed straight to port without a
pilot. This security is what we are paying for today.[4]

Such being my view, you will understand that I see an
element of absurdity in the definition of man put forth
by Linnaeus and the eighteenth century: *homo sapiens.*

[4] This is one of the reasons why I said that I am not a *progressivist.*
This is why I prefer to renew in myself, at frequent intervals, the
emotion aroused in me in my youth by Hegel's words at the beginning of his *Philosophy of History:* "*When we contemplate the
past, that is, history,*" he says, "*the first thing we see is nothing
but—ruins.*"

In passing, let us seize the opportunity to see, from the altitude
of this vision, the element of frivolity, and even of vulgarity, in
Nietzsche's famous imperative: "*Live dangerously.*" Which, furthermore, is not Nietzsche's but the exaggeration of an old Italian
Renaissance saying, Aretino's famous motto: *Vivere risolutamente.*
Because Nietzsche does not say "*Live on the alert,*" which would
have been good, but "*Live dangerously.*" And this shows that despite his genius, he did not know that the very substance of our life
is danger and hence it is rather affected, and supererogatory, to
propose as something new, added, and original that we should
seek and collect danger. An idea, furthermore, which is typical
of the period that called itself "*fin de siècle,*" a period which will
remain in history—it culminated about 1900—as that in which man
felt himself most secure and, at the same time—with its stiff shirts
and frock coats, its *femmes fatales,* its affectation of perversity, and
its Barresian cult of the "I"—as the epoch of vulgarity par excellence. In every period there are ideas that I should call "fishing"
ideas, ideas that are expressed and proclaimed precisely because it
is known they will not happen, that are thought only as a game, as
*folie;* some years ago, for example, there was a rage in England for
wolf stories, because England is a country where the last wolf was
killed in 1668 and which hence has no genuine experience of wolves.
In a period that has no strong experience of insecurity—such as the
*fin de siècle* period—they play at the dangerous life.

Let all this be taken as going to show that thought is not a gift
to man but a laborious, precarious, and volatile acquisition.

Because if we take this expression in good faith, it can mean only that man in fact knows—in other words, that he knows all that he needs to know. Now nothing is further from the reality. Man has never known what he needed to know. So if we understand *homo sapiens* in the sense that man knows some things, a very few things, but does not know the remainder, since this remainder is immense it would seem to me more appropriate to define him as *homo insciens, insipiens,* as man the unknowing. And certainly, if we were not now in such a hurry, we could see the good judgment with which Plato defines man precisely by his ignorance. Ignorance is, in fact, man's privilege. Neither God nor beast is ignorant—the former because he possesses all knowledge, the latter because he needs none.

It is clear, then, that man does not exercise his thought because he finds it amusing, but because, obliged as he is to live immersed in the world and to force his way among things, he finds himself under the necessity of organizing his psychic activities, which are not very different from those of the anthropoid, *in the form* of thought —which is what the animal does not do.

Man, then, rather than by what he *is*, or by what he *has*, escapes from the zoological scale by what he *does*, by his conduct. Hence it is that he must always keep watch on himself.

This is something of what I wanted to suggest in the epigram—which seems to be merely an epigram—that *we do not live in order to think* but *we think in order to succeed in subsisting or surviving.* And you see how this attributing thought to man as an innate quality—which at first seems to be a homage and even a compliment to his species—is, strictly speaking, an injustice. Because there is no such gift, no such gratuity; there is only a laborious fabrication and a conquest which, like every conquest—

be it of a city or of a woman—is always unstable and fugitive.

This consideration of thought has been necessary as an aid to understanding my earlier statement that man is primarily and fundamentally action. In passing, let us do homage to the first man who thought this truth with complete clarity; it was not Kant nor Fichte, it was that inspired madman Auguste Comte.

We saw that *action* is not a random fisticuffs with the things around us or with our fellow men; this is the infrahuman, this is *alteración. Action* is to act upon the environment of material things or of other men in accordance with a plan preconceived in a previous period of meditation or thought. There is, then, no genuine action if there is no thought, and there is no authentic thought if it is not duly referred to action and made virile by its relation to action.

But this relation—which is the true one—between action and contemplation has been persistently ignored. When the Greeks discovered that man thought, that there existed in the universe the strange reality that is thought (until then men had not thought, or, like the *bourgeois gentilhomme,* had done so without knowing it), they felt such an enthusiasm for the charms of ideas that they conferred upon intelligence, upon the *logos,* the supreme rank in the universe. Compared with it, everything else seemed to them ancillary and contemptible. And as we tend to project into God whatever appears to us to be the best, the Greeks, with Aristotle, reached the point of maintaining that God had no other occupation but to think. And not even to think about things—that seemed to them as it were a debasement of the intellectual process. No—according to Aristotle, God does nothing but think about thought—which is to turn God into an intellectual, or, more precisely, into a modest professor of philosophy.

But I repeat that, for them, this was the most sublime thing in the world and the most sublime thing that a being could do. Hence they believed that man's destiny was solely to exercise his intellect, that man had come into the world to meditate, or, in our terminology, to be in himself (*ensimismarse*).

This doctrine has been given the name "*intellectualism*" —that idolatry of the intelligence which isolates thought from its setting, from its function in the general economy of human life. As if man thinks because he thinks, and not because, whether he will or no, he has to think in order to maintain himself among things! As if thought could awaken and function of its own motion, as if it began and ended in itself, and was not—as is the true state of the case—engendered by action, with its roots and its end in action! We owe innumerable things of the highest value to the Greeks, but they have put chains on us too. The man of the West still lives, to no small degree, enslaved by the preferences of the men of Greece— preferences that, operating in the subsoil of our culture, for eight centuries turned us from our proper and genuine Western vocation. The heaviest of these chains is "*intellectualism*"; and now, when it is imperative that we correct our course and find new roads—in short, succeed —it is of the greatest importance that we resolutely rid ourselves of this archaic attitude, which has been carried to its extreme during these last two centuries.

Under the name first of *raison*, then of *enlightenment*, and finally of *culture*, a radical prevarication of terms and the most indiscreet deification of intelligence were effected. Among the majority of almost all the thinkers of the period, especially among the Germans—for example, among those who were my masters at the beginning of the century—*culture, thought,* came to fill the vacant office of a God who had been put to flight. All my work, from its first stammerings, has been a battle against this attitude, which many years ago I called the *"bigotry of culture."* The bigotry of culture, because it presented us with culture, with thought, as something justified by itself, that is, which needs no justification but is valid by its own essence, whatever its concrete activity and its content may be. Human life was to put itself at the service of culture because only thus would it become filled with worthy substance. From which it would follow that human life, our pure existence, would in itself be a mean and worthless thing.

This way of reversing the true relation between *life* and *culture*, between *action* and *contemplation*, brought it about that, during the last century—hence until a very short time ago—there was an overproduction of ideas, of books and works of art, a real *cultural inflation*. The result has been what—jokingly, because I distrust "isms" —we could call a "capitalism of culture," a modern aspect of Byzantinism. There has been production for production's sake, instead of production in view of consumption, in view of the necessary ideas that the man of today needs and can absorb. And, as occurs in capitalism, the market was glutted and crisis has ensued. Let no one tell me that the greater part of the immense changes that have recently occurred has taken us by surprise. For twenty years I have been announcing them and prognosticating them. To mention no other subject than the one we are now treating, reference may be made to my essay, formally and programmatically entitled "The Reform of Intelligence." [5]

But the most dangerous aspect of the intellectual aberration that this "bigotry of culture" signifies is not this; it consists in presenting culture, withdrawal into one's self, thought, as a grace or jewel that man is to add

[5] [See *Obras completas*, Vol. IV.]

to his life, hence as something that provisionally lies outside of his life and as if there were life without culture and thought—as if it were possible to live without withdrawing into one's self. Men were set, as it were, before a jeweler's window—were given the choice of acquiring culture or doing without it. And it is clear that, faced with such a dilemma, during the years we are now living through men have not hesitated, but have resolved to explore the second alternative to its limits and are seeking to flee from all taking a stand within the self and to give themselves up to the opposite extreme. That is why Europe is in extremities today.

The intellectualist aberration, which isolates contemplation from action, was followed by the opposite aberration—the *voluntarist* aberration, which throws contemplation overboard and deifies pure action. This is the other way of wrongly interpreting the foregoing thesis, that man is primarily and fundamentally *action*. Undoubtedly every idea—even the truest—is susceptible of misinterpretation; undoubtedly every idea is dangerous; this must be admitted with all formality and once and for all, but upon condition that we add that this danger, this latent risk, is not limited to ideas but is inseparable from everything, absolutely everything, that man does. This is why I have said that the essence of man is purely and simply *danger*. Man always travels among precipices, and, whether he will or no, his truest obligation is to keep his balance.

As has happened more than once in the known past, now again—and I refer to these years, almost to this century—once again peoples are plunging into *alteración*. The same thing that happened in Rome! Europe began by letting itself be overwhelmed by pleasure, as Rome was by what Ferrero has called "luxury"—an excess, an extravagance, of commodities. Then pain and

terror took their turn. As in Rome, social conflicts and
the consequent wars stupefied men's souls. And stupefaction, the extreme form of *alteración*—stupefaction,
when it persists, becomes stupidity. It has aroused some
attention that, for quite a long time now and with the
insistence of a leitmotiv, I have referred in my writings to
the insufficiently recognized fact that, even in Cicero's
time, the ancient world was becoming stupid. It has been
said that his master Posidonius was the last man of antique
civilization who was able to set himself before things and
think about them effectually. The capacity to take a
stand within the self, to withdraw serenely into one's
incorruptible depths, was lost—as it threatens to be lost
in Europe if something is not done to prevent it. Nothing
is talked about but action. The demagogues, impresarios
of *alteración*, who have already caused the death of
several civilizations, harass men so that they shall not
reflect, see to it that they are kept herded together in
crowds so that they cannot reconstruct their individuality in the one place where it can be reconstructed, which
is in solitude. They cry down service to truth, and in its
stead offer us: *myths*. And by all these means they succeed
in throwing men into a passion, in putting them, between
ardors and terrors, *beside*, that is, *outside of, themselves*.
And clearly, since man is the animal that has succeeded in
putting himself *inside himself*, when man is *beside himself*
his aspiration is to descend and he falls back into animality.
Such is the spectacle—always the same—of every period
in which pure action is deified. The interval is filled with
crimes. Human life loses value, is no longer regarded,
and all forms of violence and spoliation are practiced—
especially of spoliation. Hence whenever the figure of
the pure man of action rises above the horizon and becomes dominant, the first thing for us to do is to lock
everything up. Anyone who would really like to learn

what effects spoliation produces in a great civilization can see them set forth in the first book of major importance to be written on the Roman Empire. I refer to the book by the great Russian savant Rostovtzeff, who for many years has been teaching in the United States—*Social and Economic History of the Roman Empire.*

Torn in this way from its normal connection with contemplation, with being within one's self, *pure action* permits and produces only a chain of stupidities which we might better call "stupidity unchained." So we see today that an absurd attitude justifies the appearance of an opposing attitude no more reasonable; at least, reasonable enough, and so on indefinitely. Such is the extreme to which political affairs in the West have come!

This being the situation, it would seem sensible that, whenever circumstances give us even the slightest respite, we should attempt to break this enchanted circle of *alteración,* which hurries us from one folly to another; it would seem sensible that we should say to ourselves—as, after all, we often say to ourselves in our more ordinary life whenever our surroundings overwhelm us, when we feel lost in a whirlpool of problems—that we say to ourselves: "Quietly now!" What is the meaning of this adjuration? Simply that of inviting us to suspend for a moment the action which threatens to preoccupy us and make us lose our heads; to suspend action for a moment so that we may withdraw into ourselves, review our ideas of the circumstance in which we are placed, and work out a plan of strategy.

Hence I consider it neither extravagant nor insolent if, having come to a country that still enjoys a serene horizon,[6] I think that the most fruitful work that it can do, for itself and for the rest of mankind, is not to add to the

---

[6] [The reference is to Argentina, where this chapter was delivered as a lecture in 1939.—Editor's note.]

world's state of *alteración*, still less to be affected more than need be by the fact that others have succumbed to it, but to take advantage of its own fortunate situation to do what others cannot now do—to withdraw and think a little. If now, in places where it is possible, no store of new human projects—that is, of ideas—is created, we can have little confidence in the future. Half of the unhappy things that are taking place today are taking place because no such projects were in readiness, just as I prophesied that they would take place, as long ago as 1922 in the Prologue to my *Invertebrate Spain*.

Without a strategic retreat into the self, without vigilant thought, human life is impossible. Call to mind all that mankind owes to certain great withdrawals into the self! It is no chance that all the great founders of religions preceded their apostolates by famous retreats. Buddha withdraws to the forest; Mahomet withdraws to his tent, and even there he withdraws from his tent by wrapping his head in his cloak; above all, Jesus goes apart into the desert for forty days. What do we not owe to Newton! Well, when someone, amazed that he had succeeded in reducing the countless phenomena of physics to such a precise and simple system, asked him how he had succeeded in doing so, he replied ingenuously: *Nocte dieque incubando*, "turning them over day and night"—words behind which we glimpse vast and abysmal withdrawals into the self.

In the world today a great thing is dying; it is truth. Without a certain margin of tranquillity, truth succumbs. With which we now close the circle begun by our opening words. It was to give them their full meaning that I have said what I have said.

Hence, over against the incitements to *alteración* which today reach us from every point of the compass and from every angle of life, I believed that before plunging

into this course of lectures, I should by way of prologue
set before you a sketch of this doctrine of withdrawal
into one's self—even though it has been a hurried sketch,
even though I have been unable to dwell on any of its
parts as I should have wished to do and have had to pass
many of them over entirely. For example, I have not been
able to point out that contemplation, withdrawal into
one's self, like everything human, has sex, that there is a
masculine form of it, and another that is feminine. Which
cannot be otherwise, since woman is not *him*self but *her*-
self.

Similarly, the man of the East withdraws into himself
in a different way from the man of the West. The Occi-
dental does it in clarity of mind. Remember Goethe's
lines:

> I own allegiance to the race of those
> Who from the dark aspire to clarity.
>
> *Ich bekenne mich zu dem Geschlecht*
> *Der aus dem Dunkel ins Helle strebt.*

Europe and America mean the attempt to live by clear
ideas, not by myths. Because clear ideas were not to be
found today, the European feels lost and demoralized.

Machiavelli—not to be confused with *Machiavellianism*
—tells us that when an army is demoralized and scatters,
losing its formations, there is only one salvation: "*Ritornare al segno*," "*to return to the banner*," to take shelter
under its folds, and regroup the scattered hosts beneath
that sign. Europe and America must also "*ritornare al
segno*" of clear ideas. The new generations, who delight
in the strong body and the pure act, must integrate themselves in the clear idea, in the strictly constructed idea,
which is not redundant, which is not flabby, which is
necessary to life. Let us return—I repeat—from myths to
clear and distinct ideas, as they were called three centuries

ago, with programmatic solemnity, by the keenest mind
that the West has known: René Descartes, "that French
cavalier who set out at such a good pace," as Péguy put it.
I know very well that Descartes and his rationalism are
completely of the past, but man is nothing positive if
he is not continuity. To excel the past we must not allow
ourselves to lose contact with it; on the contrary, we must
feel it under our feet because we have raised ourselves
upon it.

Out of the immense jungle of themes that will need to
be elucidated if we are to aspire to a new dawn, I have
chosen one that seems to me greatly urgent: "What is
the social, what is society?"—a theme, if you like, that
is comparatively humble, and so of course scarcely brilliant, but above all of the utmost difficulty. But it is of
the utmost urgency. It is the root of those concepts—state,
nation, law, freedom, authority, collectivity, justice, and
the rest—that today put mortals into frenzy. Without
light on this theme, all these words represent nothing but
myths. We are going to look for a little of that light.
You must expect nothing more, of course. I can only give
what I have. Let others who can do more do their more,
as I do my little.

# 2
# Personal Life

ONCE again, man has lost himself. For this is nothing new, nothing accidental. Man has been lost many times throughout the course of his history. Indeed it is of the essence of man, in contradistinction to all other beings, that he can lose himself, lose himself in the jungle of his existence, within himself, and thanks to this sensation of being lost can react by setting energetically to work to find himself again. His ability to feel lost and his discomfort at feeling lost are his tragic destiny and his illustrious privilege.

Let us set out, then, to discover, in unimpeachable and unmistakable form, facts of such a characteristic complexion that no other denomination than that of "social phenomena" in the strict sense will seem to us to fit them. There is only one way to accomplish this most rigorous and decisive operation of finding that a type of facts is a reality or phenomenon that is definitely and determinedly different beyond any possible doubt or error, and hence is irreducible to any other type of facts. We must go back to an order of ultimate reality, to an order or area of reality which because it is *radical* (that is, of the root) admits of no other reality beneath it, or rather, on which all others must necessarily appear because it is the basic reality.

This radical reality, on the strict contemplation of which we must finally found and assure all our knowledge of anything, is our life, human life.

Whenever and wherever I speak of "human life," unless I make a special exception, you must avoid thinking of

somebody else's life; each one of you should refer it to
your own life and try to make that present to you.
Human life as radical reality is only the life of each
person, is only *my life*. In deference to idiom, I shall
sometimes call it "our life," but you must always understand that by this expression I refer to the life of each
individual and not to the life of other people nor to a
supposed plural and common life. What we call "other
people's lives"—the life of one's friend, of one's sweetheart—is something that appears in the scenario that is
*my* life, the life of each, and hence supposes that life. The
life of another, even of one nearest and dearest, is for me
mere spectacle, like the tree or the cliff or the wandering
cloud. I see it, but I *am* not it, that is, I do not live it. If the
other has a toothache, his face, the shape taken by his
contracted muscles, are patent to me, I see the spectacle
of someone suffering pain, but his toothache does not
pain me, and what I have of it in no way resembles what
I have when my own teeth ache. Strictly, my neighbor's
toothache is in the last analysis a supposition, hypothesis,
or presumption of my own, it is a presumed pain. My
pain, on the contrary, is unquestionable. Properly speaking, we can never be sure that the friend who presents
himself to us as suffering from toothache is really suffering from toothache. All that is patent to us of his pain
is certain external signs, which are not pain but muscular
contraction, wandering gaze, the hand to the cheek—
that gesture which is so incongruous with what provokes
it, for it looks exactly as if the toothache were a bird and
we were putting our hand over it to keep it from flying
away. Another's pain is not radical reality, but reality in a
sense that is already secondary, derivative, and dubious.
What we have of his pain with radical reality is only its
aspect, its appearance, the spectacle of it, its signs. This
is all of it that is actually patent and unquestionable to us.

But the relation between a sign and the thing signified, between an appearance and that which appears in it or simulates it, between an aspect and the thing manifest or "aspected" in it, is always finally questionable and ambiguous. There are those who to gain some private end feign the entire *mise en scène* of a toothache to perfection without suffering it. But we shall see that, on the contrary, our own individual life does not tolerate fictions, because when we feign something to ourselves we of course know that we are feigning. And so our intimate fiction never succeeds in fully establishing itself, for being at bottom aware that it is not genuine, we do not succeed in completely deceiving ourselves, we see through the fraud. This inexorable genuineness of our life, the life, I repeat, of each one of us, this genuineness that is evident, indubitable, unquestionable to itself, is my first reason for calling our life "radical reality."

But there is a second reason. Calling it "radical reality" does not mean that it is the only reality, nor even the highest, worthiest or most sublime, nor yet the supreme reality, but simply that it is the root of all other realities, in the sense that they—any of them—in order to be reality to us must in some way make themselves present, or at least announce themselves, within the shaken confines of our own life. Hence this radical reality—my life—is so little "egoistic," so far from "solipsistic," that in essence it is the open area, the waiting stage, on which any other reality may manifest itself and celebrate its Pentecost. God himself, to be God to us, must somehow or other proclaim his existence to us, and that is why he thunders on Sinai, lashes the money-changers in the temple court, and sails on the three-masted frigate of Golgotha.

It follows that no knowledge of anything is sufficient —that is, sufficiently profound or radical—if it does not begin by searching the sphere that is our life to discover and define where and how that thing makes its appearance in it, looms, springs up, arises, in short exists in it. For this is the proper meaning of the word *exist*—a word that originally, I take it, had strong connotations of struggle and belligerence, for it designates the vital situation in which suddenly, as though sprung from the ground, an enemy appears among us, shows himself or makes himself apparent, energetically blocking our way, that is, resisting us and at the same time affirming himself, making himself firm, before us and against us. Existing includes resisting; so it includes the fact that anything that has existence will affirm itself if we try to suppress it, annihilate it, or consider it unreal. Hence, whatever has existence or arises before us is reality, since reality is everything that, like it or not, we have to reckon with, because, like it or not, *it is there*, it ex-ists, re-sists. A terminological wrongheadedness that verges on the intolerable has for the past few years seen fit to use the words "exist" and "existence" in an abtruse and unverifiable sense precisely the opposite of that which the age-old word bears and expresses in itself.

Today some writers attempt to make the term designate man's mode of being. But man who is always "I"—the I that each of us is—is the only being that does not exist, but *lives* or is alive. Precisely all the other things that are not man, not "I," are the things that *exist*, because they appear, arise, spring up, resist me, assert themselves in the ambit that is my life. Be this said in passing and in all haste.

Now, innumerable attributes can be posited of this strange and dramatic radical reality, our life. But I shall now single out only the most indispensable one for our theme.

And it is that life is not something that we have bestowed on ourselves; rather, we find it precisely when we find ourselves. Suddenly and without knowing how or why, without any previous forewarning of it, man sees and finds that he is obliged to have his being in an unpremeditated, unforeseen ambit, in a conjunction of completely definite circumstances. Perhaps it will not be irrelevant to point out that this observation—which is the basis of my philosophical thought—was made, just as I have now made it, in my first book, published in 1914. Provisionally and to make it easier to understand, let us call this unpremeditated and unforeseen ambit, this most definite circumstance in which we always find ourselves in our living—let us call it "world." Now, this world, in which in living I am obliged to be, allows me a choice. *Within it* I may choose to be in one place or another. But it is granted to no one to choose the world in which he lives; it is always this one, this present world. We cannot choose the century or the day or the date when we are to live, nor the universe in which we are to move. To live or to be alive or, what is the same thing, to be a man, does not admit of any preparations or preliminary experiments. Life is fired at us point-blank. I have said it before: where and when we are born, or happen to find ourselves after we are born, there and then, like it or not, we must sink or swim. At this moment, every one of you finds himself submerged in an ambient that is an interval in which he must willy-nilly come to terms with that abstruse element, a lecture in philosophy, with something of which he does not know whether it interests him or not, whether he understands it or not, which is portentously devouring an hour of his life—an irreplaceable hour, for the hours of his life are numbered. This is his circumstance, his here and his now. What will he do? For something he *must* do; either listen to me, or, on the contrary, dismiss me and attend to his own meditations, think of his business or his clients, remember his sweetheart. What will he do? Get up and go, or remain, accepting the fate of spending this hour of his life, which might have been so delightful, in the slaughterhouse of lost hours?

Because, I repeat, there is no escape: we have something to do or have to be doing something *always;* for this life that is given us is not given us ready-made, but instead every one of us has to make it for himself, each his own. This life that is given us is given us empty, and man has to keep filling it for himself, occupying it. Such is our occupation. This is not the case with the stone, the plant, the animal. Their being is given them predetermined and decreed. The stone, when it begins to be, is given not only its existence; its behavior is also determined for it beforehand—namely, to be heavy, to gravitate toward the earth's center. Similarly the animal is given its behavioral repertory, directed by its instincts without any intervention on its part. But man is given the necessity of having always to do something upon pain of succumbing; yet what he has to do is not present to him from the outset and once and for all. Because the strangest and most confounding thing about this circumstance or world in which we have to live is the fact that within its inexorable circle or horizon it always presents us with a variety of possibilities for action, a variety in the face of which we are obliged to choose and hence to exercise our freedom. The circumstance, I repeat—the here and now in which we are inexorably inscribed and imprisoned—does not at every moment impose on us a single act or activity but various possible acts or activities, and cruelly leaves us to our own initiative and inspiration, hence to our own responsibility. In a little while, when you go out into the street, you will have to decide what direction, what route, you will take. And if this happens to you on such a commonplace occasion, much more happens at those solemn decisive moments of life in which the choice to be made is nothing less, for example, than a profession, a career—and career means road and direction. Among the few personal notes that Descartes left at his death there is one, dating from his youth, in which he copied an old line of Ausonius, which in turn reproduces an ancient Pythagorean saying and which runs: *Quod vitae sectabor iter?* "What way, what road shall I choose for my life?" But life is nothing except man's being; so that here we have the most extraordinary, extravagant, dramatic, and paradoxical thing about the human condition—namely, that man is the only reality that does not simply consist in being but must choose its own being. For if we analyze the commonplace thing that is going to occur in a little while—the fact that each of us will have to choose and decide the direction of the street he is going to take—you will see that the choice of such a seemingly simple act will be made only with the intervention of the entire choice that you have already made, the choice that at this moment, as you sit here, you carry secretly in your inmost selves, in your most hidden depths: the choice of a type of humanity, of a way of being man, that you seek to realize in your living.

In order not to lose our bearings, let us summarize what has been said so far: Life in the sense of human life, hence in the biographical not the biological sense—if biology is taken to mean the psychosomatic—life is the fact that someone whom we call man, as we could and perhaps should call him X (you will soon see why), finds himself having to be in the circumstance or world. But our being as "being in the circumstance" is not still and simply passive. To be, that is, to continue being, it has always to be doing something, but what it has to do is not imposed on it or predetermined for it; it has to choose and decide for itself, untransferably, for itself and before itself, upon its own sole responsibility. Nobody can take its place in deciding what it is going to do, for even submitting to another's will has to be its own decision. This obligation to choose, and hence willy-nilly to be free, to be on its own account and at its own risk, proceeds from the fact that the circumstance is never one-sided, it always has several, often many sides. In other words, it invites us to different possibilities of acting, of being. So we spend our lives saying to ourselves: "on the one hand," I would do, think, feel, want, decide *this*, but "on the other hand" . . . Life is many-sided. Every moment and every place opens different roads to us. As the ancient Indian book says: "Wherever a man sets his foot, he treads a hundred paths." So life is a permanent crossroads, a constant perplexity. This is why I am always saying that to my mind the best title for a book of philosophy is the one borne by a book of Maimonides': *More Nebuchim*—"Guide for the Perplexed."

When we want to describe a situation of the utmost extremity in our life, where circumstances appear to offer us no way out and hence no choice, we Spaniards say that we are "between the sword and the wall." Death is certain, there is no escaping it! Could there be less choice? Yet it is clear that the expression invites us to choose *between* the wall *and* the sword. Terrifying and proud privilege that man at times enjoys and suffers under—choosing the pattern of his own death: death of a coward or death of a hero, an ugly or a beautiful death!

Escape is possible from every circumstance, even the most extreme. What there is no escaping is having to do something and above all having to do what in the last analysis is the most difficult and painful of things—choosing, preferring. How many times have we not told ourselves that we should prefer not to prefer? From which it follows that what is given me when life is given me is simply "things to do." Life, as we all know only too well, "takes a lot of doing." And the most important thing is to make sure that what we choose to do in each case is not *just anything*, but the thing that has to be done— done here and now—that it is our true vocation, our genuine "thing to do."

Among all the characteristics of radical reality or life which I have mentioned, and which are a very small part of those that would have to be described to give any adequate idea of it, the one that I now want to emphasize is the one expressed in a great platitude: namely, that life is untransferable and that each man has to live his own; that no one can take over his task of living for him; that the toothache he suffers from has to hurt him and he cannot transfer even a fraction of the pain from it to anyone else; that he can delegate no one to choose and decide for him what he will do, what he will be; that no one can replace him or surrogate for him in feeling and wanting; that, finally, he cannot make his neighbor think for him the thoughts that he has to think in order to orient himself in the world (in the world of things and in the world of men) and thus find his right line of conduct— hence, that he must be convinced or not convinced, must see truths and see through nonsense, on his own account, without any possible substitute, deputy, or proxy.

I can repeat mechanically that two and two make four, without knowing what I am saying, simply because I have heard it countless times; but really to think it on my own account—that is, to acquire the clear certainty that "two and two veritably make four and not three or five"—*that* I have to do for myself, by myself, I alone— or, what is the same thing, I in my solitude. And as the same is true of my decisions, volitions, feelings, it follows that since human life in the strict sense is untransferable, it is essentially *solitude, radical solitude.*

But let there be no misunderstanding here. In no sense would I suggest that I am the only thing that exists. In the first place, you will have noticed that, even though "life" in the proper and original sense is that of each one of us, hence *my* life, I have used that possessive pronoun as little as possible, just as I have scarcely used the personal pronoun "I." If I have done so occasionally, it has been merely to make it easier for you to get a preliminary view of what this strange radical reality human life is. I have preferred using the terms "man," "the living being," or "each one of us." In another lecture you will see the reason for this reservation. But actually, and after a few detours that we shall make, what we are dealing with is clearly life, *my* life and *myself*. This man— this self, this "I"—is finally in radical solitude; but—I repeat—this does not mean that he alone is, that he is the sole reality, or at least the radical reality. What I have thus termed is not only I, nor is it man—it is life, man's life. Now, this includes an enormous number of things. European thought has traveled beyond the philosophical idealism that was dominant from the year 1640, in which Descartes proclaimed it—the philosophical idealism for which there is no reality except the ideas of my "I," of an "I," of my *moi-même*, of which Descartes said, *"moi qui ne suis qu'une chose qui pense."* For this philosophical idealism, things, the world, my body itself, would be only ideas of things, imagination of a world, fantasy of my body. Only the mind would exist and everything else would be a tenacious and exuberant dream, an infinite phantasmagoria secreted by my mind. Life would thus be the easiest thing imaginable. To live would be for me to exist within myself, floating on the sea of my own ideas, without having a need to reckon with anything but my own ideas. This is what has been called idealism. I should encounter nothing. I should not have to be in the world, the world would be in me, like an endless reel of film unwinding within me. Nothing would disturb me. I should be like God who floats, alone and unique, on himself, with no shipwreck possible because he is at once the swimmer and the sea in which he swims. If there were two Gods, they would confront each other. This conception of the real has been superseded by my generation and, within my generation, very concretely and vigorously by myself.

No, life is not my mind, my ideas, being all that exists; it is the very contrary. From the time of Descartes Western man had been left without a world. But *to live* means having to be outside of myself, in the absolute "outside" that is the circumstance or world; it is having, like it or not, constantly and incessantly to face and clash with whatever makes up that world: minerals, plants, animals, other men. There is no getting out of it. I have to tackle all that. Willy-nilly I have to come to some kind of terms with all that. But this—finding myself amid all that and having to come or fail to come to terms with all that— this finally happens to me alone and I have to do it alone without any possibility that *on the decisive plane*—note that I say "on the decisive plane"—anyone can lend me a hand.

This means that we are a long way from Descartes, from Kant, and their Romantic successors—Schelling, Hegel, from what Carlyle called "transcendental moonshine." But, needless to say, we are even farther from Aristotle.

We are, then, far from Descartes, from Kant. We are even farther from Aristotle and St. Thomas. Is it perhaps our duty and our destiny—not only those of us who are philosophers but all of us—to keep going farther and still farther? I shall not answer that question now. I shall not even tell you from *what* we must, willy-nilly, get far-

ther and farther. Let that large question mark stand here,
for everyone to do as he pleases with—use it as a lasso
to catch the future, or just hang himself with it.

The radical solitude of human life, the being of man,
does not, then, consist in there really being nothing except himself. Quite the contrary—there is nothing less
than the universe, with all that it contains. There is, then,
an infinity of things but—there it is!—amid them Man in
his radical reality is alone—alone *with* them. And since
among these things there are other human beings, he is
*alone with* them too. If but one unique being existed, it
could not properly be said to be alone. Uniqueness has
nothing to do with solitude. If we were reflecting on
the Portuguese *"saudade"*—*saudade*, of course, is the
Galician-Portuguese form of *"solitudinem,"* "solitude"—
we should say more about solitude and we should see
that solitude is always *solitude from* someone; that is, it
is a being left *alone* and a lacking. And this is so true
that the word by which the Greeks expressed "mine" and
"solitary"—*monos*—comes from *mone*, which means "to
remain"—understanding "to *remain without*"—without
others. Whether because they have died, whether because they have gone away, in any case because they have
left us—have left us . . . alone. Or alternatively, because
we leave them, flee from them and go to the desert and
into retirement to lead the life of *mone*. Whence *mona-
chos*, *monastery*, and *monk*. And in Latin *solus*, as Meillet
(whose extreme strictness in phonetics and whose lack of
talent in semantics obliges me to weigh my spontaneous
etymological findings against his observations) is inclined
to think—*solus* comes from *sed-lus*, that is from the one
who remains sitting when the rest have gone away. Our
Lady of Solitude is the Virgin who remains *solitary* of
Jesus, who has been killed; and the sermon preached in
Holy Week and called the "Sermon on Solitude" medi-

tates on the most sorrowful of Christ's words: *Eli, eli—lamma sabachthani*—"My God, my God, why hast thou forsaken me? Why hast thou left me solitary of thee?" This is the expression that most profoundly declares God's will to become man—to accept what is most radically human in man, his radical solitude.

And this is the moment to mention Leibniz. I need not say that I shall not spend even a moment expounding his doctrine. I shall confine myself to remarking for those who know Leibniz well that the best translation of his most important term—*monad*—is not unit nor yet unicity. Monads have no windows. They are shut up in themselves—this is idealism. But in its ultimate sense, Leibniz's conception of the monad would be best expressed by calling the monads "solitudes." In Homer too a centurion thrusts a lance into Aphrodite's body, and the delicious blood of Olympian woman gushes out, and she goes running to her father Zeus, whimpering like any pampered girl. No, no—Christ was man above all and before all because God left him alone, solitary—*sabachthani*.

In proportion as we take possession of life and come to know it, we observe that when we came to it, everyone else had gone away and that we have to live our radical living . . . alone, and that only in our solitude are we our truth.

From this substrate of radical solitude that is irremediably our life, we constantly emerge with a no less radical longing for companionship. Could we but find one whose life would wholly fuse with, would interpenetrate ours! We make all sorts of attempts to attain this. One of them is friendship. But the greatest of them all is what we call love. Genuine love is nothing but the attempt to exchange two solitudes.

Belonging to and forming an essential part of the solitude that we are, are all the things and beings in the universe which are there about us, forming our environment, articulating our circumstance; but which never fuse with the "each" that one is, which on the contrary are always *the other*, the absolutely other—a strange and always more or less disturbing, negative, and hostile and at best unconcurring element, which for that reason we are aware of as what is alien to and outside [*fuera*] of us, as foreign [*forastero*]—because it oppresses, compresses, and represses us: the world.

We see, then, that in the face of any idealistic and solipsistic philosophy, our life poses these two terms with identical value as reality: the somebody, the X, the Man who lives; and the world, environment, or circumstance in which, like it or not, he has to live.

It is in this world, environment, or circumstance that we must look for a reality that in all strictness, in contradistinction to all others, we can and should call "social."

Man, then, finding himself alive, finds himself having to come to terms with what we have called environment, circumstance, or world. Whether these three words will gradually take on separate meanings for us is something that does not concern us now. At this moment, they mean the same thing to us, namely the foreign, alien element "outside of himself," in which man has to work at being. That world is a great thing, an immense thing, with shadowy frontiers and full to bursting with smaller things, with what we call "things" and commonly distinguish in a broad and rough classification, saying that in the world there are minerals, plants, animals, and men. What these things are is the concern of the various sciences—for example, biology treats of plants and animals. But biology, like any other science, is a particular activity with which certain men concern themselves *in* their lives, that is, after they are already living. Biology and any other science, then, supposes that before its operations begin all these things are already within our view, exist for us. And this fact that things *are* for us, originally and primarily in our human life, before we are physicists, mineralogists, biologists, and so on, represents what these things are in their radical reality. What the sciences afterwards tell us about them may be as plausible, as convincing, as true as you please, but it remains clear that they have drawn all of it, by complicated intellectual methods, from what in the beginning, primordially and with no further ado, things were to us in our living. The Earth may be a planet in a certain solar system belonging to a certain galaxy or nebula, and may be made of atoms, each one of which in its turn contains a multiplicity of things, of quasi-things or guess-what things called electrons, protons, mesons, neutrons, and so on. But none of this knowledge would exist if the earth did not exist before it as a component of our life, as something with which we have to come to terms and hence something that is of import to us, matters to us —that matters to us because it confronts us with certain difficulties and provides us with certain facilities. This means that on this pre-existent and radical plane from which the sciences set out and which they assume, the Earth is none of these things that physics and astronomy tell us it is, but is what firmly holds me up, is terra firma, in contradistinction to the sea, in which I sink (the word *terra*, according to Bréal, comes from *tersa*, "dry"), it is what I sometimes have laboriously to climb, because it inclines upward, sometimes easily descend because it inclines downward, it is what parts and separates me from the woman I love or forces me to live close to someone whom I loathe, it is what makes some things far from me and others near me, some *here* and others *there* and others *yonder*, and so on and so on. These and many similar attributes are the genuine reality of the earth, just as it appears to me in the radical ambit of my life. Please observe that all these attributes—supporting me, making me go up or down hill, making me tire myself in crossing it to where what I need happens to be, separating me from those I love, and so on—all refer to me; so that the Earth in its primordial appearance consists entirely in utilitarian references in respect to me. You will find the same if you take any other example—tree, animal, ocean, river. If we leave out of consideration what they are in reference to us, I mean, their *being for* some use of ours—as means, instruments or, vice versa, as impediments and difficulties for our ends—they are left being nothing. Or, to put it differently: everything that composes, fills, and makes up the world in which man finds himself at birth possesses no independent condition *of itself,* possesses no being of its own, *is nothing in itself*—but is simply something *for* or *something against* our ends. We ought not to have called them "things," then, in view of the meaning that the word bears for us today. A "thing" means something that has its own being, independently of me, independently of what it *is for* man. If this is the case with every-thing in the circumstance or world, it means that the world in its radical reality is a body of somethings with which I, man, can or must do this or that—that it is a body of means and impediments, facilities and difficulties which, in order to live in any real sense, I encounter. Things are not originally "things," but something that I try to use or avoid in order to live and to live as well as possible; are, therefore, that with which I occupy myself and by which I am occupied, with which I act and oper-ate, with which I succeed or fail to do what I want to do; in short, they are concerns to which I am constantly attending. And since "to do" and "to occupy oneself," "to have concerns" is expressed in Greek by "practice," *praxis*—things are radically *pragmata* and my relation to them is *pragmatic*. Unfortunately, at least so far as I am aware, our language does not have a word that adequately expresses what the word *pragma* does. We can only say that a thing, as *pragma*, is not something that exists by itself and has nothing to do with me. In the world or circumstance of each one of us there is nothing that has nothing to do with us and in turn we have to do with whatever forms part of this same circumstance or world. This is composed exclusively of references to me, and I am remanded to whatever it contains, I depend on it, for better or for worse; everything is favorable or adverse to me, caress or friction, flattery or injury, service or harm. A thing as *pragma*, then, is something that I manipulate for a particular end, that I deal with or avoid, that I must count upon or discount; it is an instrument or an impediment *for:* a task, a chattel, a gadget, a deficiency, a failure, an obstacle; in short, it is a concern to be attended to, something that to a greater or less degree is of import for me, that I lack, that I have too much of, hence an *importance*. I hope, now that I have accumulated all these various expressions, that the difference will begin to be clear if you contrast in your minds the idea of a world of things and the idea of a world of concerns or importances. In a world of things we play no part: it and everything in it is *of itself*. But in a world of concerns or importances, everything consists solely in its reference to us, everything plays a part in us, that is, everything is of import to us and *is* only to the extent to which and in the way in which it concerns, is of import to, and affects us.

Such is the radical truth concerning what the world is—because it expresses the world's "consistency" or that in which it originally consists as element in which we have to live our life. Everything else that the sciences tell us about this world is and was at best a secondary, derivative, hypothetical, and questionable truth—for the simple reason, I repeat, that we begin to practice science after we are already living in the world and hence when for us the world is already this that it is. Science is only one of the countless activities, actions, operations that man *practices* * in his life.

Man *practices* science as he *practices* patience, as he *attends to* his affairs [*hacienda*], as he *practices* poetry, politics, business, *makes* journeys, *makes* love, *makes believe*, *marks* time, and above all, man *conjures up* illusions.

All these locutions represent the most ordinary, familiar, colloquial kind of speech. Yet now we see that they are technical terms in a theory of human life. To the shame of philosophers it must be said that they have never seen the radical phenomenon that is our life. They have always turned their backs on it, and it has been the poets and novelists, but above all the "ordinary man," who has been aware of it with its modes and situations. Hence this series of terms represents a series of titles announcing great philosophical themes on which much would need to be said. Think of the profound problem expressed in the locution "mark time" [*hacer tiempo*]—nothing less than waiting, expectation, and hope. What is hope in man? Can man live without it? Some years ago Paul Morand sent me a copy of his biography of Maupassant, with a dedication that read: "I send you this life of a man 'qui n'espérait pas,' who did not hope." Was Morand right? Can there be such a thing—literally and formally—as human living that is not hoping? Is not the primary and most essential function of life expectation, and its most

* [This and all the italicized verbs in the following passage are expressed in Spanish by the verb *hacer*, "to do, to make." They thus echo and carry on the idea that "we have something to *do* or have to be *doing* something *always;* for this life that is given us is not given us ready-made, but instead every one of us has to *make* it for himself, each his own" (p. 43, above).—*Translator*.]

visceral organ hope? As you see, the subject is immense.

And what of that other mode of life in which man *makes believe, pretends*—is it any less interesting? What is this strange, ungenuine *doing* to which man sometimes devotes himself precisely for the purpose of really *not doing* even what he is *doing*—the writer who is not a writer but who *pretends* he is a writer, the woman who is scarcely feminine but who *pretends* she is a woman, *pretends* to smile, *pretends* disdain, *pretends* desire, *pretends* love, incapable of really *doing* any of these things?

# 3

# Structure of "Our" World

WE find ourselves committed to the difficult task of discovering with unimpeachable clarity, that is, with veritable evidence, what things, facts, phenomena among all those that exist are entitled by their difference from all others to be termed "social." The question concerns us above all because we urgently need to be clear as to what society and its modes are. Like every strictly theoretical problem, this is at the same time an appallingly practical problem, one in which we are up to our necks today and indeed—why not say it?—drowning. We take it up not out of mere curiosity, as we take up an illustrated magazine, or as, forgetting our manners, we look through a crack in a door to see what is happening on the other side, or as the scholar, who is so often blind to real problems, goes through bundles of documents simply from an itch to pry and probe into the details of a life or event. No: in this present task of discovering what society is, the lives of all of us are at stake; hence it is the most genuine possible problem, hence society, to use our former terminology, is of tremendous "importance" to us. And my saying that our lives are at stake is not a figure of speech, sheer or bad rhetoric. Every one of us *l'a échappé belle*, has had the narrowest of escapes. In sober truth, the vast majority of men today, ourselves included, can and should most definitely regard themselves as "survivors," because during these last years all of us have been at the point of death—"for social reasons." In the atrocious events of these years, which are by no means over and done with today, what has chiefly acted as their decisive cause has been the confusion under which our contemporaries labor in regard to the idea of Society.

To carry out our intention with the utmost strictness we have made our way back to the plane of radical reality (radical because in it all other realities must appear, dawn, bud, arise, exist)—that is, human life. We said of it, in sum:

(1) That human life in the proper and original sense is each individual's life seen from itself, hence that it is always *mine*—that it is personal.

(2) That it consists in man's finding himself, without knowing how or why, obliged, on pain of succumbing, always to be doing something in a particular circumstance —which we shall call the circumstantiality of life, or the fact that man's life is lived in view of circumstances.

(3) That circumstance always offers us different possibilities for acting, hence for being. This obliges us, like it or not, to exercise our freedom. We are forced to be free. Because of this, life is a permanent crossroads and constant perplexity. At every instant we have to choose whether in the next instant or at some other future time we shall be he who does this or he who does that. Hence each of us is incessantly choosing his "doing," hence his being.

(4) Life is untransferable. No one can take my place in the task of deciding what I am to do, and this includes what I am to suffer, for I have to accept the suffering that comes to me from without. My life, then, is constant and inescapable responsibility to myself. What I do —hence, what I think, feel, want—must *make sense,* and *good sense,* to me.

If we put together these attributes, which are those that are of most interest for our theme, we find that life is always personal, circumstantial, untransferable, and responsible. And now please take careful note of this: if later we come upon a life, whether in ourselves or in others, that does not possess these attributes, this will without any doubt or extenuation mean that it is not human life in the proper and original sense—that is, life as radical reality; it will be life, and, if you please, human life, in another sense, it will be another kind of reality, different from the former, and in addition secondary, derivative, more or less dubious. It would be amusing if in our search we should come upon forms of life that, since they are ours, we should have to call human but that, because they lacked these attributes, we should have also and at the same time to call non-human or in-human. At the moment we do not really understand what this possibility may mean, but I speak of it now so that we may be on the alert.

But for the present let us make firm our knowledge that the properly human in me is only what I think, want, feel, and perform with my body, I being the *creating subject of all this*, that is, of what happens to me as *myself;* hence, my thinking is human only if I think something on my own account, being aware of what it means. *Only that is human in doing which I do because it makes sense to me, that is, which I understand.* In every human action, then, there is a *subject* from whom it emanates and who is thereby its agent, author, or *responsible* for it. A consequence of this is that my human life, which puts me in direct relation with everything about me—minerals, plants, animals, other men—is, essentially, *solitude, aloneness.* My toothache, I said, can pain me *alone.* The thought that I truly think and do not just repeat mechanically because I have heard it, I am obliged to think for myself *alone* or in my solitude. Two and two truly make four— that is, evidently, intelligibly—only when I retire *alone* for a moment and think it.

If we are to study elemental phenomena for a beginning, we should begin with the most elemental of the elemental. Now, the elemental in a reality is what serves as the base for all the rest of it—its simplest component, and, in addition to being simple and basic, the one that we most often do not see, its most hidden, arcane, subtle, or abstract component. We are not accustomed to contemplating it and so we find it difficult to recognize it when someone else expounds it to us and tries to make us see it. In the same way, confronted with a good tapestry we do not see the threads, precisely because the tapestry is made up of them, because they are its elements or components. What we are accustomed to is things, but not the ingredients of which they are made up. To see the ingredients we have to stop seeing their combination, which is the thing—just as, to see the pores in the stones of which a cathedral is built, we have to stop seeing the cathedral. In practical daily life, what concerns us is manipulating already finished and compounded things; hence it is their shape that is familiar to us, that we know and understand. Inversely, to become aware of their elements or components we have to go counter to our mental habits and in imagination, that is, intellectually, break things down, cut up the world so that we can see what is inside it, its ingredients.

Given human life, we are *ipso facto* given two terms or factors that are equally primary and, furthermore, inseparable: Man living, and the circumstance or world in which Man lives. For philosophical idealism since Descartes, only Man is radical or primary reality, and even so it is Man reduced to *une chose qui pense, res cogitans*, thought or ideas. The world has no reality of its own, it is only an ideated world. For Aristotle, on the contrary, originally only things and their combination in the world possess reality. Man is simply a thing among things, a piece of the world. Only secondarily, because he possesses reason, does Man have a special and pre-eminent role: to reason on all other things and the world, to think what they are, to make the Truth about the world shine in the world by virtue of the word that speaks, that declares or reveals, the truth of things. But Aristotle does not tell us why man possesses reason and speech—*logos* means both—nor does he tell us why the world, in addition to things, contains that other extraordinary thing, the Truth. For him the existence of this reason is simply a fact of the world like any other, like the giraffe's long neck, volcanic eruptions, and the bestiality of beasts. In this decisive sense I say that for Aristotle, Man, reason and all, is neither more nor less than a thing, and hence that for Aristotle there is no other radical reality than things or *being*. If the others were idealists, Aristotle and his disciples are realists. But to us it appears that since, although he is said to possess reason, to be a rational animal, the Aristotelian man, even when he is a philosopher, does not explain *why* he possesses reason, why there is in the universe someone who possesses reason—it follows that he does not give any reason for this enormous accident, whence it follows again that he is without reason. It is obvious that an intelligent being who does not understand why he is intelligent, is not intelligent; his intelligence is only presumptive. To take one's stand beyond—or, if you prefer to put it the other way round, on the hither side, ahead of— Descartes and Aristotle is not to abandon them or to disdain their authority. It is the very reverse: only he who has absorbed them both and has them both within him can escape from them. But this escape does not signify any superiority in respect to their personal genius.

By setting out from human life as radical reality, then, we take a leap beyond the millennial controversy between idealists and realists, and find that two things are equally real, equally primary in life—Man and World. The World is the net of concerns or importances in which Man is willy-nilly entangled, and Man is the being who willy-nilly finds himself fated to swim in this sea of concerns and irremediably obliged to find all this important. The reason is that life is of import to itself, matters to itself—nay, more, it finally consists in nothing but mattering to itself, and in this sense we should say, with all terminological formality, that "life is what matters." Hence the world in which it has to run its course, to be, consists in a system of importances, concerns, or *pragmata*. The world or circumstance, we said, is thus an immense pragmatic or practical reality—not a reality made up of things. "Things" in present-day parlance means anything that has its being by and in itself, hence that is independent of us. But the components of the vital world are only those that are for and in my life—not for themselves and in themselves. They *are* only as facilities and difficulties, advantages and disadvantages whereby the I that each one of us is can succeed in being. They are, then, in effect, instruments, utensils, chattels, means that serve me—their being is a being for my ends, aspirations, needs; or else they prove to be obstacles, lacks, impediments, limitations, privations, stumbling-blocks, obstructions, reefs, quagmires. And for reasons that we shall see later, being "things" *sensu stricto* is something that comes afterwards, something secondary and in any case highly questionable. But since our language has no word that adequately expresses what things are for us in our life, I shall continue using the term "things" so that we may understand one another with the fewest possible lexicological innovations.

We have now to investigate the structure and contents of this environment, circumstance, or world in which we have to live. We said that it is composed of things as *pragmata*, that is, that in it we find ourselves with things.

But this finding ourselves with things, encountering them, in itself requires certain investigations, and we shall now proceed to anatomize it rapidly, but step by step.

(1) And the first thing that needs to be said seems to me to be this: if the world is composed of things, these will have to be given me one by one. For example, one thing is an apple. Let us suppose that it is the apple of Paradise rather than the apple of discord. But in this scene in Paradise, we at once discover a curious problem: is the apple that Eve gives to Adam the same apple that Adam sees, finds, and receives? For when Eve offers it, all that is present, visible, patent, is half an apple; and what Adam finds, sees, and receives is likewise only half an apple. What is seen, what is strictly speaking present from Eve's point of view is something different from what is seen and present from Adam's. For every corporeal body has two faces, and as is the case with the moon's two faces, only one of them is present to us. Here, to our surprise, we become aware of something that, once we have observed it, is a great truism—namely, that so far as seeing goes, what is strictly called *seeing*, no one has ever seen what he calls an apple, because an apple according to all accounts has two faces, but only one of them is ever present. Furthermore, if there are two beings seeing it, neither of them sees the same face of it, but another and more or less different one.

Of course I can walk around the apple or turn it in my hand. In such a movement, aspects—that is, different faces —of the apple are presented to me, each continuous with the one before. When I am seeing, really seeing, the second face, I remember the one I saw before and add it to the one I am seeing now. But of course this adding of the remembered to the actually seen does not enable me to see all the sides of the apple at once. The apple, then, as a total unit, hence as what I mean when I say "apple," is never present to me, hence does not *exist for me* with radical evidence, but only and at most with an evidence of the second order—the evidence supplied by mere memory, in which we preserve our earlier experiences concerning a thing. Hence to the actual presence of what is only part of a thing we automatically add the rest of it; this "rest," then, we will say is not presented but is *compresented* or compresent. You will see that this idea of the com-present, of the compresence attached to any presence of any thing —an idea that we owe to the great Edmund Husserl— will cast much light for us on the way in which the things of the world appear in our life and on the world in which things are.

(2) The second point to be noted is this:

At this moment we find ourselves in this hall, which is a thing in whose interior we are. It is an interior for two reasons: because it surrounds or envelops us on all sides, and because its form is closed, that is, continuous. Its surface is present to us without interruption, so that we see nothing else; it has neither holes nor openings, breaks, gaps, or fissures that allow us to see other things that are not itself or the objects inside it, chairs, walls, lights, and so on. But let us imagine that when we leave this building here, when my lecture is over, we should find that there was nothing beyond, that is, outside; that the rest of the world was not around it, that its doors gave not on the street, the city, the Universe, but on Nothing. Such a discovery would shock us with surprise and terror. How is this shock to be explained? How—if, all of us being here, only this hall was present to us and (supposing I did not make the observation that I just made) none of us was thinking of whether or not there was a world outside these doors—that is, whether, in the absolute sense, a "without" existed? There can be no doubt about the explanation. Adam too would have suffered a shock of surprise, although a slighter one, if it had turned out that what Eve gave him was only half an apple, the half that he could see, but lacking the other compresent half. For while this hall is present to us *sensu stricto*, the rest of the world outside it is compresent to us; and as in the case of the apple, this compresence of what is not patent but an accumulated experience tells us that even though it is not in sight, it exists, it *is there*, and we can and must reckon with its possible presence—it is a knowledge that has become habitual for us, that we carry within us habitualized. Now, what acts in us through acquired habit we do not especially notice, we have no particular, present consciousness of it, just because it *is* habit. In addition to the pair of notions *present* and *compresent* we must also distinguish another pair: what exists for us now in a definite, deliberate act; and what exists for us habitually, is constantly in existence for us, but in this veiled, unapparent, and as it were, dormant form of habituality. So be so good as to fix this second pair in your memories: actuality and habituality. The present exists for us in actuality; the compresent in habituality.

And this leads us to a first law concerning the structure of our environment, circumstance, or world: namely, that the vital world is composed of a few things that are present at the moment and countless things that are latent, hidden at the moment, that are not in sight, but we know or believe we know—in this case it makes no difference which—that we could see them, that we could have them present to us. Note, then, that I am now calling latent only that which at each instant I do not see but of which I know that I have seen it before or could, in principle, see it later. From the balconies of Madrid we see the expressive, graceful notched profile of our Guadarrama range, it is present to us. But we know, from having heard it or read it in trustworthy books, that there is also a

Himalayan range, which merely with a little effort and a good supply of checks in our pockets we can *half* see; whereas, so long as we do not make the effort and—as usual—do not have the supply of checks at our command, the Himalayas are there latent for us, but forming a real part of our world in this peculiar form of *potentiality*.

To this first structural law of our world—which consists, I repeat, in the observation that at any moment our world is composed of a few present things and a great many latent ones—we will now add a second law, which is no less evident: namely, that a thing is never present to us by itself but, on the contrary, we always see a thing standing out against other things to which we pay no attention and which form a ground against which what we do see stands out. Here it is clear why I call these laws structural laws: they define for us not the things that are in our world but the structure of our world; to speak strictly, they describe its anatomy. Thus this second law tells us: The world in which we have to live always has two distances and organs—the thing or things that we see attentively, and a ground against which they stand out. For you will observe that the world always holds out one of its parts or things to us as a promontory of reality, leaving, as an unheeded ground to the thing or things to which we are attending, a second distance that functions as the ambit *in which* the thing appears to us. This ground, this second distance, this ambit is what we call "*horizon*." Every thing that we notice, to which we pay attention, which we look at and concern ourselves with, has a horizon from which and within which it appears to us. I am now referring only to what is visible and present. The horizon too is something that we see, that is *there for us*, patent, but it almost always exists for us and we see it as something not attended to because our attention is held by this, that, or the other thing which at any instant in

our life is playing the role of protagonist. *Beyond* the
horizon is the part of the world that is not now *present* to
us, the part of it that is *latent* for us.

This somewhat further complicates the structure of
the world for us, because now we have three planes or
distances in it: as foreground the *thing* that is occupying
us, as middle distance the *horizon* of vision, in which the
thing appears, and as far distance the *now latent beyond*.

Let us look more closely at the schema of this most
elementary anatomical structure of the World. As you
see, we are beginning to observe a difference in the meanings of "environment" and of "world," which we have
so far been using as synonyms. "Environment" is the part
of the world that at every moment comprises my horizon
of vision and that, therefore is present to me. Of course,
as we know from our first observation, present things
present only their faces, not their backs, which remain
only compresented; we see only their obverse and not
their reverse. Environment [*contorno*], then, is the patent
or semipatent world *around* us [*en torno*]. But in addition to this, beyond our horizon and our environment the
world at any particular moment contains a latent immensity made up of pure compresences; an immensity that,
in each situation of ours, is a hidden, eclipsed immensity,
concealed by our environment and enveloping it. But I
repeat once again, this world that is latent *per accidens*,
as they say in the seminaries, is not mysterious or arcane
or incapable of being present, but is made up of things
that we have seen or can see but that at any actual moment are hidden, concealed from us by our environment.
Yet in this state of latency and eclipse, they act on our
life as habituality, just as, without our being aware of it,
the "without" of this hall is acting on us now. The horizon is the dividing line between the part of the world that
is patent and the part of it that is latent.

To expedite matters and make the subject easier, I have throughout this exposition referred only to the visible presence of things, because vision and the visible are the clearest form of presence. Hence it is that, from the days of the Greeks, almost all terms pertaining to knowledge and its factors and objects are taken from ordinary words referring to seeing and looking. "Idea" in Greek is the view that a thing presents, its aspect—which in Latin comes in turn from *spec-*, to see, to look. Hence "spectator," he who contemplates; hence "inspector"; hence "respect," that is, the side of a thing that is viewed and considered; "circumspection," the attitude of the wary man who looks all around, not even trusting his own shadow, and so on.

But my having chosen to refer only to visible presence does not mean that it is the only kind of presence; very different characters are no less present to us. Once again I repeat that when I say things are present to us, I say something that is scientifically incorrect, I am speaking loosely. It is a philosophical sin that I commit with great pleasure in order to facilitate entrance into this radical way of thinking about the basic and primordial reality that is our life. But I ask you to note that the expression is inaccurate. What is really present to us is not things; it is colors and the figures that colors form; resistances to our hands and limbs, greater or less, of one sort or another, that is, hard and soft, the hardness of the solid, the yielding resistance of the liquid or fluid, of water, the air; odors pleasant or unpleasant: ethereal, aromatic, delightful, stinking, balsamic, musky, pungent, fetid, repellent; sounds that are murmurs, noises, hummings, hisses, squeaks, buzzes, bangs, crashes, thunderings—and so on through eleven classes of presences that we call "sense objects," for it should be noted that Man does not have only five senses, as tradition avers, but at least eleven, which the psychologists have taught us to differentiate very clearly.

But to call them "sense objects" is to replace the direct names of the patent things that *prima facie* constitute our surroundings by other names that do not designate them directly but that purport to indicate the mechanism through which we notice or perceive them. Instead of saying things that are colors and figures, sounds, odors, and so on, we say "sense objects," sensible things that are visible, tangible, audible, and so on. Now—and this is to be remembered—that colors and shapes, sounds, and so on, exist for us *because* we possess bodily organs that perform the psycho-physiological function of causing us to sense them, of producing the sensations of them in us—be it as plausible, as probable as you please, it is still only a hypothesis, an attempt on our part to explain this marvelous presence to us of our environment. What is unquestionable is that these things *are there*, surround us, envelop us, and that we have to exist among them, with them, despite them. We here have, then, two truths, both primary and basic, but very different in quality or order. That chromatic things and their forms, that sounds, resistances, hard and soft, rough and smooth, *are there*—is an unquestionable truth. That all this is there *because* we possess sense organs and these are what physiology—using a term worthy of Molière's doctor—calls "specific energies," is a probable, but only a probable, truth, that is, a hypothesis.

But this is not what now concerns us; rather it is to point out that the existence of these so-called sensible things is not the primary and unquestionable truth to be stated about our environment; it does not declare the primary character that all these things present to us, or, to express it differently, that these things *are to us*. For by calling them "things" and saying that they *are there* around us, we imply that they have nothing to do with us, that in themselves and primarily they are independent of us, and that if we did not exist they would remain the same. Now, this is more or less a supposition. The primary and unquestionable truth is this: All these figures of color, of chiaroscuro, of noise and sound, of hardness and softness, are all this in reference to us and *for* us, in active form. What do I mean by that? What is this action on us in which they primarily consist? Quite simply, in being indications, *signals*, for our conduct of our life, in informing us that something with certain favorable or adverse qualities that we must take into account is there, or, vice versa, that it is not there, that it is lacking.

The blue sky does not begin by being up there so high and quiet and blue, so impassive and indifferent to us; it begins originally by acting on us as a very extensive repertory of signals that are useful for our life; its function, its action, which makes us heed it and therefore see it, is its active role as a semaphore. It makes signals to us. To begin with, the blue sky signals fair weather to us; then too, it is our first diurnal clock, with its traveling sun that, like a laborious and faithful employee of the city, like a municipal service (if, for once, a gratuitous one), daily makes its journey from East to West; and by night the constellations signal the seasons of the year and the millennia to us—the Egyptian calendar was based on the millennial changes of Sirius; and in short, it tells us the time. But its telling, signaling, warning, suggesting activity does not stop here. It was not some superstitious primitive, but Kant himself, and not very long since as these things go, who in 1788 summed up all his proud knowledge by saying: "There are two things that flood the soul with ever-new amazement and veneration which only increase the oftener and the more persistently we meditate on them: the starry sky above me and the moral law within me."

That is, in addition to the sky's signaling all these useful changes to us—these useful but trivial changes of weather,

hours, days, years, millennia—apparently its moving noc-
turnal presence, with the stars trembling in some impenetrable agitation, signals to us the gigantic existence of the
Universe, of its laws, of its profundities, and the absent
presence of someone, of some all-powerful Being who
calculated it, created it, ordered it, adorned it. There is
no question that Kant's phrase is not simply a phrase but
that it beautifully describes an essential phenomenon of
human life: in the dark of a clear night the star-filled sky
winks at us with countless eyes, seems to want to tell us
something. We understand what Heine is suggesting when
he says that the stars are golden thoughts in the mind of
night. Their winking too, minute in each separate star
and immense in the entire vault, is a permanent stimulus
for us to transcend the world that is our environment and
find the radical Universe.

# 4

# The "Other Man" Appears

---

IT has been necessary for me to show you that the "some-things" that are present in the vital world and that go to make up the positive and negative concerns and importances with which we have to deal were pure sensible presences and compresences—colors, shapes, sounds, odors, resistances, and so on—and that their presence acts on us in the form of signals, indications, symptoms. To do this, I chose the example of the sky. But this example of the sky belongs particularly to visibility. And if it is true that the visible and the act of seeing afford greater clarity as examples in a first approach to our doctrine, it would be a grave mistake to suppose that sight is the most important "sense." Even from the psycho-physiological point of view, which is ancillary, it seems more and more probable that touch was the original sense from which the others were gradually differentiated. From our more radical point of view it is clear that the decisive form of our intercourse with things is in fact touch. And if this is so, touch and contact are necessarily the most conclusive factor in determining the structure of our world.

Now as I said, touch differs from all the other senses or modes of presence by the fact that in it two things are always present at once and inseparably: the body that we touch, and our body with which we touch it. The relation, then, is not between a phantom and ourselves, as in pure vision, but between a foreign body and our own body. Hardness is a presence in which all at once something that resists and our body become present to each other; for example, our hand, which is resisted. In it, then, we simultaneously feel the object pressing on us and our compressed muscle. Hence it would be right to say that in contact we feel things inside us, that is, inside our bodies, and not, as in sight and hearing, outside us, or as in tasting and smelling we feel them in certain parts of our corporeal surface—the nasal cavity and the palate. To realize this is instantly to take a great step forward: we learn that our environment, the world, is composed, above all and fundamentally, of presences, of things that are bodies. And they are so because they come into contact with the closest of all things to man, to the I that is each of us, namely, his body. Our body brings it about that all other bodies are bodies and that the world is a body. For what is called a "pure spirit," bodies would not exist, because it could not come into contact with them, feel their pressures, and vice versa. It could not manipulate things, move them, shape them, pulverize them. The "pure spirit," then, cannot possess human life. It would move through the world as a phantom. You will remember Wells's story in which he tells of beings that have only two dimensions and hence cannot enter our world, in which everything has at least three dimensions—a world, then, that is made up of bodies. The two-dimensional beings witness the spectacle of human life, they see, for example, a criminal making ready to murder a sleeping old woman, but they cannot interfere, they cannot warn her, and they suffer and are afflicted because their being is phantasmal.

Man is, then, first of all, someone who is in a body and who in this sense—but please note, only in this sense—*is* only his body. And this simple but irremediable fact will determine the concrete structure of our world and, with it, of our life and destiny. Man finds himself shut up in his body for life. The Pythagoreans were quite right to play on words in this connection—to pun not in order to raise a smile, but gravely, sadly, dramatically, in melancholy. Since the Greek for "body" is *soma* and for "tomb" is *sema*, they said, over and over again, *soma sema*—body-tomb, body-prison.

The body in which I live infused, shut up, inexorably makes me a spatial person. It puts me in a place and excludes me from all other places. It does not allow me to be ubiquitous. At every moment it fixes me to one spot like a nail and exiles me from everything else. Everything else, the other things in the world, are in other places, and I can only see them, hear them, and sometimes touch them from where I am. Where I am, we call *here*—and the Spanish word itself, *aquí*, with its acute accent and its lightning drop, in only two syllables, from the extreme breadth of the *a* to the extreme sharpness of the *i*, with its vertical accentuation, marvellously expresses the hammer stroke of destiny that nails me—*here*.

But this automatically entails something new and determinative for the structure of the world. I can change my place, but whatever place it may be, it will be my "here." Apparently *here* and *I, I* and *here*, are inseparable for life. And since the world, with all the things in it, must *be for me* from "*here*," it automatically becomes a perspective—that is, its things are near to or far from *here*, to right or left of *here*, above or below *here*. This is the third structural law of man's world. Do not forget that what I call man is simply "each one of us," hence that we are talking about the world of and for each one of us —not about the objective world of which physics tells us. What a physical world is, we do not know, nor even what is an objective world, hence a world that is not only the world of each but the world common to all. This third structural law is not without significance. At least, this sudden appearance on our horizon of the "near" and the "far" is no small matter. Because "near" and "far" signify distances, the close and the remote arise, and perhaps what is close to me I hate, and what is remote is the woman I love. But in addition, this distance, which is remoteness, is not geometrical nor is it the distance of physical science; it is a distance that, if I need or want to overcome it, I have—and, above all, primitive man had —to travel over it, at a great expenditure of his strength and time. Today overcoming distances does not mean expending these two things; instead, we expend money, obtaining which entails an expenditure of time and effort —expenditures that are measured in "work-hours."

We shall see that the Other Man also has his *here*—but this here of the Other is not mine. Our "heres" are mutually exclusive, they are not interpenetrable, they are different; with the result that the perspective in which the world appears to him is always different from mine. Hence our worlds do not adequately coincide. For the present, I am in mine and he in his. And this is a fresh reason for radical solitude. Not only am I outside of the other man, but my world is outside of his: we are, mutually, two "outsides" [*fueras*], and hence radically strangers [*forasteros*].

"Far" means what is at a considerable distance from my *here*. What is "far" is *yonder*. Between the "here" and the farness of the "yonder" there is a third term—*there*— that is, what is not here in me but is close by [*próximo*]. May the "there" be where we find . . . our neighbor [*prójimo*]? The *here*, demonstrative adverb of place, derives linguistically from a personal pronoun.

Man's being a body entails, then, not only that all things are bodies, but also that all things in the world are situated in relation to me. All things, even those that are not corporeal! Because if there are such things—though so far in our analysis we have not come upon them—they will, we shall see, be obliged to manifest themselves by means of bodies. Homer's images are not corporeal and would not exist, would not be, for us if they had not been written on certain pieces of parchment. From the fact that things are directly or indirectly bodies and are situated in relation to me, near or far, to right or left, above or below in respect to *here*—in respect to the *here* that is the *locus*, the place of my body—it follows that they are distributed and each one is situated in, exists in, or belongs to a region of the world. Things, then, are grouped in spatial regions, belong to this side or that side of my world. There are things, objects, or human beings, for example, that belong to the side of my world that I call the North, and others that belong to the side that I call the East. This ascription to a particular region, this localization of the constituent things of man, is such that even Christianity is obliged to situate God, must, so to speak, domicile Him in a place in space, and therefore qualifies God by attributing to Him, as something essential to Him, something that defines and fixes Him, a place where He normally is, when it prays daily: "Our Father who art in heaven." There are many fathers, but God is distinguished by being the father who lives on high, in the region of the fixed stars or firmament. And, conversely, it domiciles the Devil at the other extreme, in the lowermost, the most *infer-ior* region, namely, *Inferno*. The Devil thus proves to be the opposite to God. The primitive Greeks, too, put quite a number of things and beings in the lower or infernal region. But for them this lower region meant merely being the base or pedestal of the world, on which everything else rests for support. This basal region they called Tartarus. To be sure, since—as they could hardly help doing, even with their primitive mentality—they wondered how Tartarus in its turn was supported, they imagined that an animal with a very broad and tough carapace held it up. This animal was the turtle [*tortuga*] which in Italian and Portuguese still keeps its Greek name in less corrupted form—*tartaruga*. Our Spanish *tortuga* is in fact nothing but the Greek word *tartarougos*—he who holds up Tartarus.

But none of this, of course, is a genuine or radical phenomenon. It represents some of those imaginary interpretations with which man's mind reacts before the things of the world and their primary perspective and localization in respect to his person. To this end he invents imaginary things, which he situates in imaginary regions. I have referred to all this because it shows how much it is of man's essence to feel that he is in a regionalized world in which he encounters each thing as *belonging to* a region. But in this course of lectures we have no reason to concern ourselves with these imaginary locales and localizations of a world that is not the primary and real world of life, but an idea or image of the world.

In taking our inventory of the vital world, then, we have come upon that nearest of all things to each of us, our body, and, in collision or friction with it, all other bodies and their localization in perspective and regions. But their appearing on the inventory in this fashion must not make us forget that, at the same time—hence, not before or after, but at the same time—to us, things are instruments or impediments *for* our life, that their being does not consist in their each being of and in itself, but that they possess only a *being for*. Let us be clear in regard to this notion of "being for," since it expresses the original being of things as "things in life," concerns and importances. The concept of a thing undertakes to tell us what a thing is, its *being;* that being is stated for us or made manifest to us in the thing's definition. So far, so good. Now call to mind the children's game in which they accost a grownup, and to catch him, ask, "What is a rattle?" The grownup, not immediately finding words to define a rattle, almost instinctively makes the motion of turning a rattle in his hand, a motion that looks rather ridiculous, whereupon the children laugh. But the truth is that this motion is like an acted charade whose meaning is *something for* turning, hence, something with which something is to be *done*. This is its *being for*. And so too if we are asked what a bicycle is, before we answer in words our feet produce an embryonic pedaling motion. Now, the verbal definition that would afterwards state the being of the rattle, of the bicycle, or of the sky, the mountain, the tree, and so on, will only express in words what those same motions signify, and its content would be, and is, no more than telling us something that man does or undergoes with a thing; hence, every concept is the description of a vital episode.[1]

[1] The primary condition of things, then, consists in serving us *for* (or hindering us *from*). To be sure, metaphysics was born—far away in Greece, in the first third of the fifth century—as a search for the being of things, but taking their being as what they are— in our terminology—on their own account and not merely as what they *are for* us. It is the being of things in and for itself. This science, which a Cartesian at the close of the seventeenth century named "ontology," has for twenty-five centuries now been doggedly sweating and wearing itself out in a stubborn effort to find this being of things. But the stubbornness of the effort shows that this being of things which is the object of its search has not yet really been found. Which would be no little reason for suspecting that they have no such being, but which is indubitably more than reason enough for concluding that it is very doubtful if they possess it, whereas it is obvious that they do not display it. Otherwise it would be perfectly evident and familiar to us. Many years ago this led me to the audacious opinion that the being of things, as a being proper to them, apart from man, is only a hypothesis, as all scientific ideas are. With this, we turn the whole of philosophy upside down—a terrible undertaking which, fortunately, we can spare ourselves in this talk, since its subject is not ontology. I will merely say that among the many answers that have been given to the question "What *are* things," the one that has had the greatest success historically is the answer that Aristotle gave when he said they are substances, hence, that things ulti-

But here we are not concerned with what things *are* absolutely—always supposing that things are absolutely. We are confining ourselves, methodically and strictly, to describing what things are patently (hence, not hypothetically) *there,* in the ambit of the radical primary reality that is our life; and we find that in that ambit the being of things is not a supposed being in themselves, but their evident *being for,* their serving us or hindering us, and so we say that the being of things as *pragmata,* concerns or importances, is not substantiality but serviceability or servitude, which includes its negative form, unserviceability, being a difficulty, a hindrance, a harm to us.

Now, if we analyze this serviceability of things—to make matters simpler we will confine ourselves to the positive, that being sufficient for our purpose—if we analyze this serviceability, we find that each thing serves for another that in its turn serves for a third, and so on in a chain of *means for*—until we come to an end in man. For example, the thing that we call sulfur serves for making gunpowder, which serves for loading rifles and cannons, which serve for making war, which serves —well, what does war serve for? But this chain of services or *"means for"* which ends with war is not the only role of sulfur and of its first utilization for making gunpowder. Because gunpowder also serves for charging shotguns and rifles that serve for hunting, a very different activity from making war—the hunt, which serves for a human end that I have tried to set forth in a rambling Prologue to the book on the Art of Venery by that great hunter the Conde de Yebes,[2] a man who has hunted in

mately consist in substantiality. But everyone knows too that this answer long ago ceased to satisfy the Western mind, and that others had to be sought.

[2] ["Prólogo a 'Veinte años de Caza Mayor,' del Conde de Yebes," *Obras completas,* Vol. VI.]

every kind of place and has dozed off at every kind of
function in the best society, a man, then, who hunts
marmots in the woods and imitates them in the drawing-
room. But to return to our subject: With these two series
of articulated services that start from sulfur and the gunpowder manufactured from it, we find a third: gunpowder is an ingredient of rockets, and rockets are first and
foremost an ingredient of popular festivals. And festivals
are one of the great things that there are in this world,
and that we find and find ourselves in.

So then, things as positive or negative services are articulated together to form architectures of serviceability
—such as war, hunting, festivals. Within the world, like
little separate worlds, they form what we call the world
of war, the world of hunting, and so on, just as there is
the world of religion, of business, of art, of literature, of
science. I call them "pragmatic fields." And this, for the
present, is the last structural law of the world that I will
propound, namely: Our world, the world of each one of
us, is not a *totum revolutum*, but is organized in "pragmatic fields." Each thing belongs to one or more of these
fields, in which it interlinks its *being for* with that of
others, and so on successively. Now, these "pragmatic
fields," or "fields of concerns and importances," being,
in one way or another, directly or indirectly, fields of
bodies, are more or less precisely and exclusively localized, that is, consigned, at least for the most part, to spatial
regions. We could, then, instead of "fields," say "pragmatic regions," but it is better to speak particularly of
fields, employing this term from recent physics, which
expresses an ambit constituted by pure *dynamic* relations.
Our practical or pragmatic relation with things, and theirs
with us, even though finally corporeal, is not material but
dynamic. In our vital world there is nothing material: my
body is not matter, nor are the things that come into col-

lision with it matter. It and they, we might say to sim-
plify, are pure impact and hence pure dynamism.

Man lives in an immense ambit—the world, his world,
the world of each, occupied by "fields of *pragmata*"
more or less localized in particular regions. And each
thing that appears to us, appears to us as belonging to
one of these fields or regions. Hence, no sooner do we
become aware of it than, like a flash, there is in us as it
were a movement that makes us refer it to the field, region, or let us now say, *to the side of life* to which it
belongs. And since things have names—among the things
that we encounter in the world are the names of these
same things—I have only to utter a word and you will
say to yourselves either in definite words or wordlessly:
*that*, the thing named, belongs to this or that side of *life.*
If I now say "clothes," the ladies who are listening to me
will turn their minds, like a ship its prow, toward *the
side* of their life that is fashion in dress; if I say "Mar-
shall Plan," everyone, without any need for reflection and
without being at present concerned with the subject, will
automatically push, so to speak, the word they have heard
toward a certain "side" of their lives labeled "international politics." I said: "push, so to speak." But now I
shall drop the "so to speak"; for in fact there is no meta-
phor here, there is an actual reality. By the use of quite
elementary techniques of the physiological laboratory it
can be shown that hearing a word sets up a very slight
muscular contraction in us, observable with registering
instruments, a contraction that begins and is, as it were,
the germ of a movement of pushing something—in this
case, the word—in a particular spatial direction. Here is
an interesting subject for psychologists to investigate. All
of us carry in our imaginations a *diagram of the world* to
whose quadrants and regions we refer all things, including, as I said, those that are not directly corporeal but,

as they are called, "immaterial," such as ideas, feelings, and so on. Now, it would be interesting and curious to determine toward what region of this imaginary diagram each individual pushes the words that he hears or speaks.[3]

The world of our life, and hence our life in it, are constituted by an orientation of different *sides* which I have called "pragmatic fields." And here we have a momentary occasion to see indirectly, and therefore clearly, although I shall make no long analysis of it, what is the genius of the poet—nay more, what poetry itself is. I have long maintained in my writings that poetry is a mode of cognition, or, to put it differently, that what poetry says is true. The difference between poetic and scientific truth arises from secondary characteristics— secondary in comparison with the fact that they both say things that are true, that is, these things are actually and truly to be found in the world about which they talk.

[3] I had an aunt who, every time she uttered the word "devil," cast an angry look and fiercely thrust the point of her chin in the direction of the earth's center. It was plain that, for her, Hell was quite clearly and definitely situated there and, somewhere near it, the Devil, just as if she were seeing him. Similarly, if the laboratory experiment I mentioned were made on me, it is almost certain that when I heard, for example, "Paris Conference" and directed it toward the side of my life that is "international politics," my muscles would push the word in the direction of an oblique line intersecting the horizon and running downward and to one side. This would be a curve pantomiming—we are, and above all our bodies are, perpetual pantomime—the mental phenomenon in me that consists in detesting all politics and regarding them as a thing that is always and irremediably evil but at the same time inevitable and essential in every society. I permit myself the indulgence of stating this phenomenon in me without further explanation or documentation, because elsewhere in this course I hope to show, with all perspicuity and clarity, what politics is, why the universe contains a thing so strange, so unsatisfactory, and yet so indispensable. We shall then see how and why all politics, even the best, are necessarily bad—at least in the sense in which, good as they are, an orthopedic appliance or a surgical operation is bad.

The great novelist Marcel Proust had not the slightest scientific idea that human life and its world were really structured in an articulation of *sides*. Nevertheless, in the first volumes of his fluvial novel he tells us of an adolescent whose sensibility was prematurely developed, an adolescent who is Proust himself. The boy spends his summers at the Palace Hotel in a little Norman town, a fashionable summer resort. His parents take him for walks in the afternoon; sometimes they set out to the left, sometimes to the right. To the left is the house of a Monsieur Swann, a not very intimate friend of the family, a man of Jewish descent, without illustrious ancestry, but who possesses the rare talent of personal elegance, together with certain erratic vices. To the right stands the summer estate of the Guermantes, one of the most ancient noble families of France. For an adolescent whose alert hypersensitivity registers the slightest differences and subjects every real fact that comes its way to a vegetable luxuriance of fanciful amplifications, the two names "Swann" and "Guermantes" represent two worlds, that is, in our terminology, two different pragmatic fields; for the fact that Swann, even though a Jew, even though born without titles of nobility, insinuates one dimension of his life into the "Guermantes" world only makes the difference between the two worlds more marked. Swann and Guermantes, then, are like two opposite cardinal points, like two quadrants in the boy's whole great world, and from them his soul, in alternating gusts, receives the most various kinds of stimuli, incentives, warnings, enthusiasms, sorrows. And hence it is that, with a stroke of genius, Proust entitles two of his volumes, one *"Du Côté de chez Swann,"* "on Swann's side," and the other "the Guermantes' side." Now, in the light of what I expounded in the preceding lecture and what follows from this one, I ask you are not these two titles, bestowed by poetic intuition, really two technical terms in the scientific theory of life? It would be a very good thing if every one of us would learn for himself from what *sides* of his life the winds of his living blow most insistently, vigorously, and abundantly!

With this, we can say that we have completed our study of the formal structure possessed by the world in which each one of us lives. Observe that this world, so far as its structure is concerned, is very little like the physical world; I mean, the world that physics reveals to us. But mark that we do not *live* in that physical world, we merely think it, imagine it. For if I said earlier that for many years I have been maintaining that poetry is a form of knowledge, I now add that for just as many years I have been trying to make other people realize that physics is a form of poetry, that is, of fancy, and, I must even add, of a changeable fancy that today imagines a different physical world from yesterday's and tomorrow will imagine another, different from today's. Where each one of us in fact lives is in this pragmatic world, an immense organism of fields of concerns, of regions and of sides, and, in all essentials, unchanged since primordial man.

The time has now come when, turning our attention from this formal structuration of the world, we must cast a glance at its content, at the things that are in it, that appear, show themselves, issue, arise, in short ex-ist, in it, so that we may discover which among them we can and must call social and society. Here our theme compels us not to linger along the road, despite the interesting questions that will spring into view. We can quickly pass without a stop over what obviously cannot claim to be social or what, at least, is not evidently and fully so. For the things in the world are by ancient tradition classified as mineral, vegetable, animal, or human. Ask yourselves, each of you, if your own behavior in the presence

of a stone can be called social. Evidently it cannot. The
evidence becomes overwhelming if—passing to the other
extreme of the series—we compare it with our behavior
in the presence of man. The difference is plain. An adult
human being's every action toward or upon something
obviously takes into account his earlier experiences in
connection with that something, so that his action starts
from the qualities that, according to his knowledge, the
thing possesses. In our example, he knows that stone is
very hard but not as hard as steel; and if what he wants
to do, for some purpose of his own, is to break it to
pieces, he knows that he can do so by merely hitting it
with a hammer. He has, then, before him, to orient his
action, these two attributes of stone: that it is hard but
brittle, not very difficult to break. Now add the other
qualities that we have learned from our dealings with
stone. Among them there is one that is decisive for our
theme. We know that a stone is not aware of our action
on it, and that its behavior while we are hitting it is
reduced to splitting, to breaking, because that is its mechanical and inexorable condition. Our action upon it
evokes no corresponding action on its part upon or toward us. It has absolutely no capacity for action. Nor,
strictly speaking, should we call what happens to it from
us *passion*—in the sense of suffering. The stone neither
acts nor suffers; certain mechanical effects are produced
in it, and that is all. Hence, in our relation with the stone
our action has only one direction, it runs from us to the
stone, and there simply ends. The same thing is true, at
least macroscopically, with plants, with only the difference that exists between the attributes of a vegetable and
a mineral. But as soon as we begin dealing with an animal, the relation changes. If we want to do something to
an animal, our plan of action is affected by our conviction that I exist for the animal and that it expects some

action of mine on it, gets ready for it, and prepares its reaction to this expected action of mine. Hence there is no doubt that, in my relation with the animal, the act of my behavior toward it is not, as it was in the case of the stone, unilateral; instead, my act, before being performed, when I am planning it, already reckons with the probable act of reaction on the animal's part, so that even in the state of pure project my action moves toward the animal but returns to me in the reverse direction, expecting the animal's response. Hence it makes a round-trip journey, which is simply the anticipatory representation of the real relation that will take place between us—the animal and myself. When I go up to a horse to saddle him, I reckon from the first with his possible kick, and when I approach a sheepdog I reckon with his possible bite, and in either case I take my precautions.

Observe the new type of reality that, in the presence of what are not stones and plants, appears in our world when we encounter the animal. If, seeking to describe the real relation in the presence of a stone, we say, "We —the stone and I—are two," our statement is improper. The reason is that in this plural "we are" (which in this case is a dual, or plural of two only) we unite and equal the stone and the plant in being. Now, the stone *is* a stone *to me*, but to the stone I absolutely *am not*. There is no possibility, then, of community—the community expressed by this dual plural—between the stone and me. But in the case of the animal the reality is different. Not only is the animal an animal to me, and a particular animal (note that my behavior differs according to its species: I do not behave in the same way in the presence of a linnet and in the presence of a Miura bull)—the animal not only *is to me*, but I also *am to it*, that is, to it I am another animal. The animal's behavior toward us could be summarized and symbolized by saying that the animal is forever calling us animals. There seems to be no doubt that what takes place in the donkey when the driver belabors its back with his stick would have to be expressed in some such terms as: "What a brute! this animal that, in the world of fable where even we donkeys talk, we call 'man'! How different from that other animal that comes into the stable and licks me and I call him 'dog'!"

At any rate, it is certain that saying "we—the animal and I— are" has some degree of meaning that was absolutely lacking in "we—the stone and I—are." The animal and I are "we" because we mutually are *to each other,* because I know very well that in response to my action on the animal the animal will respond to me. This relation, then, is a reality that we must term "mutuality or reciprocity." In distinction from the stone and the plant, the animal appears to me as a thing that responds to me and in this sense as something that does not simply exist for me but that, since I also exist for it, *co-exists* with me. The stone exists but does not *co-exist.* Co-existence is an intertwining of existences, is two beings inter-existing, not simply "being there" without having anything to do with each other.

Now, is not this what we began by calling "social *intercourse*"? Does not the word "social" naturally point to a reality consisting in the fact that man conducts himself in confrontation with other beings which, in their turn, conduct themselves with respect to him—hence, to actions in which, in one way or another, there is the reciprocity in which not only am I a broadcasting center of actions toward another being but that other being is also a broadcasting center of actions toward me, so that in my action there must already be an anticipation of its action, my action reckons with its because its action also reckons with mine—in short, to put the same thing in another way, that the two actors mutually respond to each other, that is, cor-respond? The animal "responds" to my presence by its acts; it sees me, comes to me or runs from me, loves me or fears me, licks my hand or bites me, obeys me or attacks me—in short, *reciprocates to me* in its way. But this way, experience has shown me, is extremely limited. After all, it is only to a small number of my acts that the animal responds, cor-responds, and then with a very small repertory of acts of its own. Furthermore, I can establish a scale that will register the extent of this repertory for each species. Such a scale will therefore also tabulate the amount of co-existence that I can enjoy with the animal. It would show us how slight, even at best, this co-existence is. I can train or tame the animal and then imagine that it cor-responds to a larger number of my gestures and other acts; but I soon observe that in the tamed state the animal does not respond from itself, from its spontaneous center, but becomes a pure mechanism, that it is a machine into which I have put a few discs, like the phonographic answers that the parrot grinds out, always the same, according to program. Conversely, to co-exist more largely with the animal, the only thing that I can do is to reduce my own life, to elementalize it, to becloud my intelligence and befuddle my common sense until I become almost another animal. Such is the case with those elderly ladies who live for years on end alone with a dog, think of nothing else, have no other companion, and end by even coming to look like their dogs. To co-exist with the animal, we must do what Pascal counsels us to do in respect to God: *il faut s'abêtir.*

I repeat my question. Can we recognize a social fact in the relation of a man with an animal? We cannot answer out of hand. Of course an affirmative answer seemed precluded by the limitation of the co-existence between man and animal, as well as by a certain confused, ambiguous, vague character that we perceive in the mode of being of even the most intelligent beasts. The truth is that, not only in this order but in all orders, the animal confounds us. We do not really know how to deal with it, because we do not see its condition clearly. Hence in our conduct toward it we spend our lives alternating between treating it humanly, or, on the contrary, vegetably and even minerally. It is easy to understand the variations in attitude toward the animal through which man has passed in the course of history—from seeing almost a God in it, like the primitive and the Egyptians, to thinking, like Descartes and his disciple the gentle and mystical Malebranche, that the animal is a machine, a somewhat more complicated stone.

Whether our relation with it is social or not, we can only determine by comparing it with facts that are unquestionably and completely social. In cases like this, it is the complete, transpicuous, obvious case that enables us to understand cases that are confused, defective, ambiguous.

These considerations have delimited the group of unique phenomena among which something that is social can plainly and irrefutably appear. Of the contents of the world, our analysis has to deal only with the things that we call "men."

How do those things that I call "other men" appear in my vital world? The question has only to be asked, for all of us to feel a change of mood. So far, we have been relaxed and placid. Now, hearing that our horizon of reflection, the horizon of themes that are being developed in these lectures, is about to be invaded by "other men," we feel, we do not quite know why, a slight uneasiness, rather as if a subtle electric current had run through our backbones. Think it as absurd as you please, it remains a *fact*. We come from a vital world in which, until now, there have been only stones, plants, and animals; it was a paradise, it was what we call nature, the country. And although we have said a hundred times that the vital world we are analyzing is the world of each one of us, the concrete world of his life, we have spoken of it only abstractly. I have not tried to describe the separate world of each of us, nor that of any one of us, nor even mine. We are talking about the superlatively concrete in abstract and general terms. This is the paradox inseparable from a theory of life. Life is the life of each; but its theory, like all theories, is general. Theory provides the empty and abstract frames into which each can put his own autobiography. Well, what I now want to emphasize is that, even though we are still speaking abstractly, the mere announcement that other men are going to make their appearance in our analysis suffices to put us all on the alert, challenging "Who goes there!" We are no longer carelessly relaxed, but on guard and cautious. So terrifying, it seems, are other men! Earlier, in the world as mineral, vegetable, animal world, nothing troubled us. This is the peace that we feel in the country. Why do we feel it? We shall soon see; but Nietzsche put the gist of it in a few words: "We feel so tranquil and at ease in pure Nature because Nature entertains no opinion about us." Here lies the hypersuspicious origin of our uneasiness. We are about to talk of beings—men—characterized by the fact that we know that they entertain an opinion about us. It is this that has put us on guard, with our souls alert; on the gentle horizon of the paradisal world looms a danger—*the other man*. And there is no doubt about it: more or less and little by little, he is going to become animate. And we shall all be to some degree confounded.

Now indeed, in the area that my horizon encloses, appears the *Other*. The "other" is the other man. As a sen-

sible presence, all that I have of him is a body, a body
that displays its peculiar form, that moves, that manipulates things in my sight, that in other words exhibits external or visible "behavior," to use the term of the American psychologists. But the surprising thing, the strange
and finally mysterious thing, is that, though there are
present to us only a figure and some bodily movements,
in or through this presence we see something that is essentially invisible, something that is pure inwardness,
something that each of us knows directly only of himself—his thinking, feeling, desiring, operations that, by
themselves, cannot be presences to other men, that are
non-external and that cannot be exteriorized directly because they do not occupy space or possess sensible qualities, so that, over against all the externality of the world,
they are pure inwardness. But we have already found
something of the same sort in the case of the animal's
body; when we see it, not only does it signal to us, like
all other colors and resistances, a certain corporeality, it
is also the sign of something completely new and different—namely, an incorporeality, a *within*, an *intus* or *intimacy* or inwardness in the animal, where it shapes its response to us, prepares its bite or its butt, or, on the contrary, its gentle, tender coming to rub itself against our
ankles. I said that our intercourse with the animal has an
element of co-existence. This co-existence arose because
the animal responds to us from an inner center that is
there in it, that is, from its inwardness. All co-existence is
a co-existence of two inwardnesses, and the extent of it is
precisely the extent to which these two inwardnesses in
one way or another become present to each other. If
through the animal's body we glimpse, presume, suspect
this inwardness of the animal, this happens because it
signals it to us by its shape, movements, and so on. Now,
when a body is the *sign* or *signal* of an inwardness that is

as it were contained and shut up inside it, this means that the body is *flesh*, and this function of signaling its inwardness is termed "expression." Flesh, in addition to having weight and motion, expresses, *is* "expression." The expressive function of the zoological organism is the most puzzling of the problems with which biology is concerned, now that biologists have renounced concerning themselves with biological life *itself* on the ground that it is too much of a problem.

I shall not pause to go into this highly suggestive subject, the expressive function—in a certain sense, suggestive by antonomasia, for in it lies the cause of all suggestion—because I have treated it at length in my essay "On Expression as Cosmic Phenomenon." [4] And the aspect of it that more especially concerns the appearance of the *other man* to each of us will be discussed later.

Suffice it to say for the present that the body of the other, at rest or in motion, is an unstinting semaphore that is constantly sending us the most various signals or indications or suggestions as to what is going on in the *within* that is the other man. This within, this inwardness or intimacy, is never present, but is compresent, like the side of the apple that we do not see. And here we have an application of the concept "com-presence," without which, as I said, we could not explain how the world and everything in it exists for us. Certainly, in this case the function of com-presence is more amazing. For in the case of the apple the part of it that is hidden at any moment has been present to me at other times; but the inwardness that the other man *is* has never made itself, nor can ever make itself, present to me. And yet, I find it there—whenever I find a human body.

The physiognomy of that body, its mimicry and its

[4] ["Sobre la expresión fenómeno cósmico," Vol. VII of "El Espectador," in *Obras completas*, Vol. II.]

pantomime, its gestures and words, do not make patent but *manifest* that there is out there an inwardness like my own. The body is a superlatively fertile "expressive field" or "field of expressiveness."

For example, I see that a body is looking. The *eyes,* "windows of the soul," show us more of the other man than anything else—because looks are acts that come from *within* as few others do. We see *at what* it is looking and *how* it is looking. Not only does the look come from within, but we observe from what depth the body looks. This is why nothing so delights the lover as the first look. But here caution is in order. If men knew how to *measure* the depth from which a woman's look comes, many mistakes and much grief would be avoided.

For there is the first look that is merely conceded, like an alms—only just deep enough to be a look at all. But there is also the look that comes from the utmost depths, drawing its very root with it from the abyss of the feminine being, a look that emerges laden as it were with seaweed and pearls and the whole submerged landscape, the essentially submerged and hidden landscape, that this woman is when she truly is—that is, when she is profound, abysmal woman. This is the *saturated* look, overflowing with her own desire to be looked into, whereas the first look was asthenic, was scarcely a look but mere seeing. If man were not vain and did not interpret some inadequate gesture on a woman's part as proof that she was in love with him, if he suspended judgment until *saturated* gestures appeared in her, he would not suffer the painful surprises that are so frequent.

I repeat, from the depth of radical solitude that is properly our life, we now and again make an attempt at interpenetration, at *de-solitudinizing* ourselves by tentatively showing ourselves to the other human being, desiring to give him our life and to receive his.

# 5

# Inter-Individual Life. We, You, I

---

We started from human life as radical reality. By radical reality—the present occasion bids me remind you—we did not understand the only nor even the most important and certainly not the most sublime reality, but purely and simply that primary and primordial reality in which all others, if they are to be realities to us, must appear and hence have their root in it or be fixed in it. In this sense of radical reality, "human life" means strictly and exclusively the life of each individual, that is, always and only my life. This X that lives it and that I habitually call "I," and the world in which that "I" lives, are patent to me, present or compresent, and all of this—my being who I am, and this being my world, and my living in it —all these are things that happen to me and solely to me, or to me in my radical solitude. If, by chance (I added), something that must also be called "human life" apart from mine appears in this world, you may be absolutely sure that it will be "human life" in another sense, neither radical nor primary nor patent, but secondary, derivative, and more or less latent and hypothetical. Now, when bodies of human form appear and are present to us, we observe in them as compresent other quasi-I's, other "human lives," each with its own world, which as such does not communicate with mine. What is decisive in this step and this appearance is that whereas my life and everything in it, being patent to me and being mine, are immanent in character (hence the truism that my life is immanent to itself, that it is all within itself), the indirect

94

presentation, or compresence, of the alien human life
startles and confronts me with something transcendent to
my own life, and which therefore is in it without properly *being*.

What is certainly patent in my life is the notification,
the signal, that there are other human lives; but since
human life in its radicality is only *mine*, and these will be
lives of others like myself, each the life of each, it follows that, because they are others, all their lives will be
situated outside of or beyond or *trans*-mine. Hence they
are *trans*cendent. And here please note that for the first
time there appears to us a type of realities that are not
such in the radical sense. The life of another is not patent
reality to me as my own life is; the life of the other—I
deliberately put it in loose terms—is only a presumption
or a presumed or assumed reality; as probable, as plausible, as likely as you please, but not radically, unquestionably, primordially "reality." But this brings us to the
realization that one property of the radical reality that is
my life is that it contains within it many presumed realities, or realities of the second order—a fact that opens to
my life an immense field of realities different from it. For
by calling them, loosely, presumed—we could also say
"probable"—I do not deprive them of the character and
value of realities. I deny them only the quality of being
*radical* or unquestionable realities. So it appears that the
attribution of reality allows and even demands a scale or
gradation or hierarchy and that there will be, as with
burns, first-degree realities, second-degree realities, and
so on—the reference, however, being not to the content
of the given reality but to its pure character of being
reality. For example: The world described to us by physics (the model science, that is, among those that man today has at his disposal), the physical world, undoubtedly
possesses reality; but what, or what degree of, reality?

It goes without saying: a reality of the sort that I have called presumed. We need only remember that the figure of the physical world into whose reality we are now inquiring is the result of physical theory, and that this theory, like all scientific theories, is in motion; it is essentially changing because it is questionable. To the world of Newton succeeds the world of Einstein and De Broglie. The reality of the world of physics, being a reality that so quickly and easily succeeds to and supplants itself, can be only a reality of the fourth or fifth degree. But it is of course—I repeat—a reality. By reality I mean *everything with which I have to reckon*. And today I have to reckon with the world of Einstein and De Broglie. The medicine that undertakes to cure me is dependent on that world; so too are most of the machines by which we live today; so too, quite concretely, is my future, the future of my children, of my friends, for never in all history has the future so depended on theory—on the theories of nuclear physics.

In order not to confuse all these presumed realities with radical reality, we shall call them interpretations, or ideas of ours about reality—that is, presumptions or probabilities.

And now comes the great change in optics, or shift in perspective, that we are called upon to make. But this new perspective, from which we shall gradually begin to speak—except for an occasional reference or momentary return to our earlier one—this perspective, which is new in these talks, is precisely the one that is normal in everyone. The abnormal, the unusual perspective is the one we have been using. I shall soon clear up the meaning of these two perspectives. But in order to do so, I must go on for a little with what I was saying. And I was saying that the appearance of the other man—with the suspicion or compresence that he is an "I" like my "I," with a life like mine and hence not mine but his, and a world of his own in which he radically lives—is the first case, in this inventory of my world, in which I encounter realities that are not radical but mere presumption of realities, that strictly speaking are ideas about or interpretations of reality. The other man's body is radical and unquestionable reality to me; but that a quasi-I, a quasi-human-life lives in his body is already an interpretation on my part. The reality of the other man, of this other "human life," is, then, of the second degree in comparison with the primary reality that is my life, that is my I, that is my world.

This statement, aside from its value in itself, has that of making me realize that in my life there is an immense quantity of presumed realities—which, I repeat, does not mean that they are necessarily false, but only that they are questionable, that they are not patent and radical. I have given you my great example—the so-called physical world, which physical science presents to us and which is so different from my vital and primary world, in which there are neither electrons nor anything remotely resembling them.

Now—and this is the new thing in comparison with all that has gone before—normally we live these presumptions or second-degree realities as if they were radical realities. The other man as such, that is, not only his body and his gestures, but his "I" and his life, are normally as much realities to me as my own life is. In other words, I live, equally and simultaneously, my life in its primary reality and a life that consists in living, *as primary*, many realities that are such only in the second, third—and so on up—degree. Nay, more: normally, I am not aware of my genuine life, of what it is in its radical solitude and truth, but instead, I presumptively live presumed things, I live among interpretations of reality

which my social environment and human tradition have
been inventing and accumulating. Of these, some deserve
to be regarded as genuine, and these I call second-degree
realities—but the phrase, "deserve to be regarded as genuine," must always be understood with due caution, not
simply taken at face value. Being inter-pretations, they
can, after all, be erroneous and propose to us realities that
are frankly illusory. And in fact, the vast majority of the
things that we live are not only presumptive but illusory;
they are things that we have heard named, defined, evalu-
ated, justified in our human environment; things, that is,
which we have heard from others and which, without
further analysis, conditions, or reflection, we accept as
genuine, true, or probable. The theme that I am here
pointing out for the first time will be the backbone of the
rest of our discussions. But for the present let us leave
it in this first simple, popular, and obviously confused
appearance.

But if what I say is true—and whether it is or not will
appear in the following pages—our normal life consists
in our occupying ourselves with *pragmata*, with things
or concerns and importances that are not properly such
but are new irresponsible interpretations put forth by
others or by ourselves. I mean that, since our life consists in always doing something with or about these
pseudo-things, it would inevitably be a pseudo-doing
[*hacer*], precisely the pseudo-doing that appeared to us
earlier as that very common but very profound expression "*hacer que hace*" [pretend],* that is, we habitually
pretend to live, but we do not actually live our genuine
life, the life that we should have to live if, freeing ourselves from all these interpretations accepted by the other
people among whom we find ourselves and who are
commonly called "society," we from time to time made

* [Cf. above, pp. 55–56.—*Translator*.]

energetic and clear contact with our life as radical reality. But this, we said, is what we are in radical solitude. What it comes down to, then, is man's need for a periodical and thorough going over the accounts of the enterprise that is his life and for which only he is responsible. This accounting he can make by resorting from the perspective in which we see and live things so far as we are members of society, to the perspective in which they appear when we *withdraw* to our solitude. In solitude, man is his truth; in society, he tends to be his mere conventionality or falsification. The genuine reality of human living includes the duty of frequent withdrawal to the solitary depths of oneself. This withdrawal, in which we demand that the mere seeming probabilities, if not sheer enchantments and illusions, in which we live shall show us their credentials of genuine reality, is what is known by the manneristic, absurd, and confusing name of *philosophy*. Philosophy is withdrawing, *anabasis*, settling accounts with oneself, in the fearsome nakedness of oneself before oneself. Before another, we are not, cannot be, wholly naked; if the other looks at us, his look already to some extent covers us from our own eyes. This is the extraordinary phenomenon of the blush, in which the naked flesh appears to cover itself with a rosy cloth in order to hide. We shall have to talk seriously about nakedness when we come to discuss confusion.

Philosophy, then, is not a science but, if you like, an indecency, since it consists in baring things and oneself, stripping them to stark nakedness—to what they are and I am—and that is all. Hence, if philosophy is possible, it is genuine knowing—which the sciences never are in the strict sense; rather, they are mere techniques, useful for the delicate manipulation, the refined exploitation of things. But philosophy is truth, the terrible and desolate, solitary truth of things. Truth means things laid open, and that is the literal meaning of the Greek word for truth—*a-letheia, aleuthein*, that is, to bare. As for the Latin word, *veritas, verum*, with its cognates *verdad, verity*, it must have come from an Indo-European root *ver*— meaning "to say"—whence *ver-bum*, word—but not an ordinary kind of saying, but the most serious and solemn, a religious declaration in which we call God to witness what we say—in short, the oath. But the peculiar property of God is that when we call him to witness in this relation of ours with reality which consists in declaring it— that is, in saying what it really is—God does not represent a third party between reality and myself. God is never a third party, because his presence is composed of essential absence. God is he who is present precisely as absent, is the vast absent one who shines in all presence—shines by his absence; and his role in this "being called to witness" which is the oath consists in leaving us alone with the reality of things, so that between them and ourselves there is nothing and no one that veils, covers, dissembles, or hides them; and this absence of anything between them and ourselves—is truth. Hence Master Eckhart, the greatest of European mystics, calls God "the silent wilderness that is God."

That this resort (in which philosophy consists) from our conventional pseudo-living to our most genuine reality demands a more rigorous intellectual technique than that of any other science is another matter. It only means that philosophy is *also* a philosophical technique, but philosophy knows very well that it is such only secondarily and because it needs a technique to undertake its perpetual and primordial mission. True enough, in the middle of the last century and at the beginning of this one, philosophy, under the pseudonym of Positivism, claimed to be a science, that is, it tried to "be scientific"; but we need not take this too seriously—it was really only a brief attack of modesty that came over the poor creature!

Philosophy, then, is the criticism of conventional life—including, and most particularly, of his own life—which man finds himself needing to undertake from time to time, haling his conventional life before the judgment-seat of his genuine life, of his inexorable solitude. Or we could also say that it is the double entry he must carry so that the business, the concerns, the things to which he has directed his life shall not be too greatly illusions, but instead, tested by the touchstone of radical reality, each of them shall be relegated to the degree of reality that befits it.

In these lectures, we summon before this judgment-seat of the reality of the genuine human life all the things that are commonly called "social," in order that we may see what they are in their truth—that is, we proceed by constantly resorting from our conventional, habitual, daily life and its constituent perspective to our primary reality and its unwonted, difficult, and severe perspective. This is what we have done step by step, from our most elementary observation concerning the apple. Haled before this judgment-seat, the apple that we believed we saw turned out to be slightly fraudulent; it has a half that is never present to us at the same time as the other half, and hence the apple as patent, present, seen reality does not exist, it is not such a reality. Then we observe that the greater part of our sensible world is not present to us, but rather that the part of it that is at each moment present to us hides the rest and leaves it only compresent, as the room in which we are conceals the city from us, yet we live in the room as being in the city, and the city in the country, and the country in the World, and so on and so on.

But the chief criminal, summoned to our tribunal *in*

*absentia,* was the other man, with his present body and his present gestures, but whose character of man, of another "I," of another human life, we found to be mere interpreted reality, the great presumption and probability.

For the true theme·of our studies, he is the decisive reality, because, searching for clear facts that we could upon sufficient evidence call social, our path led from failure to failure—our behavior with neither the stone nor the plant had the slightest appearance of sociality. When we confronted the animal, it seemed that something like a social relation between us and it, and between animals themselves, did appear. Why? Because when we do something to the animal, our action must reckon with the animal's foreseeing it, more or less correctly, and preparing to respond to it. Here, then, we have a new type of reality: an action—my action—a component of which is, by anticipation, the action that the other being will perform in answer to mine—and meanwhile the other being is going through the same process as I am. It is a curious action, then, which emanates not from one but from two—from the animal together with me. It is a genuine collaboration. I foresee the mule's kick, and its kick "collaborates" in my behavior toward the mule, inviting me to keep my distance. In this action we reckon with each other, that is, we exist mutually or co-exist, I and my collaborator the mule. The supposition, as you see, is that there is another being of which I know beforehand that it will more or less probably respond to my action. This obliges me to anticipate its response in my plan of action, or, what comes to the same thing, makes me in turn respond to it in advance. It does the same: our actions, then, interpenetrate—they are mutual or reciprocal. They are properly inter-action. A whole line of linguistic tradition gives this meaning to sociality, to the social. Let us accept it for the time being.

However, our total relation with the animal is at the same time limited and confused. This suggested to us a very natural methodological reservation—that we should look for other facts in which the reciprocity would be clearer, unlimited and evident, that is, in which the other being that responds to me should in principle be *capable of responding to me as much as I respond to it*. Then the reciprocity will be clear, full, and evident. Now, this happens to me only with the other man; what is more, I regard him as the "other" precisely because I believe that he is my peer in the sphere of power to respond. Please observe that "other"—*alter* in Latin—is properly the term of a pair and only of a pair. *Unus et alter*—the *alter* is the counterpart, the mate, the match to the *unus*. Hence in our Spanish the relation of the *unus*—I—with the *alter*—other—is amazingly termed *alternar*. To say that we do not frequent [*alternar con*] someone is to say that we have no "social relations" with him. We frequent neither the stone nor the vegetable.

So now we can set it down that man, aside from the man that I am, appears to us as the other, and this means (I want you to take this in all strictness), the "other" means, he whom I can and must—even against my will—frequent, since even if I should prefer that the other did not exist, because I loathe him, it turns out that I irremediably exist for him, and this obliges me, willy-nilly, to reckon with him and with his intentions toward me, which perhaps are malevolent. This mutual "reckoning with," *reciprocity*, is the first fact that we can classify as *social*. Whether this classification is final or not may be left for the further development of our meditations. But reciprocity in action, inter-action, is possible only because the other is like me in certain general characteristics; he possesses an "I" that in him is what my "I" is in me— or as they say, "he has what it takes"; that is, he thinks, feels, desires, has his purposes, concentrates on achieving them, and so on, just as I do. But of course, I discover all this because in his gestures and motions I observe that he responds to me, reciprocates to me. It follows that the other, *Man*, originally appears to me as the reciprocator and nothing besides. Whatever else man proves to be is secondary to this attribute and comes afterwards. Observe, then: being the other does not represent an accident or adventure that may or may not befall Man, but is his original attribute. I, in my solitude, could not call myself by a generic name like "man." The reality represented by this name appears to me only when there is another being who responds or reciprocates to me. Husserl says very well: "The meaning of the term 'man' implies a reciprocal existence of one to the other, hence *a community of men*, a *society*." And conversely: "It is equally clear that men cannot be apprehended unless there are (really or potentially) other men around them." Hence—I add— to speak of man outside of and apart from a society is to say something that is self-contradictory and meaningless. And here we have the explanation for my reservations when, speaking of life as radical reality and radical solitude, I said that I ought not to speak of Man but of X or of the living being. We shall soon see why it was also inadequate to call him "I." But I had to make this radical perspective easier to understand. Man does not *appear* in solitude—although his ultimate truth is solitude; man appears in sociality as the Other, frequenting the One, as the reciprocator.

Language shows us that there was a time when men did not distinguish, at least not generically, between human beings and beings not human, because they thought that the latter heard them and answered them. That is, the stone, the plant, and the animal were also "reciprocators." The proof is the fact that all the Indo-European languages have expressions of the type, "By what name is such and such a thing called?" Apparently, if a thing's name is known, it can be called; it perceives our *call* and comes running, that is, it gets into motion, reacts to our action of naming it. *Ap-pello* is "to make something move"; and similarly *calo* in Latin, *kio*, *kelomai*, in Greek. In Spanish "*llamar*" ["to call"], the *clamare* that is *calo* survives. Exactly the same semantic values—"to call" and "to make move"—are found in the German word "*heissen.*"

But now I must correct a possible error in perspective to which the unavoidable order of our inventory of what is to be found in the world may give rise. We begin by analyzing our relation with the stone, continue with the plant and then with the animal. Only after all this do we confront the fact that Man appeared to us as the Other. The error would lie in supposing that this sort of chronological order into which due analytical order has led us purports to be the real order in which the contents of our world successively appear to us. The real order is precisely the reverse. The first thing that appears to each of us in his life is other men. Because every "each" is born into a family, which itself never exists in isolation; the idea that the family is the social cell is a mistake that belittles that marvelous human institution the family—and it *is* marvelous even though it is troublesome, for there is nothing human that is not *also* troublesome. The living human being, then, is born among men and they are the first thing that he encounters; that is, the world in which he is going to live begins by being "a world composed of men"—in the sense that the word "world" bears when we speak of a "man of the world" or say "one must know the world" or "what will the world say to that?" In our life the human world precedes the animal, vegetable, and mineral world. We see all the rest of the world, as through prison bars, through the world of man into which we are born and in which we live. And since one of the things that these men in our immediate environment do most intensely and frequently is to talk to one another and to me—by their talk they instill into me their ideas about all things, and so I see the whole world through these accepted ideas.

This means that the appearance of the Other is a fact that always remains as it were hovering in the immediate background of our life, because when we first become aware that we are living, we already find ourselves not only with others and among others, but accustomed to others. Which leads us to formulate this first social theorem: Man is *a nativitate* open to the other, to the alien being; or, in other words: *before each one of us became aware of himself*, he had already had the basic experience that there are others who are not "I," the Others; that is, again, Man, being *a nativitate* open to the other, to the *alter* who is not himself, is *a nativitate*, willy-nilly, whether he likes it or not, an *altruist*. But this word and this whole theorem must be understood without adding to them what is not said in them. When it is stated that man is *a nativitate*, and hence always, open to the Other, that is, disposed in his acts to reckon with the Other as alien and different from himself, it is not stated whether he is open favorably or unfavorably. The statement concerns something previous to good or bad feeling toward the other. Robbing or murdering the other implies being previously open to him neither more nor less than does kissing him or sacrificing oneself for him.

Being open to the other, to others, is a permanent and constitutive state of Man, not a definite action in respect to them. The definite action—doing something to them, whether *for* them or *against* them—supposes this previous and inactive state of openness. This state is not yet properly a "social relation," because it is not yet defined in any concrete act. It is simple co-existence, matrix for all possible "social relations." It is simple presence within the horizon of my life—a presence which is, above all, mere compresence—of the Other, singular or plural. In this presence not only has my behavior toward him not condensed into any action, but—and this observation is extremely important—my pure knowledge of the Other has not become concrete either. For the time being he is for me only the most abstract kind of reality—"he who can respond to my acts toward him." He is man in the abstract.

This relation of mine with the other is the starting-point for two different though connected lines of progressive concretion or definition. One consists in my gradually coming to know more about the other, to know him better; I decipher his physiognomy, his gestures, his acts, in increasing detail. The other consists in my relation with him becoming active, in my acting on him and he on me. In practice, the former usually follows upon the latter.

So let us begin with this second line.

If, in the presence of the other, I make a pointing gesture indicating with my forefinger an object in my environment, and I see the other move toward the object, pick it up, and hand it to me, I infer from this that the world that is only mine and the world that is only his seem, nevertheless, to have a common element—the object that, with slight variations—namely, its shape as seen from his point of view and from mine—exists for us both. And as this happens in connection with many things, although sometimes both he and I make mistakes in supposing that we share a common perception of certain objects, and as it happens not only with one other man but with many other men, bit by bit there arises in me the idea of a world beyond mine and his, a presumed, inferred world, common to all. This is what we call the "objective world," in contrast to the world of each of us in his primary life. This common or objective world becomes better defined in the course of our conversations, which for the most part deal with things that appear to be approximately common to us. To be sure, every now and again I discover that our agreement about this or that thing was an illusion; some detail in the behavior of others suddenly shows me that I see things, at least some things —quite a number of things—differently; and this annoys me and makes me plunge back into my own exclusive world, into the primary world of my radical solitude. Yet the proportion of agreements reached is sufficiently high to enable us to understand one another in respect to the main outlines of the world, to render collaboration in the sciences possible, and a laboratory in Germany utilizes observations made in a laboratory in Australia. In this way we keep building up—for what is involved here is not something patent, but a construction or interpretation —the image of a world that, being neither only mine nor only yours but, in principle, the world of all, will be *the* world. But this brings to light a great paradox: it is not *the* unique and objective world that makes it possible for me to co-exist with other men but, on the contrary, it is my sociality or social relation with other men that makes possible the appearance, between them and me, of *something like* a common and objective world; the world that Kant had called *allgemeingültig*—"universally valid," that is, valid for all—thereby referring to human subjects and basing the objectivity or reality of the world on their unanimity. And this is what follows from my earlier remark, when I said that the part of my world that first appears to me is the group of men among whom I am born and begin to live, the family and the society to

which my family belongs—that is, a human world
through which and influenced by which the rest of the
world appears to me. Obviously both Kant and Husserl,
who gave this train of reasoning its purest and most
classic form, like all idealists tend rather to utopianize this
unanimity. The truth is that we men are at one only in
our vision of certain gross and coarse components of the
world, or, to express my thought more accurately, the
list of men's agreements about things and the list of their
disagreements will come to the same and offset each
other. Nevertheless, this incomplete body of agreements
suffices to make Kant's and Husserl's idealistic reasoning
valid, for it is what leads us to believe, as in fact we do,
that all men live in one and the same world. This is what
we may call the natural, normal, and everyday attitude in
which we live. And, because of it, because of *living with*
others in one present world—hence *our* world—our living is co-living, *living together*.

But if there is to be living together, there must be an
advance from that simple state of being open to the other,
to the *alter*, which we called man's basic *altruism*. To be
open to the other is a passive thing. What is necessary is
that, on the basis of an opening, I shall act on him and he
shall respond or reciprocate to me. What we do does
not matter—I can bandage his wound or I can give him
a blow to which he answers and reciprocates by another.
In either case we live together and in reciprocity with
respect to something. The form "we live" very well expresses this new reality, the relation "we"—*unus et alter*,
I and the other together do something and in doing it
*we* are. If I called being open to the other *altruism*, this
mutual being to each other should be called *nostrism*, or
*nostrity*, "we-ity." It is the first form of concrete relation with the other, and hence the first *social* reality—if
we choose to use this word in its most usual sense which

is, at the same time, that of almost all sociologists, including some of the best of them, such as Max Weber.

With the rock there is no *nostrity*. With the animal there is a very limited, confused, diffused, and dubious *nostrity*.

As we together live and are the reality "we"—I and he, that is, the Other—we come to know each other. This means that the Other, until now an undefined man, of whom I only know, from his body, that he is what I call my "like," my "fellow," hence someone able to reciprocate to me and with whose conscious response I have to reckon—as I continue to have dealings with him, good or bad, this Other becomes more definite to me and I increasingly distinguish him from the other *Others* whom I know less well. This greater intensity in dealings implies *closeness*. When this closeness in mutual dealing and knowing reaches a high point, we call it "intimacy." The Other becomes close to me and unmistakable to me. He is not just some or any other, indistinguishable from the rest—he is the Other as unique. Then the other is *You* to me. Note, then, that "You" is not simply a man, but a unique, unmistakable man.

It is, then, within the ambit of living together opened up by the relation "we" that the "you"—or unique human individual—appears to me. You and I, I and you, we act on each other in frequent interaction of individual to individual—both reciprocally unique. One of the things that we do, and that is the most typical reciprocity and *nostrity*, is to talk. And one of the things we talk about is *him* or *them*—that is, about others who are not in the relation of "we" with you and with me. Whether absolutely or occasionally, now and for this purpose he or they are those who remain outside of this closeness that is our relation. And here we come upon a peculiarity of the Spanish language which is worthy of reflection, like everything pertaining to common speech. The Portuguese and the French instead of *nosotros* ["we," but literally "we others"] say *"nos"* and *"nous,"* by which they express merely the common living and the closeness between those to whom the *nos* and the *nous* refer. But we Spaniards say *nosotros*—and the idea expressed is remarkably different. To express communities and collectivities, *nostrities*, languages have the plural. But many languages are not satisfied with only one form of plural. There is the inclusive plural which, like *nos* and *nous*, only includes; but in contradistinction to it there is the exclusive plural, which includes many and various things but gives notice that it excludes others. Now, our Spanish plural *"nos-otros"* is exclusivistic. It means that we do not announce simply the pure community of the I and the you and perhaps other you's, but a community between the two or more than two of us—I, you, and certain other you's—a community in which you and I together form a particular collective unit, *in contradistinction to, outside of*, and in a way *against*, others. In our *nos-otros*, while we do declare that we are very much united, we above all recognize that we are other than the Others, than *They*.

We noted man's fundamental *altruism*, that is, that he is *a nativitate* open to the other. Next we saw that the Other and I enter into the relation *We*—within which the other man, the indeterminate individual, becomes defined as a unique individual and is the *You*, with whom I talk of that distant creature *He*—the third person. But now I must go on to describe my struggle with the *You*, in collision with whom I make the most stupendous and dramatic discovery: I discover myself as being I and . . . only I. Contrary to what might be supposed, the first person is the last to appear.

# 6

## More about Others and "I." Brief Excursion toward "Her"

---

OUR real environment has a center—the "here" in which my body is—and a periphery delimited by a line that we call "horizon," that is, which includes whatever is within view. The word "horizon" comes from the Greek *horizein* —to bound, to set up marks that enclose and delimit a space. For us, these concepts and names are technical terms with which we have been familiarized by what has been said in the previous lectures; with these, and with many others that I think I have managed to make familiar too, we are gradually acquiring a common capital of notions and words that enable us to understand one another, and therefore to move on toward questions that are really more difficult, subtle, and refined, but which thanks to our stock of concepts will be considerably easier and more accessible. These preparatory notions will serve as finely pointed forceps which will make it possible for us to grasp, that is, comprehend, some quite delicate and tenuous things. This means that we are now fully philosophizing. In a way the philosopher and the barber are of the same guild; the barber cuts hair and the philosopher splits hairs.

But I mentioned the notion of horizon again just now in order to show you that, like everything belonging to the strictly corporeal world, it leads us to employ its notion—the notion of horizon—in the incorporeal order. And just as I earlier pointed out that the actual structura-

tion of the corporeal world into spatial regions gives rise
to a corresponding imaginary and ideal diagram in which
we situate incorporeals—I now say that when he analyzes,
meditates on a theme, man also has a horizon, which, like
the corporeal horizon, shifts as our meditation, our analysis advances, and that, as it shifts, new things keep enter-
ing it and appearing to our sight, bringing with them new
problems. To meditate is to sail a course, to navigate,
among problems many of which we are in the process of
clearing up. After each one looms another, whose shores
are even more attractive, more suggestive. Certainly, it
requires strength and perseverance to get to windward
of problems, but there is no greater delight than to reach
new shores, and even to sail, as Camoëns says, "through
seas that keel has never cut before." If you will now open
a bank-account of attention for me, I foretell sun-smitten
landscapes and promise archipelagoes.

Every step, I said, brings new things within our horizon. It was thus that a great quarry entered our horizon
of meditation—the Other—that is to say, the other man,
no less! All that is present to us of him is a body, but a
body that is flesh; and flesh, over and above other signals
similar to those that other bodies send us, possesses the
enigmatic gift of signalling an *intus* to us—a *within*, an
inwardness. To some degree, this already occurred with
the animal. The body of what will be another Man, or
the Other, to us is a superlatively rich "field of expressiveness." Its countenance, its silhouette, its whole form
are already the expression of an invisible someone to
whom they belong. And so are its purposeful movements,
its coming and going, its manipulation of things.

I see a human body running, and I think: *he* is in a
hurry or training for a cross-country race. In a place
where there are a great many marble slabs, I see a body
digging a large hole in the ground; I think: *he* is a grave-

digger and is digging a grave. If I am a poet, I set out from there and give my imagination rein: perhaps it is the grave for Yorick, the fool of Denmark; perhaps Hamlet will come and pick up the skull and speak his vague, tremulous words.

More important than all this—and here is the curious thing—are the Other's useless movements, those that serve no apparent end at all—his gestures, which reveal more of him to us. The Other Man appears to us above all in his gesticulation, and there are good grounds for saying that a man *is* his gestures, to the point that, if someone scarcely makes gestures at all, this absence or lack is, in its turn, a gesture because it is either a *restraint* of gestures, or it is a gesticulatory dumbness, and these two things manifest, declare, or reveal to us two very peculiar inwardnesses, two different modes of being the other. In the first case we observe the suppression of the gesture that was already forming, that was about to be discharged, and we observe the Other's degree of success or failure in suppressing the germinating gesture. Think how many of the other man's intimate concerns have been revealed to us by "ill-suppressed gestures."

In contrast to these, I mentioned the case of the person who makes no gestures or few, of the mute in gesture. When such a man is before us, we say that his mien is inexpressive, that it "tells us nothing." And since, aside from individual cases, there is a certain type or style of gesticulation that belongs to the collectivity, we should find that there are peoples among whom a rich and highly flavored expressiveness is normal—Southern Europeans— and others, the peoples of Northern Europe, for whom the normal thing is an almost complete—I say only *almost* complete—inexpressiveness. Think of the number of times that we have suffered before the inert cheek of a German or an Englishman, a cheek that does not quiver, that does not vibrate, that looks like a desert, a desert of soul, that is, of inwardness! Some considerations on this phenomenon and the reasons for it—by which I mean why in some cases there is such an abundance of expression and in others inexpressive dumbness—can be found in some essays of mine that, though written long ago, I still consider valid: "On Expression as Cosmic Phenomenon" and "Vitality, Soul, Mind." [1]

I had earlier to confine myself to discussing the look—which is so expressive because it is an act that comes directly from an inwardness, with the straight-line accuracy of a bullet, and then too because the eye, with the superciliary socket, the restless lids, the white of the sclera, those marvelous actors the iris and pupil, is equivalent to a whole theater with its stage and its actors. The muscles of the eye—the orbicular and palpebral, the *levator*, etc.—the muscular fibers of the iris, are miraculously subtle in function. All this makes it possible for every look to be so minutely differentiated even in the single dimension of the inward depth from which it was sent. In this order there are the minimum look and the maximum look, or, as I termed them with special reference to the man-woman relation, the "conceded look" and the "saturated look." But the dimensions in which looks differ, and hence can be classified and measured, are very numerous. To cite only a few examples of species in this fauna of looks: there is the look that lasts but an instant and the insistent look; the look that slips over the surface of the thing looked at and the look that grips it like a hook; the direct look and the oblique look, whose extreme form has its own name, "looking out of the corner of one's eye"—the height of obliqueness. Differing from the various oblique looks,

[1] ["El Espectador" Vol. VII and "El Espectador" Vol. V, respectively; both in *Obras completas*, Vol. II.]

although the direction of the visual axis is also on the bias, is the sidewise glance. Each of these classes of looks tells us what is going on within the other man, because each of them, that is, every act of looking, is engendered by a particular intention, an intention that, the less conscious it is in the looker, the more genuinely revealing it is to us. Looks, then, constitute a vocabulary; but, as is the case with vocabularies, the isolated word may often be ambiguous, and only in its place in the entire sentence, and with the latter in the context of the composition or the conversation, is it adequately clear. This need for a context if either gestures or words are to make their meaning clear, is very justly emphasized by the great psychologist Karl Bühler in his *Theory of Expression*.

The sidewise glance—if it is simply that—does not express a wish to conceal our very look itself, this latter being a most curious case and one that shows how revealing, how incriminating our looks are, since sometimes men deliberately try to hide them, thus making their looking a clandestine act, like robbery and smuggling. Hence both Spanish and English very aptly term this look "furtive" or "stolen"—the look that wants to see but not to be seen. There are stolen looks whose robbery is of the sweetest. This reminds me of a popular song, which runs:

> Don't look at me, because
> If we look at each other, *they* look
> And if they look, why then
> We have to hold back.
> So let's quarrel, and then
> When *they* aren't looking
> We'll look at each other.

So much for the stolen look. But there is another, much more complicated look—in my opinion the most complicated of all—perhaps for the same reason the most effec-

tive, the most suggestive, the most delicious and enchant-
ing. It is the most complicated because it is at once
furtive and the very opposite of furtiveness, a look that,
more than any other, wants to make it obvious and known
that it is looking. This double nature, which delectably
contradicts and *undoes* itself, gives it its power of enchant-
ment; in short it is the look with eyes partly shut, or as
the French so aptly put it, *les yeux en coulisse*. It is the
look of the painter when he steps back from the canvas to
judge the effect of the brushstroke he has just made. It
is furtive because, the lids being almost three-fourths
closed, it seems to be trying to hide itself; but it is the
very opposite, because, compressed by the narrow crevice
that the lids leave, the look shoots out like a well-aimed
arrow. It is the look of eyes that are as it were asleep but
which behind the cloud of sweet drowsiness are utterly
awake. Anyone who has such a look possesses a treasure.
Paris, so sensitive to these human things, to these *humanities*, has always been in a state of subjugation to anyone
who had *les yeux en coulisse*. For example, while the
mistresses of the great Bourbons were always unpopular—
Mademoiselle de Lavallière, Louis XIV's Montespan, la
Pompadour of Louis XV—the latter monarch's last sweetheart enjoyed immense popularity not only, or so much,
because she was the first royal favorite to come from the
People, but because la Dubarry looked at the world with
her *yeux en coulisse*. And when anyone looks at Paris in
that fashion, Paris is hypnotized and succumbs. In the same
way, when I was a lad and visited Paris for the first time,
the great city was at the feet of Lucien Guitry—the
man with *les yeux en coulisse*.

But let us linger no longer in this world of looks, which
I wished only to touch upon in passing, as an example of
the fact that the only part of the Other Man which is

actually present to us is his body, but that his body, being flesh, is a field of expressiveness, an almost inexhaustible semaphore of signals.

Let us now make clear to ourselves the *exact* situation that we have reached. When, among minerals, plants, and animals, a being appears to me consisting in a certain corporeal form that I call human—even though only that corporeal form is *present* to me, something that is invisible in itself and, more generally still, imperceptible, becomes *com-present* to me in it, namely, a human life, something, then, that is similar to what I am, since I am nothing but a "human life." This com-presence of something that cannot be present by itself is unquestionably based on the fact that this body which is flesh makes peculiar signals to me that point toward an inwardness; it is an expressive field of "inwardnesses." Now, this thing that I call an "inwardness" of life is properly and directly known to me—that is, is patent, present, evident to me—only in the case of my own. Hence to say that in the body in human form another inwardness renders itself com-present to me is to say something too contradictory or at least very hard to understand. Because originally there is no inwardness except my own. What do we mean when we say that an Other is before us, that is, an other like myself, another Man? For this implies that the new being —neither stone nor plant nor merely an animal—is I, *ego* —but at the same time is other, *alter*—that it is an *alter ego*. This concept of *alter-ego*—of an I that I am not but that is precisely another, hence not-I, has every appearance of being like a square circle, the prototype of the contradictory and impossible. And yet the thing itself is indubitable. There, before me, is another being that appears to me as being also an *I*, an *ego*. But so far I, *ego*, means for us no more than "human life," and human life, we said, is properly, originally, and radically only the life of each of us, hence, *my life*. Everything that it contains, namely, the man that I am and the world that I experience, possesses (as we shall soon see) the character of being mine, of belonging to me or being *my* I, *my* world. And lo! in *my world* appears a being that presents itself to me, though in the form of compresence, as being also "human life," hence with a life of its own—not my life—and hence too with a world of its own that, originally, is not *my* world. The thing is immense and amazing, despite the fact that we meet it every day. The paradox is stupendous, for it turns out that within the horizon of my life—which life consists solely in what is mine and only mine, and hence is such radical solitude—another solitude appears to me, another life, in the strict sense incommunicable with mine and having its world, a world alien to mine, an *other* world.

The world of my life appears to me as distinct from me because it resisted me; to begin with, resisted my body— the table resists my hand. But my body itself, although the closest thing in my world to me, likewise resists me; it does not just let me do whatever I please: it brings me pain, sickness, fatigue; and hence I distinguish it from myself, while, on the other hand, I moderate my unreasonable projects, the extravagances of my fantasy—hence, contrary to what is usually thought, the body is the policeman of the mind. Despite all these resistances and *negations of myself* which my World is to me, they are mine, patent to my life, belong to it. So we cannot simply say that my world is the not-I. In any case it will be a not-I that is *mine*, and hence only comparatively a not-I. But in a man's body which, as such, belongs to my world, I have the intimation and the declaration of a being—the Other—and a World—his world—which are absolutely alien, absolutely foreign to me, strange to me and to everything that is mine. Now there is reason indeed to speak of a not-I. The pure not-I, then, is not the world but the other Man with his *ego* outside of mine and his world that does not communicate with mine. This world of the other is unattainable to me, inaccessible, if we are to speak strictly. I cannot enter it because I cannot enter directly, because I cannot make the other's "I" patent to myself. I can suspect it, and the suspicion, which is patent to me and which I find in my own or primordial world, is what makes compresent for me the actual and strict not-I that the other and his world are for me. Here is the immense paradox: that, with the being of others, there appear in *my world* worlds alien to me *as such*, worlds that present themselves to me as unpresentable, that are accessible to me as inaccessible, that become patent as essentially latent.

Hence the unparalleled importance in human life, which is always my life, of the compresent presence of the Other Man. Because he is not other in the trivial sense in which the stone that I see or touch is another thing than I or another thing than the tree, and so on. No—when the Other Man appears to me, there appears to me what is other than my whole life, than my whole universe, hence the radically other, the inaccessible, the impenetrable, which nevertheless exists, exists like the stone that I see and touch. Let it not be said that the comparison is faulty because the stone is, exists, for me *because* I see it and touch it, and the inaccessible, as its name indicates, is something to which I have no access, that I cannot see or touch but that always remains outside, latent, beyond everything that is within my reach. But this is precisely the point: I do not say that, with the Other Man, the inaccessible *is* accessible to me; on the contrary, I say that, with him, I discover the inaccessible *as such*, the inaccessible in its inaccessibility, exactly as, with the apple, there is given me, in compresence, the half of it that I do not see—that I do not see but that is *there for me*.

It was Husserl who most accurately formulated—please note that I only say "formulated"—the problem of how the Other Man appears to us; the passage occurs in the last book that he published before his death, the "Cartesian Meditations." [2]

Husserl says: "In my own intentionality" (an expression that *for our present purposes* means the same as "my life as radical reality") "there constitutes itself" (in our terminology, "appears") "an I, an *ego* not as 'myself' but as 'reflecting' itself in my own 'ego.' But this second *ego* is *not simply there*, nor, properly speaking, is it given to me 'in person' " (in our vocabulary, "is present to me"); "it is constituted as 'alter ego' and the *ego* that this expression '*alter ego*' designates as one of its moments is myself, in my own being. 'The other,' by his constitutive meaning, refers to myself, 'the other' is a 'reflection' of myself, and yet, properly speaking, is not a reflection; he is my *analogue*, and yet not an analogue in the usual sense of the term." Observe how Husserl, in order to define the Other in his simplest and most primary character, hence, without yet describing any particular Other but simply the Other in the abstract and in general—observe how he finds himself forced to employ constant contradictions; the Other is I since he is an I—but an I that is not I, hence something different from my I, which of course, is well known to me. Hence he tries to express that strange reality the other by saying that it is not "I" but something "analogous" to my I—but that it is not analogous either, for after all, it contains many components that are identical with me, hence with "I." He then continues: "If, first, one delimits the *ego* in its proper being" (in-

[2] [*Méditations Cartésiennes*, Paris 1931, pp. 78–79.]

stead of *ego*, we should put, "my life"), "and if one em-
braces in an over-all view the content of this *ego*" (I add,
"of this 'my life'") "and its articulations . . . the following question necessarily arises: how does it come about
that my *ego*" (my life), "within its own being, can, in
some manner, constitute 'the other' precisely as being
foreign to it," (to my life or my *ego*) "that is, give it
an existential meaning that places it outside of the concrete
content of the 'myself' that constitutes it?" (of my life
which is the reality in which it appears).

Husserl was the first who clearly defined the radical
and not merely psychological problem that I call "The
Appearance of the Other." Husserl's development of the
problem, is, in my opinion, much less successful than his
definition of it, although there are many admirable discoveries in his development. As many people are un-
acquainted with Husserl's thought—which has been of
the greatest influence in this last half-century, the dividing
line of which we shall shortly cross to the second half of
the century—it would be useless for me to undertake a
critical examination of his theory of the Other here. Such
a thorough criticism of Husserl's doctrine has no bearing
on my exposition of my own, for the simple reason that
his fundamental principles oblige him to explain by what
means the appearance of the Other is brought about,
whereas for our part, setting out as we do from life as
radical reality, we do not need to explain the mechanisms
by virtue of which the Other Man appears to us, but only
*how* he appears; we need only make it clear *that* he *is*
*there* and *how* he *is there*. One point in this theory of
Husserl's, however, I must needs repudiate, and that is its
starting point. I have to repudiate it because perhaps in
the whole of Husserl's exact, careful work ("I go slowly,
step by step," he once told me)—work that has no equal
for scrupulousness in the whole history of philosophy

(unless it be, in a very different style, the work of Dil-
they)—in all his work, I say, I find no other error so
serious precisely because of the carelessness that it reveals.
It is this: According to Husserl, the Other Man appears to
me because his body signals an inwardness that therefore
remains latent but is given in the form of a compresence,
as the city is compresent to us around every house, precisely because the house, being closed, hides the city's
presence from us. But an inwardness is not, like the city,
something that I can see by going out from where I am;
it is by nature hidden—even for mere compresence, it
needs a body. How then does it come about that, seeing
a human body, I believe that I have before me an inwardness *like* mine, an *I* like mine—I do not say the same as
mine, but at least similar to it? Husserl answers: by an
analogical transposition or projection. Now, there is
analogy when there are four terms that correspond two
and two: for example, John has bought a hunting preserve
from Peter and George has bought a house from Fred-
erick; John and George, then, have done not the same
thing but an analogous thing, namely, buying something
from somebody. In every analogy, there must be a common term.

In our case the analogical transposition would, according to Husserl, consist in this: if my body is body—flesh
because I am in it—in the Other's body there must likewise be another "I": an *alter ego*. The basis of this analogy, the common term—common in the sense of similar—
would be my body and the body of the Other. Husserl's
idea, in effect, is this: my body is the thing in the world
that is closest to me, so close that in a certain sense it is
indistinguishable from me since I am where it is, namely,
"here," *hic*. But I can move elsewhere, and in so doing
move the *here* elsewhere—so that I can transport my body
to the place that, from *here*, *hic*, is a there, *illic*. Now,

from my *here* something appears to me "there," *illic—a body like mine*, that differs from mine only in the aspect conferred on it by its distance from *here*—hence, by its being *there*. But this difference does not make this body of the Other different from mine, because having moved or being able to move to this place that is now *there, illic*, I know that *from there, illinc*, the body is seen *here* with some changes. If I could actually be simultaneously *here and there*, I should see my body there just as I see the Other's body.

In this description of how the Other's body is originally (we are still discussing the original way in which things appear) given to me, there are two errors. One of them is colossal; the other is scarcely less so, but though we cannot accept it, we can at least excuse it.

The colossal error consists in supposing that the difference between my body and the Other's is only a difference in perspective—the difference between what is seen here and what is seen *from here, hinc*—there, *illic*. But the truth is that this thing that I call "my body" is very little like the other's body. The reason is: My body is not mine only because it is the thing closest to me (so much so that I do not distinguish myself from it), namely, here. That would be only a spatial reason. My body is *mine* because it is the direct instrument of which I make use in order to deal with other things—to see them, hear them, approach them or run from them, manipulate them, and so on. It is the universal instrument or *organon* on which I count; hence for me my body is the organic body par excellence. Without it I could not live, and since it is the thing in the world whose "being for" *is to me* the most indispensable, it is my *property* in the strictest and most superlative sense of the word. All this Husserl sees perfectly well. But since he does, it is surprising that he identifies the idea of "the body that is mine" with the body of the Other, which *is to me* only through my body, my seeing, my touching, my hearing, its resisting me, and so on. The proof that they are almost completely different is that the information I receive about my body is chiefly pains and pleasures that it gives me and that appear in it, internal sensations of muscular tension or relaxation, and so on. In short, my body is felt principally from within it, it is also my "within," it is the intra-body—whereas all that I observe of the other's body is its exteriority, its alien form, its without. To be sure, I see my hands and part of my arms and some other portions of my corporeality; with one hand I touch the other or my thigh. If we carefully compare how much of my body is in fact outwardly present to me with how much of the alien body is present to me, the difference will prove to be very great. The body of the Other comes very near to being more like the bodies of certain animals that are also present to me outwardly. You will say that we have looking-glasses, in which we see ourselves outwardly, as we see the alien body. But in the first place primitive man did not have looking-glasses and, nevertheless, the Other Man existed for him, just as he does for us. You will say: there were gentle streams, quiet lakes, pools in which he could see himself. But, aside from the fact that in many places where primitive peoples live today, there are no rivers, lakes, or even pools because it scarcely ever rains, it is clear that the Other existed for them from their childhood, before they devoted themselves to contemplating their own reflected forms. In addition, it is well known that the exploration and subjugation of the so-called savage peoples was carried out not only by force of bullets but equally by force of looking-glasses. No gift more delighted the primitive than the gift of a looking-glass, because for him it was a magical object that conjured up before his eyes the image of a man—but in that man he did not recognize himself. The majority of those primitives had not seen themselves and, consequently, did not recognize themselves. In the looking-glass they saw precisely . . . another man. It is from here that we should have to start if we would rightly understand the myth of Narcissus, which could not originally have consisted in a boy's delighting in nothing but contemplating his own beauty mirrored in a fountain, but in the magical and sudden appearance of another man where there was only one—the I that was Narcissus. The original Narcissus did not see himself but another, and lived with him in the magical solitude of the forest, leaning over the spring.

But the error of supposing that I transpose my body into that of the Other and therefore observe in him an inwardness like mine is obvious on the face of it if we consider that what proclaims and reveals the other I to me, the *alter ego*, is not so much the form of the body as its gestures. The expression that is sorrow or irritation or melancholy, I did not discover in myself but *primarily* in the other and it at once signified inwardness to me— grief, annoyance, melancholy. If I try to see myself tearful, irritated, afflicted in a looking-glass, my corresponding gesture *ipso facto* ceases or at least is altered and falsified.

Here Husserl's error appears in macroscopic proportions. The appearance of the Other Man can hardly start from an act of imagination in which I transport my body from where it is to where his is—since sometimes what appears to me is not an Other that is a man in the sense of a male but an Other that is feminine, that is Woman, an Other that is not He but She. And the difference shows itself from the first appearance of another's body—which is already charged with sexuality, is a male or female body. There are cases in which the body present is epicene, and I experience a peculiar and notorious ambiguity.[3]

The appearance of the She is a particular case of the appearance of the Other, and one that shows us the inadequacy of any theory that, like Husserl's, explains the presence of the Other as such by a projection of our inward person on his body. I have pointed out that the expression "alter ego" was not only paradoxical but contradictory and hence improper. *Ego*, strictly, is something that I alone am, and if I refer it to an Other, I have to change its meaning. *Alter ego* has to be understood analogically: there is in the abstract Other *something* that is in him what the *Ego* is in me. The two *Egos*, mine and the analogical one, have in common only certain abstract components, which, being abstract, are unreal. Only the concrete is real. Among these common components is one that, provisionally, was the most important for our study —the capacity to respond to me, to reciprocate. But in the case of a woman, the striking thing is the heterogeneity between my ego and hers, because her response is not the response of an abstract Ego—the abstract Ego does not respond, because it is an abstraction. Her response is already, in itself, from the beginning and with no further ado, feminine, and I am aware of it as such. Husserl's supposition, then, proves clearly invalid; the trans-

---

[3] Let us see if I have succeeded in making Husserl and myself clear:

| Here, *hic* | There, *illic* |
|---|---|
| x-------------------------------------------:x | |
| Body A | Body B |

My body is what I feel here, and this, which is what it is to me, I call body A. The body of the Other is the body that I see there, *illic* (whence *el* ["he"] is derived). It is *His* body that I call body B. According to Husserl, since I can move from where I am and make that *there* a *here*, "in imagination I put myself in the place of the 'other body'"—these are Husserl's exact words—and then body B becomes body A. From which it appears that Body A, or my body, and Body B, or his body, would be equal, except for the difference of place.

position of my ego, which is irremediably masculine, into a woman's body could only produce an extreme case of a virago, but it is inadequate to explain that prodigious discovery, the appearance of the feminine human being, different from me.

It will be said—and this has led to many mistakes that have been not only theoretical but practical, political (suffragettes, legal equalization of men and women, and so on)—that the woman, since she is a human being, is not "completely different from me." But this error springs from another and far greater one, caused by the fact that no true idea of the relation between the abstract and the concrete has ever reached the generality of mankind. In an object we can isolate one of its components, for example, its color. This operation of isolation, in which we fix our attention on one component of the thing, thus mentally separating it from the other components with which it inseparably exists, is what we call "abstraction." But by abstracting it *from the others* we have destroyed its reality, not only because it does not and cannot exist in isolation—there *is* no color without the surface of particular form and particular dimensions over which it extends—but because its content even as color is different in accordance with this form and these dimensions of the surface. Which means that the other components act on it in turn, giving it its particular character. Similarly, to say that a woman is a being like myself *because* she is capable of responding to me, is to say nothing real, because in these words I ignore and omit the content of her responses, the peculiar *how* of her response.

As a young man, I once traveled back to Spain from Buenos Aires on a great liner. Among my fellow passengers there was a small group of American ladies, young and extremely beautiful. Although my acquaintance with them never even reached a footing of intimacy, it was

obvious that I spoke to each of them as a man speaks to
a woman who is in the full flower of her feminine attributes. One of these ladies felt rather offended in her
American dignity. Evidently Lincoln had not struggled
to win the War of Secession in order that I, a young
Spaniard, could permit myself to treat her like a woman.
In the United States of that time women were so modest
that they thought there was something better than "being
a woman." At any rate, she said to me, "I insist that you
talk to me as if I were a human being." I could not help
answering: "Madam, I am not acquainted with this person
whom you call a 'human being.' I know only men and
women. As it is my good fortune that you are not a man
but a woman—and certainly a magnificent one—I behave
accordingly." The poor creature had gone through some
college where she had suffered the rationalistic education
of the time, and rationalism is a form of intellectual bigotry which, in thinking about reality, tries to take it into
account as little as possible. In this case it had produced the
hypothesis of the abstraction "human being." It should
always be remembered that the species—and the species
is the concrete and real—reacts on the genus and specifies
it.

That the forms of the feminine body differ considerably
from those of the masculine body would not be sufficient
reason for us to discover woman in it. Indeed, the differentiating forms are those that frequently lead us to interpret her inward person mistakenly. On the contrary, any
of those parts of her body which differ least from the
parts of ours manifests—in the mode of compresence
which we have analyzed—her femininity to us. The fact
is surprising, although in the last analysis no more so than
the appearance of the masculine Other.

According to this, we should come closer to the truth
if we said that it is not the corporeal forms that we *later*

term peculiarly feminine which signal to us a strange human mode of being, profoundly different from the masculine and which we call "femininity," but rather the contrary: all the parts of her body, together and severally, make compresent to us, give us a glimpse of, the being who is instantly Woman for us, and this inner femininity, once observed, is exuded over her body and feminizes it. The observation is paradoxical but seems to me undeniable; it is not the feminine body that reveals the "feminine soul" to us, but the feminine "soul" that makes us see its body as feminine.

You will ask: What primary characters do we discern as soon as a woman is present to us, which constitute her elemental femininity for us and produce this paradoxical effect that it is they—even though they are only compresent—that impregnate her body with femininity, that make it a feminine body? There is no room to describe them all here, and it will suffice if I point out three:

(1) The instant we see a woman, we seem to have before us a being whose inward humanity is characterized, in contrast to our own male humanity and that of other men, by being essentially confused. Let us waive the pejorative connotation with which this word is usually understood. Confusion is not a defect in woman, any more than it is a defect in man not to have wings. Even less, in fact —for it makes some sense to wish that man had wings like hawks and angels, but it does not make sense to want woman to stop being "substantially" confused. This would amount to destroying the delight that woman is to man by virtue of her confused being. Man, on the contrary, is made up of clarities. Everything in him is given with clarity. You are to understand, of course, "subjective clarity," not actual, objective clarity concerning the world and his fellow human beings. Perhaps everything that he thinks is sheer nonsense; but within himself,

he sees himself clearly. Hence in the masculine inwardness everything normally has strict and definite lines, which makes the human male a being full of rigid angles. Woman, on the other hand, lives in a perpetual twilight; she is never sure whether she loves or not, will do something or not do it, is repentant or unrepentant. In woman there is neither midday nor midnight; she is a creature of twilight. Hence she is constitutionally secret. Not because she does not report what she feels and what befalls her, but because normally she cannot express what she feels and what befalls her. It is a secret for her too. This gives woman the softness of forms which belongs to her "soul" and which for us is the typically feminine. In contrast to man's angles, woman's inwardness seems to have only delicate curves. Confusion, like the cloud, has rounded forms. Correspondingly, in woman's body the flesh always tends to the most subtle curved lines, which is what the Italians call *morbidezza*. In Victor Hugo's *Hernani* Doña Sol is given a phrase that is infinitely, enchantingly feminine: "Hernani, toi qui sais tout!"—"Hernani, you who know all things!" By "know," Doña Sol does not mean acquired knowledge; in these words she appeals from her feminine confusion to Hernani's masculine clarity as to a higher substance.

(2) Because, in fact, this inwardness that we discover in the feminine body and which we shall call "woman" presents itself to us from the outset as a form of humanity inferior to the masculine. This is the second primary characteristic in the appearance of the She. In a time like ours in which, though to a diminishing degree, we suffer under the tyrannical myth of "equality," a time in which we everywhere find the mania of believing that things are better when they are equal, the foregoing statement will irritate many people. But irritation is no guarantee of perspicacity. In the presence of Woman we men imme-

diately divine a creature who on the level of "humanness" has a vital station somewhat lower than ours. No other being has this twofold condition—being human, and being less so than a man is. This duality is the source of the unparalleled delight that woman is for the masculine man. The aforesaid equalitarian mania has recently resulted in an attempt to minimize what is one of the fundamental facts in human destiny—the fact of sexual duality. Simone de Beauvoir—a distinguished writer in that capital of graphomania, Paris—has written a very long book on "The Second Sex." This estimable lady finds it intolerable that woman should be considered—and consider herself—constitutively referable to man and hence not centered in herself, as man would seem to be. Mademoiselle de Beauvoir thinks that to consist in "reference to another" is incompatible with the idea of person, which is rooted in "freedom toward oneself." But it is not clear why there must be such incompatibility between being free and consisting in reference to another human being. After all, the amount of reference to woman which constitutes the human male is by no means small. But the human male consists pre-eminently in reference to his profession. Professionality—even in the most primitive of primitive men—is probably the most masculine trait of all, to the point where "doing nothing," having no profession, is felt to be something effeminating in a man. Mademoiselle de Beauvoir's book, so prodigal of pages, leaves us with the impression that the writer, very fortunately, confuses things and thus displays in her work the characteristic confusion that assures us of the genuineness of her feminine being. On the other hand, to believe, as follows from her argument, that a woman is more a person when she does not "exist" preoccupied by man but occupied in writing a book on "the second sex," seems to us something decidedly more than simple confusion.

The duality of the sexes has as its consequence that men and women are constituted by their reference to one another—and to such a degree that any insufficiency in either men's or women's living in reference to the other sex is something that in every case requires explanation and justification. It is another matter that this reference to the other sex, though constitutive in both, has a pre-eminent place in woman, while in man its autonomy is reduced by other references. With all the qualifications and reservations that "case histories" would suggest, we may affirm that woman's destiny is "*to be* in view of man." But this formula in no way diminishes her freedom. The human being, as free, is free before and in the face of his destiny. He can accept it or resist it, or, what is the same thing, he can be it or not be it. Our destiny is not only what we have been and now are; it is not only the past, but, coming from the past, it projects itself, in openness, toward the future. This retrospective fatality—what we now are—does not enslave our future, does not inexorably predetermine what we are not yet. Our future being emerges from our freedom, a continuous spring forever flowing out of itself. But freedom presupposes plans of action among which to choose, and these plans can only be created by using the past—our own and others'—as a material that inspires us to new combinations. The past then—our destiny—does not influence us in imperative and mechanical form, but as the guiding thread of our inspirations. We are not inexorably circumscribed in it; rather, at every moment it launches us upon free creation of our future being. Hence the antique formula could not be improved: *Fata ducunt, non trahunt*, "Destiny directs, it does not drag." For, great as is the radius of our freedom, there is a limit to it—we cannot escape maintaining continuity with the past. Nothing more clearly shows us in what this ineluctable continuity with the past consists than those occasions when the plan we make and adopt consists in the radical negation of a past. Then we see that one of the methods the past employs to inspire us is to urge us to do the opposite of what it had done. This is what, since Hegel, has been termed "dialectical movement," in which each new step is only the mechanical negation of the preceding one. This dialectical inspiration is certainly the most stupid form of human life, the form in which we come nearest to behaving with an almost physical automatism. An example of it is what is today called "modern art," the inspiring principle of which is simply to do the opposite of what had always been done in art, hence, to hold up to us as art something that in essence is "non-art."

All this brief "philosophical" embroidery on past and future, destiny and freedom, comes down to opposing the tendency of certain present-day "philosophers" who invite woman to plan her "future being" by ceasing to be what she has been until now, namely, woman—all in the name of freedom and the idea of the person. Now, what woman has been in the past, her femininity, does not derive from her freedom and person having been negated, either by men or by a biological fatality; on the contrary, it is the result of a series of free creations, of fertile inspirations that have sprung as much from her as from man. For the human being, the zoological duality of the sexes is not—just as the other subhuman conditions are not— something inexorably imposed, but the very opposite—a theme for inspiration. What we call "woman" is not a product of nature but an invention of history, just as art is. This is why the copious pages that Mademoiselle de Beauvoir devotes to the biology of the sexes are so little fertile, so completely beside the point. Only when we are engaged in imagining the origin of man need we keep constantly in mind the facts which the biology of evolution presents to us today—even though we can be certain that tomorrow it will present us others. But once man is man, we enter a world of freedom and creation. Instead of studying woman zoologically, it would be infinitely more fertile to contemplate her as a literary genre or an artistic tradition.

So let us, without a blush that would be pure snobbery, go back to calling woman the "weaker sex" with perfectly quiet consciences. Indeed, let us proclaim it in a more radical sense. I said that, besides the characteristic of confusion, the other characteristic with which woman appears to us is her lower vital rank on the human plane. This last qualification serves only to introduce us to the phenomenon to be considered, but it is insufficient because it implies a comparison with man, and nothing, in its true reality, is a comparison. We are not, then, considering the fact that, in comparison with man, woman seems to us to be less strong vitally than he is. There is no occasion, at least for the present, to talk of more or less; what we must consider is the fact that, when we see a woman, what we see consists in *weakness*. This is so obvious that, for that very reason, we completely pass over it when we discuss what woman is. When Aristotle says that woman is a sick man, it is not likely that he was referring to her periodical sufferings but precisely to this constitutive characteristic of weakness. But to call it "sickness" is to go out of one's way to use a secondary expression that supposes comparing her with the healthy man.

This patent characteristic of weakness is the basis of woman's inferior vital rank. But, as it could not but be, this inferiority is the source and origin of the peculiar value that woman possesses in reference to man. For by virtue of it, woman makes us happy and *is happy herself, is happy in feeling that she is weak*. Indeed, only a being inferior to man can radically affirm his basic being—not his talents or his triumphs or his achievements, but the elemental condition of his person. The greatest admirer of the gifts that we may have does not corroborate and confirm us as does the woman who falls in love with us. And this is because, in sober truth, only woman knows how to love and is able to love—that is, to disappear in the other.

(3) The confusion of the feminine being appears to us together with its weakness and, in a way, as proceeding from it; but the weakness in its turn becomes compresent to us in the last primary characteristic of the three that I said I would describe.

The feminine ego is so radically different from our male ego that it displays the difference from the very first in something that could not be more elementary—in the fact that its relation to its body is different from the relation in which the masculine ego stands to its body.

I have already remarked on the incongruousness of Husserl's statement that in our perception of the other we identify our body with his. Our body is known to us first and above all from within, and the other's body from without. They are heterogeneous phenomena.

For it is too much overlooked that the feminine body is endowed with a more lively internal sensibility than man's; that is, our organic intracorporeal sensations are vague and as it were muffled in comparison with woman's. In this fact I see one of the roots from which—ever suggestive, charming, and admirable—the resplendent spectacle of femininity comes to flower.

The comparative hyperesthesia of woman's organic sensations brings it about that her body exists for her more than man's does for him. Normally, we men forget our brother the body; we are not aware of possessing it except at the chill or burning hour of extreme pain or extreme pleasure. Between our purely psychic I and the outer world, nothing seems to be interposed. Woman, on the

contrary, is constantly having her attention claimed by
the liveliness of her intracorporeal sensations; she is always
aware of her body as interposed between the world and
her I, she always carries it before her, at once as a shield
of defense and a vulnerable hostage. The consequences
are clear: woman's whole psychic life is more involved
with her body than man's; in other words, her soul is
more corporeal—but, vice versa, her body lives more constantly and closely with her spirit; that is, her body is more
permeated with soul. In fact, the feminine person displays
a far higher degree of interpenetration between body and
spirit than man. In man, comparatively speaking, each
normally takes its own course; body and soul know little
of each other and are not allied, rather, they act like
irreconcilable enemies.

In this observation I believe we can find the cause for
an eternal and enigmatic fact which runs through human
history from one end to the other, and of which all the
explanations so far given have been stupid or superficial—
I refer to woman's age-old propensity to adorn and orna-
ment her body. In the light of the idea that I am expounding, nothing could be more natural and at the same time
inevitable. Her native physiological structure imposes on
woman the habit of noticing, paying attention to her
body, which ends by being the closest object in the perspective of her world. And since culture is only sus-
tained reflection on that to which our attention prefers to
turn, woman has created the remarkable culture of the
body, which, historically, began in adornment, continued
in cleanliness, and has ended in courtesy, that inspired
feminine invention, which, finally, is the subtle culture of
the gesture.[4]

The result of this constant attention that woman devotes

[4] In these last three paragraphs, I have made use of my essay "La
percepción del prójimo" ["The Perception of One's Fellowman";
*Obras completas*, Vol. VI, pp. 161 ff.].

to her body is that her body appears to us from the first as impregnated, as wholly filled with soul. This is the foundation for the impression of weakness that her presence creates in us. Because in contrast to the firm and solid appearance of the body, the soul is a little tremulous, the soul is a little weak. In short, the erotic attraction that woman produces in man is not—as the ascetics have always told us in their blindness on these matters—aroused by the feminine body as body; rather, we desire woman because Her body *is* a soul.

# 7

# The Other as Danger, and the I as Surprise

---

OUR concern is to find facts that we can indubitably call social, because we hope to reach absolute certainty as to what "society" is and what all the things essentially connected with it are. We credit nothing that anyone may tell us about the social and society; we intend to discover it for ourselves, directly. All the sociologists have left us unsatisfied, even in respect to the fundamental notions of their sociologies—for the simple reason that they never took the trouble to come really to grips with the most elementary phenomena out of which the social reality arises. To this end, we have together engaged in a thorough and unhurried *battue*—together but, of course, each in his own primordial world, which is that of his life as radical reality and radical solitude. And the result was this: something to which we could properly apply the purely verbal meaning of "social relation"—at least, its commonest meaning in ordinary speech and among sociologists—appeared to us only when the living being that each of us is encountered the Other, whom he at once recognized as like himself and whom we called the Other Man. The characteristic and primary attribute of what I call the Other Man is that he responds, actually or potentially, to my action upon him, which obliges my action to reckon in advance with his reaction, that reaction of the other's in which in his turn he has reckoned with my action. We have, then, a new and *unique* reality, that cannot be confused with any other—namely, an action in which two active subjects take part—I and the other; an action into which the other's action enters, which is interpenetrated by it, wrapped in it, and which is therefore inter-action. My action, then, is social, *in this sense of the word*, when in it I reckon with the eventual reciprocity of the Other. The other, Man, is *ab initio* the reciprocator, and hence *is* social. He who is incapable of reciprocating, whether favorably or adversely, is not a human being.

Now, we must not forget the other side of this capacity of the Other to reciprocate. It is that this capacity presupposes that he is "human life" like mine, hence a life that is his, not mine, with its own exclusive I and world, which are not mine, which are outside of, beyond, transcendent to my life. Whence it follows that the only class of beings capable of responding to me—of cor-responding to me and co-living with me—the only class of beings of whom I could hope that they would make it possible for me to emerge from my solitude and communicate with them, namely other men—precisely because they are such, because they are *other* men and *other* lives like mine, are in their radical reality incommunicable with me. Between us only a relative and indirect and always dubious communication is possible. But, first and last, that is, at the beginning and at the end of my experience in respect to the Other Man, for me he is fundamentally the Being who is strange to me, the essential stranger. And when in my intercourse with him I think I may infer that a considerable part of his world coincides with mine and that hence we live in a common world, this community of ambience in which we co-exist—far from breaching our two solitudes so that, like torrents bursting their dikes, they fuse and become one in a common flowing and being—represents the very opposite. Because my partic-

ular world, that of my life in its radical reality—although
it resists me, hinders me, denies me in many of its points
and contents—is, when all is said and done, mine; and
it is mine because it is patent to me—as patent, at least, as
my life and I myself are. In this sense it belongs to me, is
intimate to me, and my relation with it is warm, as is
normal in domestic affairs. It at once represses me and
shelters me. The Germans and the English have words to
express this delicious, diffused emotion of what is intimate
and ours and homely: they say *gemütlich* and "cosy."
Spanish has no such word, but there is an Asturian region-
alism that admirably expresses it and that I am trying to
bring into use, namely the word "*atopadizo*" ["snug"].
My world is snug, including what is painful to me in it.
I cannot now enter into a strict phenomenology of pain—
which, by the way, no one has undertaken; but it would
show that our pains, which are one of the things found in
the world of each of us, our subjective world, have a
positive dimension by virtue of which, at the same time
that they exasperate us, we feel for them something
rather like affection, the diffuse but warm attitude, we
might call it, that we feel toward everything that is genuinely ours. And this is because while it pains us it is
intimate to us. How could it be otherwise, if in pain it is
always *I* who suffer the pain? I say this merely to give an
extreme example, in order to contrast with it what happens to us in the case of the objective or common world
in which we live with other men and which is what we
normally call the World, and even, if you like, the real
World. Because it, as I say, is neither mine nor yours; it
is not patent to us, but a vast conjecture that we are constantly making in our living together but which, as such, is
always doubtful, which never shows us its face, but which
we reach as it were gropingly and always suspect to be
full of enigmas, of unknown territories, of confounding

surprises, of trapdoors and pitfalls. What the other is to me as strange and foreign is projected on this world that is common to us both, that therefore, because it comes from others, is, as I said, the genuine not-I and hence for me the great strangeness and absolute foreignness. The so-called objective world, which is the world of all men as they form society, is the correlative of society and, finally, of humanity.

But there is another and still deeper reason why the common Objective World that we call the universe is absolutely strange and inhospitable to me, a reason which at any cost—I mean, at the cost of not being immediately understood—I shall briefly define. My world, you will remember, was made up of things whose being consisted in *being for* my advantage or use. This *being for* of things, we called their serviceability, which made them consist in pure reference to me—their serving me or hindering me. But this new objective world, common to you and to me and to everyone else, which is neither yours nor mine, cannot be composed of things that refer to any of us, but of things that claim to exist independently of each one of us, indifferent to you, to me, and to anybody. In short, this world is composed of things that appear to me possessing a *being* that is their own and not a mere *being for*. This is the counterpart of its being common and objective—that is, non-subjective, alien or strange to Man, who is always *you* or *he*. The *being for* of things is patent to me because their services and hindrances are patent to me; but this world which is the Universe is not patent but present to me and hence preconjectural. We live together in it; but while we are living together in the World we are living *in what is foreign to us*—there is no possible doubt about it. This is why the World is so radically an enigma to us and why there are sciences and philosophy to extract its secret, to plumb its hidden depths and dis-

cover *what it is*. For everything would seem to indicate
that someone has decreed that we should live shipwrecked
in its vast enigma! Hence man, whether he likes it or not,
with or against his will, is essentially and inevitably a
decipherer of enigmas, and all down the course of history,
through all its other noises rises the scrape of a knife that
someone is sharpening on a whetstone; it is the human
mind passing its edge back and forth over the stubborn
enigma, What is Being? To this task of making ourselves
keenly alive to the tremendous secret and infinite conun-
drum that the Universe is, and of pertinaciously attempting to solve it, we must return again and wholeheartedly
—even though not during these lectures. Nothing more
profoundly divides us from the last two centuries than
the predominant tendency of their thinkers to shun the
stirring presence of the enigma in which "we live and
move and have our being," making caution their one intellectual virtue and avoiding error their sole aspiration.
Today this seems cowardly and inconceivable to us and
we know how to listen when Hegel exhorts us to have
the courage to be wrong. And this first beginning in us of
fruition through the enigmatic, through contemplating
the enormous mystery face to face is—despite all the surface signs of our times which are interpreted as fatigue
and senescence—incontrovertible proof of youth; it is
the joy of sport, the jovial elasticity that confronts enigma
and complication—as if the soul of the West had suddenly
been endowed with an unhoped-for boyhood!

But at this date in history, it falls to us to attempt the
solution of the immense hieroglyph by setting out from
man, and we need, among other things, to discover the
truth of his social condition. That is what we are about,
and, for the present, we shall confine ourselves to it.

We have shown that the first thing I fall foul of in my
proper and radical world is Other Men, the Other singu-

lar and plural, among whom I am born and begin to live. From the beginning, then, I find myself in a human world or "society." We have not yet even the remotest idea of what society is. However, it will not involve us in difficulties to use the word now, because we are using it informally and only in a sense that does not compromise us, namely: that all men find themselves among men, even as I do.

Since this human world occupies the first distance or foreground in the perspective of my world, I see all the rest of it, and my life and myself, through Others, through Them. And since They never cease to act all about me, manipulating things and above all talking about them, that is, operating on them, I project upon the radical reality of my life all that I see them do and hear them say— whereupon my radical reality, which is so much mine and mine alone, is concealed from my own eyes by a crust made up of what I have received from other men, from their maneuvers and their opinions, and I become habituated to normally living by a presumed or probable world created by them, which I ordinarily accept as genuine without further question and regard as reality itself. Only when my docility or what Other Men do and say leads me into ridiculous, contradictory, or disastrous situations do I ask myself how much truth there is in all this—in other words, withdraw for a moment from this pseudo-reality, from the convention in which I live with them, to the genuineness of my life as radical solitude. So that to less or greater degrees and proportions and with less or greater frequency, I actually live a double life— two lives, each with its own optics and perspective. If I look around me, I seem to suspect that the same thing happens with every one of the Others, but—and this should be noted—with each in a different proportion. There is the man who scarcely lives anything but the pseudo-life of convention, yet in contrast there are extreme cases in which I seem to see that the other is energetically true to his genuine self. Between these two poles, there are all the intermediate equations, for it is a case of an equation between the conventional and the genuine, which has different figures in each man's case. Indeed, in our first moment of intercourse with the Other, without being particularly aware of it we calculate his vital equation, that is, what proportion of convention and what proportion of genuineness there are in him.

But observe that even in the case of maximum genuineness, the human individual lives the greater part of his life in the pseudo-living of the surrounding, or social, conventionality—as we shall see in greater detail in the following lectures. And as the Others are "Men," "Mankind"—I in my solitude could not call myself by a generic name like "man"—it follows that I see the World and my life and myself in accordance with their formulas; that is, I see all this as colored by other men, impregnated with their humanity, in short, humanized, the word *humanized* being used here as having a neutral value; it does not suggest whether this—the World humanized in accordance with the gospel of the human beings who are the Others—is good or bad. Only one aspect is clearly defined: that this world that is humanized for me by others is not my genuine world; it does not possess an unquestionable reality; it is only more or less probable, illusory in many of its parts; and it lays on me the duty—not an ethical but a vital duty—of submitting it to periodical purifyings so that its things shall be rated at their true value, each with the coefficient of reality or unreality that belongs to it. This technique of inexorable purification is philosophy.

Thus our analysis of the radical reality that the life of each one of us is has led us to discover that, normally, we do not live in it, but pseudo-live by co-living with the world of men, that is, by living in "society." And since this is the great theme of these present lectures, we shall attempt, step by step, tolerating neither haste nor confusion, to see how the different components of this human or social world appear to us and what its texture is.

Not long ago we made a great step forward: we observed that there is in each of us a basic *altruism* that renders us from birth open to the other, to the *alter*, as such. This other is Man, for the present the indeterminate man or individual, the undistinguished Other, about whom I know only that he is my "like" in the sense that he is capable of responding to me by his reactions, on a level approximately the same as that of my actions—which did not happen to me with the animal. This capacity for responding to me to the full scope of my actions, I call cor-responding or reciprocating to me. But if I do no more than to remain open to the Other, to realize that he is there with his I, his life, and his world, I do nothing to him and this basic altruism is not yet "social relation." For that to arise, I have to act or operate on him, in order to provoke a response in him. Then he and I exist for each other and what either of us does in respect to the other is something that takes place between *us*. The relation *We* is the primary form of social relation or sociality. Its content does not matter—it can be a kiss or a blow. *We* kiss and *we* hit. What matters here is the *we*. In it, I do not live but co-live. The reality *we* or *we-ity* can be expressed by a more ordinary term—intercourse. If the intercourse that is the *we* becomes frequent, continuous, the Other becomes more and more distinct to me in it. From being any man, my fellow-man in the abstract, the undefined human individual passes through degrees of increasing definition, becomes better and better known to me, humanly closer. The extreme degree of closeness is what I call "intimacy," "inwardness." When my intercourse with the Other is intimate, he is an individual whom I cannot confuse with any other, for whom I can substitute no other. He is a unique individual. So, within this ambit of vital reality or co-living, the We, the Other, has become a You. And since this happens to me not only with one but with a number of other men, I find the human World appearing to me as a horizon of men whose nearest circle to me is full of You's; that is, of those individuals who for me are unique. Beyond them lie circular zones occupied by men of whom I know less, and so on to the horizon-line of my human environment, the place of the individuals who to me are indeterminate, interchangeable. Thus the human world opens before me as a perspective of greater or less intimacy, of greater or less individuality or uniqueness, in short, a perspective of close and distant humanity.

This is the point we had reached, and it is from here that we must set out on a fresh advance.

Let us make it perfectly clear to ourselves what our situation is at this stage of our analysis.

I, the I that each of us is, finds itself surrounded by other men. With many of them I am in a social relation, I experience the reciprocity between them and myself which we called the reality "We," within which they increasingly become the definite individuals, known to me —that is, identifiable for me—whom we have called You's. But beyond this sphere or zone of the You's, there are those other men who are in sight within my horizon, with whom I have not entered into real association, but whom I see as like myself, fellow-men, and hence as beings with whom I have a potential sociality that one or another eventuality can make actual. It is the well-known "Who would ever have dreamed that I should become a friend of yours!" In love the case is usually more striking, for what normally happens is that we fall in love with a

woman about whom, a minute before we fell in love and
she became the most unique of women to us, we knew
nothing in particular. She was there, in our environment,
and we had never paid any attention to her; if we had
seen her it was simply as one more woman, interchangeable with many others, just as the "unknown soldier" is
undoubtedly an individual, but not a particular individual
—what the Scholastics very aptly call "the indeterminate
individual" in contrast to the "unique individual." One
of the most deliciously dramatic and confounding scenes
in life is the one—sometimes literally instantaneous—in
which the unknown woman is transformed for us, as if
by magic, into the unique woman. We are, then, in a human environment.

But now we have to come rather more seriously to
grips with the You, for we must say a little—even if only
a little—of what can be said about the way in which the
Other proceeds to change into You for us and what happens to us in respect to him when we have him completely *you-ified* before us—which is no slight thing to
have happen but rather the most dramatic thing that happens to us in life. For it turns out that, so far, all that has
appeared to us in our world is the Other and He, that is,
the so-called—I shall not stop to argue whether correctly
or incorrectly so called—third person, and the You or
second person, but so far we have had no appearance of
the first person, the I, the concrete *I* that each one of us is.
Apparently our *I* is the last character to appear in the
tragicomedy of our life. We have often referred to him,
but irresponsibly, taking him for granted, so that we
might begin to understand one another. Nevertheless, I
have several times pointed out that all the names I found
myself obliged to use for the "subject" of living were inadequate; that it was incorrect to say that Man lives.
We have already seen that original Man is the Other and

that rather than live he co-lives with us and we with him.
But co-living is already a second and presumed reality,
whereas living in radical solitude is primary and unquestionable. Similarly, as we are now about to see—and as I
pointed out once before—it is incorrect to say that *I* live;
it would only be proper to speak of X who lives, of
someone who lives, or of the living being. But let us without further ado enter upon our new task, which is decisive for a full understanding of what Society is. The matter as I see it—which is more or less the opposite of the
way it has been seen by the only men who have seriously
concerned themselves with the question—that is, Husserl
and his disciples Fink, Schütz, Löwith, and others—the
matter as I see it turns out to be rather complicated and
demands a special effort of attention.

The foregoing considerations have presented us with
the Men around each one of us, constituting a human environment, in which they appear to us some as nearer,
others as farther away, hence ranged in what I called a
"perspective of humanity"—in a being more or less
known to us or individualized, that is, intimate to us, until the series reaches the zero of intimacy. Starting from
this, I ask: What do I have before me when I describe
my relation with the other as a zero of intimacy? Obviously I know nothing about him that is unique, that
belongs to him alone. I only know of him, that, given his
corporeal appearance, he is my "like"—that is, that he
possesses the most abstract and indispensable attributes of
the human being; hence that he feels—but I am completely ignorant of what he feels, what he wants, what the
trajectory of his life may be, what he aspires to, what
norms his conduct obeys. Now, let each of you imagine
that for some reason he enters into active social relation
with such a being. That relation, we said, consists in your
performing an action, whether directed especially to him

or simply reckoning with his existence and therefore with
his eventual intervention. This obliges you, in planning
your action, to try to anticipate the action or reaction of
the other. But what basis can I find, or can you find, for
such an anticipation? Observe that the attributes just referred to, which for me put this other at the zero point
of intimacy with respect to me, come down to just this:
I know that the other will probably react to my action.
How he will react, I cannot surmise. I have no data for
surmising. So I fall back on the general experience of men
that I have acquired from my intercourse with others less
distant, whose relation to me has not been zero in intimacy but some positive figure. For somewhere in the
lumber room of our habitual knowledge, all of us have
a practical idea of man, of what his general possibilities
for behavior are. Now, this idea of possible human behavior, in this general form, has a terrible content. For I have
learned by experience that man is capable of everything—
certainly of the admirable and perfect, but also and no
less of the worst. I have known the kind, generous, intelligent man, but, beside him, I have known the thief—thief
of things and thief of ideas—the murderer, the envious
man, the knave, the fool. From which it follows that, in
the presence of the pure and unknown Other, I have to
expect the worst and suppose that his reaction will be to
hit me. And so with innumerable other adverse reactions.
The pure Other is in fact provisionally and equally my
possible friend or my potential enemy. We shall see later
that this opposed but equally likely possibility, that Man
may be friend or enemy, that he may *be for* us or *be
against* us, is the root of everything social. The traditional
phrase that man is a sociable animal, in the sense in which
it has usually been understood, has always barred the way
to a solid sociology. Sociality, sociability means to be in
social relation with others, but "social relation," as I have

already said, is equally a pretty woman giving me a kiss —how delightful!—or an unknown passerby taking it into his head to hit me—what a nuisance! The automatically optimistic interpretation of the words "social" and "society" cannot be maintained and we must have done with it. The reality "society," in its very root, signifies both its positive and its negative meanings, or, as I say for the first time in these lectures, every society is at the same time, to a greater or lesser extent, *dissociety*—which is a living together of friends *and* of enemies. As you see, the sociology toward which we are setting our course is far more dramatic than all those that have preceded it. But if this contradictory—or, better, *contrafactory*—duality of social reality has suddenly appeared to us here, please note, nevertheless, that we have not even distantly glimpsed what underlies this opposition, that X which can equally well be delightful living together and atrocious hostility. And this X, which underlies the two opposing possibilities alike, which bears them within it and, in fact, makes them possible, is precisely Society, with a capital S. But what Society is, I repeat, we have not even the remotest suspicion.

We may say, then: Of the pure other, at the zero point of intimacy, I have no direct intuition beyond that which comes to me from his momentary presence and compresence, I have nothing but the sight of his body, of his gestures, of his movements, in all of which I believe that I see a Man, but that is all. I believe that I see an *unknown* man, some random individual not defined by any particular attribute. To this I add something that is not direct intuition of him, but the general experience of my intercourse with men, a collection of generalizations concerning my instinctive intercourse with many who were closer to me, hence something purely conceptual, or let us say *theoretical*—our generic idea of Man and the human.

This comprehension, formed from two separate sources of knowledge—intuitive comprehension of each individual, and rational, theoretical comprehension, the result of my "experience of life"—will reappear in all the other more positive degrees of intimacy; I mean that they are not like the case just studied, the extreme case of zero intimacy; instead, whereas in that case intuition of the other individual is reduced to the minimum and our comprehension of him rests principally on our theoretical knowledge or general and intellectual experience of Man, in cases of greater intimacy this factor loses weight and the intuitive and individualized increases.

Let us conclude this analysis of our relation with the pure and unknown Other by drawing the immediate consequence. It is this: Since, before the other, I have to anticipate the possibility that he will be ferocious—we shall soon see that man on one of his sides is literally and formally speaking a mammal of the order carnivora—I have no choice but to *begin* my intercourse with him by a wary approach. The same is true of him in respect to me; and so the intercourse between the two of us has to *begin* by an action, useless in itself, whose only purpose is estimating each other, allowing time for us to discover our attitudes and intentions toward each other. This formally initial action, which serves only to indicate and estimate our intercourse, has been enormously important in history, and among some peoples even to this day it is carried on for fully half an hour and consists in strictly ritualized gestures and steps. Historically, this quite simple act of one man approaching another demands a whole scrupulously observed technique even when they know each other, and still more so when they are strangers. This technique of mutual approach is what we call the "salutation," of which, for peculiar reasons that will be set forth later, we today keep only the residual form.

This (besides other reasons) is why our next lecture will have to be a meditation on the salutation.

Observe that, of the pure and indeterminate other, of Man the unknown, precisely because he is such—I mean, because he is unknown to me and I cannot surmise what he is capable of and what his behavior toward me will be —I have only a concept that is at once vast and empty. In effect, not knowing what he is like, I attribute to him the potentiality of all human possibilities, including the most extreme or extremist and the most self-contradictory. There could not be a greater wealth of attributes. But at the same time, since I attribute them to him in pure and abstract potentiality, I in reality attribute nothing positive to him. It is the void of human possibilities or, to express it differently, nothing human is foreign to him, but only *in vacuo*. It is as if we had the cavities of every kind of vessel but none of the vessels.

As we continue our intercourse with him, a curious phenomenon of progressive elimination takes place in us; that is, we become convinced that this man is incapable of such and such types of behavior, some good, others inadequate or perverse. In other words, under our very eyes he gradually becomes a definite system of concrete possibilities and concrete impossibilities, and of actions that we believe we must fear from him. If we had the patience, we could make a card-index, in which each of our neighbor would have a card on which we had listed what behavior we consider possible or impossible in him. Such a catalogue might take the form of a graph which would even show the plus and minus of a quality or defect. Because, in practice, this is the most important thing in knowing our neighbor—since, except for unusual and extrapolated cases, almost all men have the same qualities, positive or negative, but each man has them in a different place or stratum of his personality, and this is what counts.

Peter and John are generous, but Peter is generous in
the deepest and most forceful stratum of his being whereas
John's generosity is all on the surface. No one will doubt
that, aside from being entertaining, it would be not a little
fertile for that great discipline, the Knowledge of Man, to
draw on a blackboard some schemas of human structures,
typical figures, to each of which a great many human individuals belong. Aristotle's best disciple, who spoke so
delectably that the master nicknamed him Theophrastus
—that is, "he of divine speech"—long ago applied himself
conscientiously to the subject, and a brief but famous extract from his work has come down to us, the *Characters*.

I said that the You becomes increasingly definite to us
when the unlimited human possibilities that we attribute
to the other *in vacuo* are constantly reduced and, as they
are reduced, gradually concrete into a definite system of
possibilities or impossibilities, which is what every *You*
is to us. This reduction and concretion or definition arises
in our frequent intercourse with him. We see him before
us in sufficient continuity, and this means the following:
in the literal sense we see his physiognomy, his gestures,
his movements, and in them we read a good deal of what
goes on within him or, to put the same thing in different
words, we glimpse him living his life. I say "we read," and
I use the word deliberately, because no other word better
expresses what happens to us in relation to him. In a particular position of his facial muscles I read "sorrow," in
another "joy," and so on. His external movements I can
generally interpret clearly, though once in a while the interpretation is doubtful. I see him enter a luggage shop
and come out with a suitcase, he goes to a travel agency;
these external acts have a vital meaning in themselves—
please note this carefully—a meaning that I understand
without having to resort to his inwardness, that is, to his

inner subjective and individual meaning. In these acts I
read the meaning: "So-and-so is going to take a journey."
What these acts do not disclose to me is the why and
wherefore of this action of going on a journey. To discover that, I have to resort to my previous knowledge of
his life, together with what his gestures at the moment
tell me. When I speak of gestures, I include language,
speech.

Outward act, physiognomy, gestures enable me to *witness* the living of the other Man who is in the process of
becoming a You for me, and all the more when he is already a familiar and accustomed You—that is, a relative,
a friend, a business or professional colleague. This *witness-
ing* is not seeing his life patent before me; it is glimpsing
it, making it compresent to myself, suspecting it. But the
strict philosophical reservation which these words express
must not blind us to the fact that, *in practice,* we do actually *see,* we witness the Other's living, within the ambit
of reciprocity represented by the reality *We.* I see his
life flow unbroken in a continuous current of vital experiences,[1] which is only interrupted in his hours of sleep
and sometimes only partially even then because while he
sleeps man often goes on living in that strangest, most
mysterious form of life which we call dreaming. I see,
then, the flowing series of my neighbor's vital experiences
as they arise in him—his perceptions, thoughts, feelings,
volitions. I do not, of course, say that I see his whole living completely, or anywhere near it; but I do see substantial parts of it. Behind these there always remain dark,
impenetrable, hidden areas of the other, holes and corners
of his being that I cannot penetrate. But the fact is that,
without trying to or wishing to, I have constantly before

[1] [*Vivencias,* representing Husserl's term *Erlebnis* (see *Obras
completas,* I, p. 257, note 1). It is defined in the following sentence.
—*Translator*]

me an image of the character, activity, experiences, and being of the You. This image is constantly changing to some extent, because as I continue to witness his living I observe that the new thing that he does never quite coincides with what the image prognosticated. This is important, because it is characteristic of all vital knowledge in contrast to scientific knowledge. I refer, for example, to facts such as this: However well we think we know someone, however certain we are of what traits make up his character, if we venture to prophesy what his behavior will be in some matter that is really of importance to us, we observe that our conviction in regard to his mode of being vacillates and we finally admit the possibility that his future conduct on this occasion may be different from what we have presumed it will be. Now, this does not occur in the case of such anticipations of knowledge as the laws of physics and in large part the laws of biology, to say nothing of mathematical laws. Reflecting on this, we discover that scientific knowledge is closed and stable, whereas our vital knowledge of other men and of ourselves is an open knowledge that is never stable, with shifting contours. The reason for this is plain: Man, whether the other or I, does not possess a fixed or settled being; his being is precisely freedom to be. This implies that, while he lives, man can always be different from what he has been until that moment—nay more, that he in fact always *is* more or less different. Our vital knowledge is open, shifting, because its subject—life, Man—is in itself a being ever open to new possibilities. Our past undoubtedly weighs on us; it inclines us to be this rather than that in the future; but it does not chain us or drag us. Only when the Man, the you, has died does he have a fixed being—what he has been, which he can now no longer alter, contradict, or add to. This is the meaning of the famous line in which Mallarmé sees the dead Edgar Allan Poe: *Tel qu'en lui-même enfin l'Éternité le change.*

Life is change; at every new moment it is becoming something different from what it was, hence it never becomes definitively *itself*. Only death, by preventing any new change, changes man into a definitive and immutable himself, makes him a forever motionless figure—that is, frees him from change and renders him eternal. This shows us a new aspect of what we were saying before. I see my neighbor's vital experiences flowing. They succeed one another, and this succession is time. To say that I see the other's life running on is the same as saying that I see his vital time, his lifetime, running on, passing, spending itself; and that is a time whose hours are numbered. But while his time runs and flows before me, my time is doing the same. While we live together, an equal portion of our two vital times is simultaneously running out; that is, our times are contemporary. The you, the you's, are our contemporaries. And as Schütz well says, this means that in my intercourse with the You's we grow old together. The life of each Man, throughout his course of existence, witnesses the spectacle of a universal aging, for obviously the old man sees the young aging too. From his birth, man does nothing but age. There is no help for it, but perhaps it is not as sad a thing as an improper but entrenched education leads us to believe.[2]

[2] If we undertook to discuss the disadvantages of immortality in this world—a thing that, though you will hardly believe me, has never been done—we should immediately see the benefits of mortality, of the fact that life is short, that man is corruptible, and that, from the moment we begin to be, death enters into the very substance of our life, collaborates in it, compresses and densifies it, makes it urgency, imminence, the need to do our best at every instant. One of the great limitations—not to say disgraces—of all the cultures that have so far existed is that none of them has taught man properly to be what he constitutively is—namely, mortal. This means that, *in sum*, my doctrine regarding death is strictly the reverse of that held by the existentialists.

The idea that the you present in my environment is my contemporary because our vital times flow parallel and we grow old together, makes me aware that there are you's who are not now, or who have never been, our contemporaries and, not being such, are not present in our environment. They are the dead. The Others are not only the living. There are Others whom we have never seen, yet who exist for us; family memories, ruins, old documents, stories, legends are a new type of indications to us —indications of lives that have gone by, anachronous to our own, that is, not contemporaneous with us. In these indications which are not actual physiognomy, gestures, or movements we must learn to read the reality of those past, deceased you's, those pre-decessors. Beyond the men within the horizon that is our environment, there are many, many more; they are latent lives—they are Antiquity. History is the effort that we make to recognize Antiquity—because it is the technique of intercourse with the dead, a curious modification of the genuine, present social relation.

I said that the Other, the pure Other, the unknown man, simply because he is such and because I do not know what his behavior toward me will be, forces me, in approaching him, to expect the worst, to anticipate his possible hostile and ferocious reaction. Expressed in other words, this is equivalent to saying that the other is formally, constitutively perilous. The word is splendid; it exactly expresses the reality to which I refer. The perilous is not deliberately evil and adverse; it can be the contrary—beneficial and fortunate. But, so long as it is perilous, the two opposite contingencies are equally possible. To put an end to doubt, we must prove it, assay it, estimate it, experience it. This—proving, assaying—is the original meaning of the Latin word *periculum*, from which "peril" comes. Note in passing that the radical *per* of *periculum* is the same that gives life to the word ex-*per*-ience, ex-*peri*ment, ex-*per*t. I have not time now to show by strict etymological methods that the original meaning of the noun "experiences" is "to have undergone peril."

The Other Man is, then, essentially perilous, dangerous, and this characteristic, which stands out in the highest degree in the case of the completely unknown person, subsists to diminishing degrees as he becomes You for us and—if we want to speak strictly—never entirely disappears. Every *other* human being is a peril, is dangerous to us—each in his way and in his particular measure. Do not forget that the innocent child is one of the most dangerous of beings—it is he who sets fire to the house with a match, he whose playing with it fires the shotgun, he who pours nitric acid into the stew, and, worst of all, it is he who is constantly putting himself in danger of falling from the balcony, breaking his head against the corner of the table, swallowing a wheel from the toy train he is playing with—thereby subjecting us to the most serious inconvenience. And if we call this being "innocent," that is, "not harmful," imagine what those who have lost their innocence will be!

This consciousness of the basic dangerousness of the Other Man is vividly present throughout history, except for brief periods during which here or there, in one or another society, it oddly enough becomes obscured, loses its vigor, and even disappears. Perhaps in the whole history of the world this last phenomenon has never occurred in such a serious form as during the first two thirds of the eighteenth century and then again from 1830 to 1914. This numbness or obtuseness to the evident and basic truth that every fellow human being is ultimately dangerous has been the chief cause of the sufferings and catastrophes that we have been undergoing for the past thirty-five years. For it caused Europeans to lose the alertness without which men cannot and have no right to live. Hence the surprise—the totally unjustified surprise —of our Europeans during these last years when, suddenly, an abyss of crime and ferocity which they had willfully refused to suspect yawned before their eyes in their several nations.

But it is not these extreme, melodramatic, and clearly ferocious forms of human dangerousness that now concern us, but precisely its minor and minimum and ordinary forms, so ordinary that although we are constantly exposed to them and because we constantly experience them, we do not recognize them under the appellation "dangers." But let us make thoroughly clear to ourselves what the habitual *basis* of our daily life is in so far as it consists in intercourse with our fellows, including those who are our nearest neighbors and even our intimates. I repeat that, simply because it is so constant and habitual with us, we are not aware of it, as people who live near a waterfall end by not hearing the noise of it. But the fact is that the basis—how shall I put it?—the ground, the plane on which this daily intercourse is conducted can only be adequately described by calling it "strife." The fact that we commonly reserve the term for intense and less frequent conflicts that rise above this level as mountains rise above sea-level, is no reason why, now that we are energetically reacting against the weight of habit that dulls us to perceiving this daily basis of our living together with others, we should not call it by the only adequate name—strife. The exemplary harmony in an exemplarily harmonious family, whose members are united by the warmest bonds of affection, is only a resultant equilibrium, a good adjustment and mutual adaptation, at which they have arrived after each of them has un-

dergone countless impacts and collisions against the others
—collisions that, comparatively speaking, may be as minor as you please but which, clearly seen, are real strife.
In this strife we have learned with what angles in the
Other's mode of being our own mode of being clashes;
that is, we have gradually discovered the endless series of
small dangers that our living with him entails, for ourselves and for him. To give only a very minor example,
there is the word, the particular word, that cannot be
spoken because it irritates or wounds or confounds or ex-
cites him, and so on.

With this we discover a final, and the most substantial,
stratum of the Other's dangerousness: it is not the possibility that he will be hostile and savage toward us even
though only to a very slight degree; it is the simple fact
that You are You—I mean, that you have a mode of being
that is your own and peculiar to you, and that does not
coincide with mine.

From *you*, that is, arise frequent negations of my being
—of my way of thinking, of feeling, of wanting and desiring. Sometimes the negation consists precisely in the
fact that you and I want the same thing, and this implies
that we have to strive against each other for it—be it a
picture, a success, a social position for the possession of
which we fight or contend, be it—as sometimes it is—a
woman. It follows that even in these cases in which the
other coincides with me, he collides with me, negates me.
These active negations that are discharged from him to
me make my living with him a constant collision; and
this collision with him in this, that, and the other thing
makes me discover my boundaries, my frontiers, dividing
me from your world and you. Whereupon we realize that
what when we were children each of us called "I" was an
abstract concept, without any definite content, just as the
concept of "I" that we have so far used in these talks has

been. Because formerly, in my radical solitude and in my childhood, I believed that the whole world was *I* or, what is the same thing, mine. Others were no more and no less *I* than *I* was; I considered them identical with myself and myself identical with them. Saying *I* signified no limitation or definition whatever. In infancy, my body itself seemed to me unbounded, seemed to extend to the horizon. I had to bump into the furniture—tables and bureaus—and bruise myself, in order gradually to discover where my body ended and other things began. Ever since there have been tables and bureaus, they have been the first dumb tutors to teach man the frontiers, the limits of his being, beginning with those of his corporeal being. Yet this world of tables and bureaus, though it was different from me, was nevertheless *mine*—because everything in it was, existed, because it was what it was for me. But what is Yours does not exist for me—your ideas and convictions do not exist for me, I see them as foreign and sometimes as opposed to me. My world is entirely impregnated with me. You yourself, before you became for me the particular You that you now are for me, were not strange to me; I believed you were like myself—*alter*, other, but myself, I, *ego—alter ego*. But now as I face you and the other *you's*, I see that there is more in the world than that vague, indeterminate *I*; there are anti-I's. All *You's* are such—because they are different from me—and when I say *I*, I am only a minute portion of the world, the tiny part of it that I now begin accurately to call "I."

Provisionally, then, the word *I* has two meanings, which we must separate and distinguish. Let us see if I can make the matter completely clear. We are going to imagine three things in succession, each of them perfectly simple.

*First*, let us imagine that absolutely nothing existed in the world except what any one of us is, but that, nevertheless, this unique human being had a language—which is obviously impossible. The function of any word is to distinguish one thing from other things. Now, in such a situation, what would be the meaning of the word *I*— which this unique and lone human being would utter? It could not signify an intention to distinguish itself from other human beings because, in our imaginary assumption, there are none. It could only signify that this unique living subject felt itself to be different from the World in which it lived and from the things in that world. It would then mean, solely and strictly, the subject that lives in the World—not the subject that lives in it in some particular way in distinction from the way another subject lives, for we assume that there is no such other.

*Second imagination.* Let us now suppose that, instead of this being the only human being, many such exist, as many as there are men today, but that each of them exists in the radical solitude of its genuine life, hence, with no communication between them. Observe that this new situation does not change the former one in the least— because, since each being has no communication with the others, it is as if it alone existed. Nevertheless, the new thing is that they would all use the word *I*, which before referred to the only existing subject and signified only him as "he who lives in his World." Now, however, it also refers to all men, but meaning the same in each case —namely, each as living, that is, feeling himself to be different from the world that surrounds him. The meaning of *I* continues to be single, because it signifies nothing different in reference to one or another. This is normally the case with the noun substantive, as the grammarians call it. "Table" applies to every table and all tables, but only in as much as they are *tables* and nothing more, and without distinguishing the pine table from the mahogany table, *this* table from *another* table.

*Third imagination.* You are at home. Somebody knocks at the door, and you ask, "Who is it?" From the other side of the door comes the answer, "I!" What meaning does this word have now, that is, what thing names itself and identifies itself in it? Obviously all men, coming to your door in succession, could say the same, and in fact everyone in his life is constantly saying "I!" Have we not here the same generic, common, and hence normal meaning of the noun substantive as we had in our second imagination? Not at all; the person who answers "I" from the other side of the door to identify himself does not give the word this generic meaning of "he who lives in the World"; on the contrary, in uttering it he excludes all others, and it is as if the extreme brevity of the word summed up the whole of his highly individual biography, which he assumes that you know. But since the same thing can happen in the case of many whom you know just as intimately as you know him, we have a type of word that is not a common and normal generic noun— that is, which signifies and names a single and exclusive reality that is always the same; on the contrary, we have a noun that signifies a different reality whenever someone else uses it. All of us who are present here say "I" with a frequency that is sometimes excessive, and yet its meaning varies in accordance with who says it, since it refers to the different and exclusive individuality that each of us is in the face of everyone else. This man wants to make known who is knocking at your door; and he is not an "I," but the unique "I" that he is in distinction from and to the exclusion of all others. There could not, then, be a more radical change in meaning in comparison with the "I" of our second imagination, which, signifying simply "he who lives in the World," is equally valid for all men, whereas here it formally excludes everyone except this particular man.

Now, the same sort of thing occurs with other words. If there are several of us in a room, we can say "here" referring to the place in which each of us is. So that this word signifies various different realities, that is, different locations in space. Grammar has had to set up a pigeon-hole or special category for these words and calls them "words of occasional meaning," words whose meaning is defined not so much by the word itself as by the occasion on which it is used—for example, by who it is, in a given situation, that uses it. I think that we could argue with the grammarians whether words like "here" or "I" have *one* occasional meaning, or whether it would not be more nearly true to say that they are innumerable different words, each with its unique and precise meaning. Because this fellow human being who answers "I" from the other side of the door makes no claim that this word, in so far as it is a common word, signifies his own little personality, because he knows only too well that all the other little personalities in the world could call themselves "I" too. What is it, then, that when you hear "I" makes you recognize who is referred to and renders its meaning exclusive? It is something that modern linguistics does not even recognize as a word—namely, not the vocable, but the voice in which it is uttered, whose tone and timbre are familiar to you. But if this is so, if the significant thing is not the vocable "I" as a word but the voice that utters it, then to identify himself, to make himself known, the man on the other side of the door could just as well have said "abracadabra," "hypotenuse," or "streptomycin," or, better yet, because these might be distracting, he could have used arbitrary combinations of meaningless syllables, that is, anything that could serve as a pretext for producing the sound of a human voice. Needless to say, students of linguistics have observed this, for it is something too obvious to escape notice, but the curious thing is that they have observed it as private individuals, not as students of linguistics—I mean, that the observation has had no effect on grammar. And indeed such an effect would have obliged them radically to revise their notion of "word" and hence their whole traditional notion of language.

We have seen, then, that the word "I" has two separate meanings. One is its generic, abstract meaning as a common noun—"he who lives in the World," or something of the sort—this being the meaning that has chiefly occupied philosophers ever since Descartes, and more especially ever since Kant, with the series of philosophies of the *I*, an *I* that never succeeded in being the concrete and unique I that each one of us is. The other meaning of the word is concrete and unique: the one that it has when somebody knocks at my door and I ask "Who is it?" and he answers "I."

I dwell on this because it is important for my doctrine that it be clearly understood. For I am now going to point out something highly unexpected—namely, that the concrete and unique I that each one of us feels himself to be is not something that we possess and know from the outset but something that gradually appears to us exactly as other things do, that is, step by step, by virtue of a series of experiences that have their fixed order. I mean, for example—and this is the strange and unexpected thing —we discover that we are *I* after and by virtue of having first known the *you's*, our *you's*, in our collision with them, in the strife that we called social relation.

This will perhaps be even clearer if I present it in the following way. Let us imagine the word *I* displayed on a blackboard in printed characters, that is in characters reproduced mechanically to obviate all graphological peculiarities. Consider what meaning this sign has for each one of us—that is, what thing it denominates—and you will see that it cannot signify any reality at all but only something abstract and general. This would come out with startling clarity if, in a theater, someone suddenly shouted, "I!" What would happen? To begin with, the entire audience would, by a reflex movement, turn their heads toward one point in the theater, the point from which the shout came. This detail is important. For the fact is that every sound, every noise, in addition to its phonic content, as if by magic always brings to our ears an indication of the locality in space where it was emitted. This phenomenon, proper to all sonority, which places it in its origin, which inexorably localizes its point of provenience, has not yet been sufficiently studied by psychologists investigating auditory sensations. Bühler rightly calls attention to it in his *Theory of Language;* in addition, he cites the well-known fact that for this reason a blindman, when in conversation with several people, is perfectly aware if one of them addresses him, without the latter's having to tell him so, simply because the voice of his interlocutor reaches him as directed to him from the person speaking to him. But if this is so, we must recognize that every word, as a *spoken* word, is first of all an adverb of place—a new observation for this future and more concrete linguistics. This, then, means that every sound reaches us with a direction, brings us, bears to us, and so to speak, fires into our ears, the particular reality that emits it. In turning our heads toward the place from which the shout "I!" came, we should simply be taking in that reality, becoming aware of it. But when the sound is precisely the word "I," what is, so to speak, introduced into our ears, and hence into our persons, is that other person who shouted it, that person himself. And if we know him and recognize his voice, when we hear him say "I" he has fired his whole autobiography at us, he displays and exhibits it to us. In the same way, of course, when we say *you* to someone we fire at him point blank the whole biography of him that we have constructed. This is the terrible thing about these two personal pronouns—willy-nilly, they are two explosions of "humanity." We can well understand Michelet's remark, *Le moi est häissable*, "The I is odious." This proves—and to spare—that the meanings of the *I* and the *you* are superconcrete, that they resume two lives in a superlatively condensed form which, for that very reason, is highly explosive. That is why their abuse is so annoying, and it is perfectly understandable that courtesy curtails their employment, to keep our personality from weighing too heavily on our neighbor, oppressing and wearing him down. Courtesy, as we shall later see, is a social technique that eases the collision and strife and friction that sociality is. Around each individual it creates a series of tiny buffers that lessen the other's bump against us and ours against the other. The best proof that this is so lies in the fact that courtesy was able to attain its most perfect, richest, and most refined forms in countries whose population density was very great. Hence it reached its maximum where that is highest—namely, in the Far East, in China and Japan, where men have to live too close to one another, almost on top of one another. Without all those little buffers, living together would be impossible. It is well known that the European in China produces the impression of a rude, crass, and thoroughly ill-educated being. So it is not surprising that the Japanese language has succeeded in suppressing those two slightly and sometimes more than slightly impertinent pistol-shots the *you* and the *I*, in which, whether I want to or not, I inject my personality into my neighbor and my idea of his personality into the You. In Japan both these personal pronouns have been replaced by flowery ceremonial phrases, so that, instead of "you," one says something like "the miracle that is here," and instead of "I" something like "the wretchedness here present." [3]

But now let us finish looping the loop of all these observations and recall that their trajectory was none other than to make us see that the Other Man, the *you*, is dangerous by nature and that our social relation with him is always, more or less, strife and collision, but that in this strife and collision with the *you's*, I gradually discover my limits and my concrete figure as a man, as *I*; my *I* continues slowly becoming apparent to me all through my life, as a vaporous reduction and contraction of that immense, diffuse, unlimited thing that it was before and still was in my childhood. My knowledge of the *you's* keeps pruning and paring down this vague and abstract *I* which yet, in the abstract, believed that it was everything. Your mathematical talent shows me that I have none. Your graceful speech shows me that I am without it.

[3] The carnival, which is moribund today, has perpetuated in the Christian societies of the West the great pagan festival dedicated to Dionysus, the orgiastic God who summons us to depersonalize ourselves and blot out our differentiating I and submerge ourselves in the great anonymous unity of nature. This is enough to make us infer an Oriental divinity in him. And indeed, according to the Greek myth, Dionysus arrived from the East as a newborn infant, in a boat without sailor or pilot. In the festival this ship, with the image of the God, was borne through streets and fields in a cart amid the intoxicated and delirious crowd. This *carrus navalis* is the origin of our Spanish word *car-naval* ["carnival"], a festival in which we put on masks so that our person, our I, will disappear. Hence the masker speaks in a feigned voice and masks himself, so that his *I* shall be other and unrecognizable. It is the great religious festival in which men play that they do not know each other, having grown a little surfeited with knowing each other too well. In this magnificent festival, the pasteboard mask and the falsetto voice give man the opportunity to rest from himself a little, from the *I* that he is, to engage in being another and, at the same time, to free himself for a few hours from the daily *you's* of his milieu.

Your strong will shows me that I am a milksop. Obviously, the reverse is also true: your faults reveal my virtues to my own eyes. Thus, it is in the world of the *you's*, and by virtue of them, that the thing that I am, my *I*, gradually takes shape for me. I discover myself, then, as one of countless *you's*, but as different from them all, with gifts and defects of my own, with a unique character and conduct, that together draw my genuine and concrete profile for me—hence as another and particular *you*, as *alter tu*. And now we see why, as I said in the beginning, we must, I think, reverse the traditional doctrine, which in its most recent and refined form is the doctrine of Husserl and his disciples; Schütz, for example.

# 8

# Suddenly, "People" Appear

AND now we ask ourselves: With these great categories—the mineral, vegetable, and animal worlds, and the *inter-individual* human world—have we exhausted the content of our surroundings? Do we come upon no other reality, which cannot be reduced to these great classes, including and especially the inter-individual class? If this were the case, it would follow that "the social," "society" was a pure phantom, an optical illusion, that strictly speaking there *would be* no society.

Well, let us see. When we go out into the street, if we want to cross from one sidewalk to the other anywhere except at a streetcorner, the traffic policeman will stop us. This action, this fact, this phenomenon—to what class does it belong?

Obviously it is not a physical fact. The policeman does not stop us like the rock that blocks our road. His is a human action; but on the other hand, it is entirely different from the action with which a friend takes our arm and leads us off for a private chat. This act of our friend's is not only performed by him, it is also born in him. It occurred to him for *such* and *such* reasons, which he clearly sees; he is responsible for it; and, in addition, he refers it to my individuality, to the uninterchangeable friend that I am to him.

And we ask ourselves: Who is the subject of this human action that we call "to forbid," to command legally? Who forbids us? Who commands us? It is not the man *police-man* nor the man *superintendent* nor the man *Chief of*

*State* who is the subject of this action of *forbidding* and *commanding*. The *forbidding* and *commanding*—we say —come from the State. If *to forbid* and *to command* are human actions (and obviously they are, since they are not physical movements nor zoological reflexes or tropisms); if *to forbid* and *to command* are *human actions*, they come from someone, from a particular subject, from a man. Is the State a man? Obviously not. And Louis XIV suffered a serious delusion when he believed that the State was himself—so serious that it cost his grandson's head. Never, not even in the case of the most extreme autocracy, has a man been the *State*. He would at most be the man who performs a particular function of the State.

But then who or what is this *State* that commands me and stops me from crossing from one sidewalk to the other?

If we put this question to someone, we shall see him begin by spreading out his arms in a swimming gesture— which is what we commonly do when we are going to say something particularly vague—and he will say: Why, the State is everything, society, the collectivity.

Let us accept this for the moment, and go on:

If this evening somebody had taken it into his head to walk through the streets of his city dressed in a helmet and coat of mail and carrying a lance, ten chances to one he would be sleeping tonight in an insane asylum or at police headquarters. Why? Because it is not one of our usages, it is not customary. On the other hand, if he does the same thing in Carnival time, he may well be awarded first prize for maskers on foot. Why? Because it is one of our usages, it is customary to wear disguises during that festival. So that, though no action could be more human than wearing clothes, we do not perform this action out of our own inspiration, we wear *one kind* of clothes or *another kind* of clothes simply because it is usual. Now, what is usual, what is customary, we do because it "is done." But who does what "is done"? Why, *people*. Very well—but, who is "people"? Why, *everybody, nobody* in particular. And this leads us to the observation that an immense part of our lives is made up of things that we do, not because we want to, not out of our own inspiration or on our own account, but simply because *"people" do them;* and, like the *State* in our earlier example, so now *people* force us into human actions that proceed from them and not from us.

But this is not all. In conducting our lives, we orient ourselves by our thoughts, by what we think things are. But if we draw up the balance sheet of these thoughts, ideas, or opinions by which and from which we live, we find to our surprise that many of them—perhaps most of them—we have never thought on our own account, with full and trustworthy evidence of their truth; we think them because we have heard them and we say them because they "are said." Here, then, we have this impersonal stranger, the implied *agent* of the passive voice,* turning up installed inside ourselves, forming part of ourselves, and *itself* thinking ideas that we only voice.

Well then, who says what "is said"? Obviously, each one of us; but we say "what we say" in the same way that the policeman stops us, we say it not on our own account but on account of this unseizable, indeterminate, and irresponsible subject, *people, society,* the *collectivity*. In the measure to which I think and speak not from my own individual conviction, but simply repeating what "is said" and "is thought," my life ceases to be mine, I cease to be the supremely individual person that I am, and I act on

* [Spanish uses not the passive but the reflexive, *"se dice,"* equivalent to the French *"on"*-construction, in which *"on"* stands for "they," "people," as is pointed out below, pp. 182–184.—*Trans.*]

society's account—I am a social automaton, I am *social-ized*.

But in what sense is this *collective* life *human* life?

Since the end of the eighteenth century, it has been arbitrarily and mystically supposed that there is a social spirit or consciousness, a *collective soul*, which the German romanticists, for example, called *Volksgeist*, or "national spirit." It has never been sufficiently emphasized that this German concept of the "national spirit," the *Volksgeist*, is simply the heir of the idea that Voltaire suggestively launched in his masterly *Essai sur l'histoire générale et sur les moeurs et l'esprit des nations*. The *Volksgeist* is "*the spirit of the nation.*"

But I repeat, this idea of the *collective soul*, of a *social consciousness*, is arbitrary mysticism. There is no such *collective soul*, if by *soul* is meant—and here it can mean nothing else—*something* that is capable of being the responsible subject of its acts, *something* that does what it does because what it does has a clear meaning for it. But then will the characteristic of *people*, of *society*, of the *collectivity* be precisely that they are soulless?

The collective soul, *Volksgeist* or "national spirit," social consciousness, has had the loftiest and most marvelous qualities attributed to it, sometimes even divine qualities. For Durkheim, society is veritably God. In the Catholic De Bonald (the actual inventor of collectivistic thought), in the Protestant Hegel, in the materialist Karl Marx, this collective soul appears as something infinitely above, infinitely more human than man. For example, it is wiser. And here our analysis, with no special effort or premeditation, with no formal precedents (at least so far as I am aware) among philosophers, drops into our hands something disquieting and even terrible—namely, that the *collectivity* is indeed something human, but is the human

without man, the human without spirit, the human without soul, the human dehumanized.

So here we have human actions of ours that lack the
primordial characteristics of the human, that have no
particular subject who creates them and is responsible
for them, for whom they have meaning. We have, then,
a human action; but it is irrational, without spirit, without soul, in which I act in the fashion of the gramophone
on which someone puts a record that it does not hear, of
the planet circling blindly in its orbit, of the vibrating
atom, the germinating plant, the nest-building bird. We
have a human activity that is irrational and soulless. A
very strange reality, this which now rises before us! It
looks as if it were something human, but dehumanized,
mechanized, materialized!

Will society, then, be a peculiar reality intermediate
between man and nature, neither one nor the other, but
a little of one and a great deal of the other? Will society
be a quasi-nature and, like nature, something blind, mechanical, somnambulistic, irrational, brutal, soulless, the
contrary of spirit, and still, by that very fact, useful and
necessary for man?—yet itself (the social, society) not
man nor men, but something rather like nature, like
matter, like a *world?* Shall we find, after all, that the name
by which it has always been informally called will prove
to have a formal meaning, that it is a *social "World"?*

# 9

# Reflections on the Salutation

---

I PROPHESIED that our voyage of discovery toward what is veritably society and the social would reach a crisis. And so it did.

You will remember that the voyage set out from the distrust inspired in us by sociologists because not one of them had devoted the necessary time and attention to analyzing the most elementary social phenomena. On the other hand, all about us—in books, the press, conversations —we find the nation, people, the state, the law and laws, social justice, and so on, being talked about in a way that is the very pattern of irresponsibility; that is, those who do the talking have not even the most rudimentary clear idea about all this. That being so, we decided that we would try, on our own account, to discover the possible truth about these realities; and to this end we felt that we must summon before us the actual things to which those words refer, shunning any and all ideas or interpretations of them which others have produced. We wanted to move back from all accepted ideas to the realities themselves. To do so, we had to withdraw to the reality that is "radical" reality precisely in the sense that in it all other realities must appear, announce their presence, or proclaim themselves. This radical reality is our life, the life of each one of us.

It is in our life that whatever can claim to be reality for us must manifest itself. The ambit in which realities manifest themselves is what we call World, our primordial world, that in which each one of us lives and which, consequently, is lived, experienced by him, and, being experienced by him, is obvious and without mysteries to him. This led us to take an inventory of what there is in this world, an inventory focused on the discovery of realities, things, facts, occurrences to which some of the imprecise verbal meanings of the words "social, sociality, society" could be applied with precision. Our investigation undertook to consider the great classes of "somethings," of things that are patent in our world, that make up our environment—minerals, plants, animals, and men. Only when we encountered men, and found them beings capable of responding to our action by their reaction with a range on the same level of response equal to our capacity for acting on them—capable, therefore, of cor-responding and reciprocating to us—only then did we seem to find a reality worthy to be called intercourse or social relation, sociality.

We have devoted several lectures to analyzing what this relation is in its most elementary, abstract, and basic structure—this social relation in which man gradually appears to and defines himself to the other man, and from being the pure Other, the unknown man, the not-yet-identified individual, becomes the unique individual— the You and the I.

But now we have become aware of something that is a constituent factor in all that we have called "social relation" in accordance with the verbal value of these words in common and current speech, something that, simply because it is so obvious, we had not particularly noticed, or, what is the same thing, of which we had not formed a separate and clear consciousness: namely, that all these actions of ours and all these reactions of others in which the so-called "social relation" consists, originate in an individual as such, myself for example, and are directed to another individual as such. Hence the "social relation,"

as it has so far appeared to us, is always explicitly a relation between individuals, an explicitly inter-individual
relation. For the present purpose it makes no difference
whether the two individuals who reciprocate to each
other are known to each other or not. Even when the
other is as unknown to me as can be imagined, my action
toward him, so far as possible, anticipates his eventual
reaction as an individual. Parents and children, brothers,
lovers, friends, teacher and pupil, business men and their
colleagues, and so on, are different categories of this inter-
individual relation. It is always a case of two men face to
face, each of them acting from his personal individuality,
that is, on his own account and for his own ends. In this
action or series of actions the one lives facing the other—
whether for *pro* or for *con*—and hence the two live together in it. The inter-individual relation is a typical
reality of human life—it is human living together. In this
action each emerges from the radical solitude that human
life primordially is and from it attempts to reach the
other's radical solitude. This takes place on a plane of reality that is already secondary, as we have gone to great
trouble to see, but that preserves the fundamental character of the human—namely, that the properly and strictly
human phenomenon is always a personal phenomenon.
The parent, as the individual that he is, directs himself to
the child as the child is such another completely personal
individual. The individual in love falls in love of himself—
that is, in the intimate genuineness of his person—with a
woman who is not woman in general, nor any woman,
but precisely *this* woman.

Our minute analysis of these social relations which, now
that we have perceived their most decisive characteristic,
we call "inter-individual relations" or co-living, appeared
to have exhausted all the realities in our world which can
lay claim to the denomination "social." And this is what

has happened to the majority of sociologists, who have not succeeded in even setting foot in genuine sociology because on the very threshold they have confused the social with the inter-individual. With which I seem already to be saying that calling this latter "social relation"—as we have so far done in accordance with common usage and adapting myself to the teaching of the greatest sociologist of recent times, Max Weber—was a sheer error. So now, once again, we must try to learn—and this time clearly—what the social is. But as we shall find, in order to see, indubitably to grasp the full strangeness of the social phenomenon, all the foregoing preparation was absolutely necessary, because *the social appears not, as has hitherto been believed and as was far too obvious, when we oppose it to the individual, but when we contrast it with the inter-individual.*

Simply observing what happens to us when we want to cross the street and the traffic policeman, with a dignified and even prescriptively hieratic gesture, stops us from doing so—this simple observation embroils us in difficulties, makes us start with surprise, and is as it were a whip-lash of light. So here, we say to ourselves, is something entirely new—an extraordinary reality, which we had not noticed until now. It is not only that; it is—I emphatically say—a reality that no one, believe me or not, had adequately observed before—even though that seems impossible, even though it is the clear and patent reality that it is, even though it is all about us and part of our daily lives. When someone had a confused and momentary glimpse of it, like the Frenchman Durkheim, he did not succeed in analyzing it and above all was incapable of thinking it, of translating it into concepts and doctrine. To anyone familiar with Durkheim's thought, I recommend that when my analysis touches the two or three momentary points at which my doctrine *appears* to coincide with

Durkheim's—I recommend that he reject the suggestion, because it would completely prevent him from understanding my concepts. Even at those two or three moments, I repeat, the similarity is illusory and misleading. You will soon see in what way my perception and analysis of the new phenomena that will now be coming into view will lead me to an idea of the social and sociality, hence to a sociology, that is the most absolutely opposed to Durkheim's that could possibly be imagined. The difference is so great that it is tremendous, literally—tremendous in the sense of making one tremble.

Our relation with the traffic policeman is almost wholly unlike what we have so far called "social relation." It is not a relation of man to man, of individual to individual, that is, of person to person. The act of starting to cross the street did originate in our completely individual responsibility. We decided it ourselves, for reasons of our individual convenience. We were the protagonists of our action; hence it was a human action in the normal sense that we have so far defined. On the contrary, the act in which the policeman stops us does not originate spontaneously in him, for personal motives of his own, and he does not address it to us as man to man. As man and individual, the good policeman would perhaps prefer to be amiable to us and let us cross, but he finds himself in the situation that it is not he who engenders his own actions; he has suspended his personal life, hence his strictly human life, and has changed into an automaton that is limited to performing, as mechanically as possible, acts laid down in the traffic regulations. So if we seek the engendering and responsible protagonist of his action, we are transferred to a code of regulations. But the code of regulations is simply the expression of a will. Whose will is it, in this case? Who wills that I shall not move about freely? This was the starting point for a series of transfers that, like a series of water-wheel buckets, finally convey us to an entity that is certainly not a man. The name of this entity is State. It is the State that prevents me from crossing the street at my own sweet will. I look about, but nowhere do I discover the State. Around me I see only men who pass me on from one to the next: the policeman to the Chief of Police, he to the Minister of the Interior, he to the Chief of State, and he, finally and irremediably, back to the State. But who or what is the State? Where is the State? Tell us! Show us! Vain hope! the State does not appear simply of itself. It is always hidden, no one knows how or where. When we think we are going to lay hands on it, what our hands feel and find is one or several or many men. We see men who govern in the name of this latent entity the State, that is, who give orders and operate hierarchically, transferring us upward or downward—from the humble policeman to the Chief of State. The State is one of the things that our ordinary language calls unquestionably social, perhaps the most social of all things. Language is always a fertile index of realities, but, of course, never an adequate guarantee. Every word shows us a thing—that is, the word says it to us, shows it to us, already interpreted, qualified. Language is in itself theory—perhaps theory that is always archaic, mummified, in some cases completely outdated. We shall find out later. But the fact is that every word is already a contracted, and as it were, saturated definition. This is why, when he shows us a thing, points it out to us, directs us to it—such is the mission of the word—the man of knowledge, and not merely of words, ought to say to himself: "Let us see!" And so we should do in the present case. The State does not let me cross the street as I please. Damn the State! The State is a social thing. Let us see! But the problem is that we don't see it; the State, a social thing, is always hidden behind men,

behind human individuals who are not and make no claim
to be social things in themselves. And since we shall find
exactly the same situation in the case of all the social
things that we shall successively encounter, we must pre-
pare ourselves to use the methods of the detective, since
actually, and for reasons that we shall see at the proper
time, the social reality, with everything that strictly per-
tains to it, is essentially something that hides, is concealed,
surreptitious. And here we have the reason, though for
the present only stated and not explained, why sociology
is the most recent among the sciences of Man and obviously the most backward and stammering.

But, in addition to the social thing, "State," which has
appeared to us as simultaneously indicated and concealed
by the policeman, we could rapidly force a number of
other social things to emerge from their accustomed hid-
ing places. We saw that if we dress as we dress, it is not
of our own doing nor by virtue of pure personal will, but
because it is usual to go about covered by a particular
form of clothing and adornment. This form leaves a
certain margin of choice to our caprice, but the principal
lines of our attire are not chosen by us, we are forced to
accept them. Here too, somebody commands us to dress
in a particular way and not in another, and here too, we
cannot discover who so commands us. We dress—we said
—because it is our "usage." Now, the "usual," the customary is something that we do because it "is done." But
who does what "is done"? Why, people. Very well—but
who is "people"? Why, *everybody* and, at the same time,
*no one in particular*. So here again we find no author of
the usage, who willed it and is responsible for the reality
that devolves to it as usage. Our coming and going in the
streets and our dressing have this most strange condition:
that we perform it ourselves, and hence it is a human act,
but at the same time it is not *ours*, we are not its active

subjects and protagonists; on the contrary it is decided, resolved on, and actually done in us by *Nobody*—the nobody who is indeterminate—and hence it is an inhuman act. What kind of anomalous reality is this—nay, more than anomalous, formally contradictory—that is at the same time human and not human, which is to say "inhuman"? But, after all, crossing or not crossing the street, dressing, belong to our external behavior. But if we draw up the balance sheet of the ideas or opinions by which and from which we live, we shall find to our surprise that the greater part of them were never thought by us with full and sufficient evidence; we think them because we have heard them and say them because they "are said." Here the impersonal reflexive pronoun *se* reappears,* with its signification of *somebody* but of somebody who is no one particular individual. This *se* in our Spanish is stupefying and marvelous. It names *someone who is no one;* as if we should say a man who is not exactly this, that, or the other man, and so on—who is therefore nobody. Do you understand this? I hope not, because it is quite hard to understand. It reminds me of Baudelaire's dandyism (dandyism is always scornful) when somebody asked him where he would best like to live and he answered, carelessly: "Oh, anywhere! Anywhere—so long as it is out of the world." In the same way, then, *se* means any man so long as he is no man. In French the thing is even clearer. For *se,* French uses *on*—"is said" is "*on dit.*" Here the impersonal is "*on*" —which, of course, is nothing but the contraction and residuum of *homo*—man; so that, explicating the meaning of "*on* dit" we have: a man who is no particular man, and since men are always particular men (they are this man, that man, the other man), a man who is not a man. To distinguish it from the personal pronouns, grammar terms this *se* an impersonal pronoun. But man, if he is truly man,

* [See page 173.—*Translator.*]

is personal; the human phenomenon—we said earlier—is always a personal phenomenon. But here we have an impersonal man—"one," *on*, *se*—who does what "is done" [*se hace*] and says what "is said" [*se dice*]—hence an inhuman man. And the momentous thing, when we ourselves do what "is done" and say what "is said," is that then the *se*, this inhuman man, this strange contradictory entity, is within us, we are he.

Such is the undeniable and unquestionable phenomenon; such is the new reality that we find inescapably before us. The thing now is to see if we are capable of understanding it, of conceiving it with complete and evident clarity. What we may not do is to elude it, deny it, because it is superlatively patent despite its secretive character.

To make the attempt, we must analyze an example of social behavior that seems to me the one that will enable us to enter most thoroughly into the entire problem.

One of us—any one of us—goes to the house of a friend or acquaintance, where he knows that he will find a gathering consisting of various other friends or acquaintances. The general reason or the pretext for the gathering is immaterial, so long as it is a private and not an official occasion. It can be simply a call on the host's saint's-day, it can be a cocktail party, it can be a so-called "social" function, it can be a gathering in which some matter is going to be discussed privately. I go to it by virtue of a voluntary act on my part, impelled by my own intention, in order to do something there that concerns me personally. This something can consist in an action or a complex series of actions. The one will do as well as the other for the case that we are considering. The important thing is to remember that all that I am going to do occurred to *me*, proceeds from my own inspiration, and has meaning for me. And even if what I am going there to do is the same thing that others have done, the fact is that

I am doing it on my own account, originally, or re-originating it in me. These acts, then, possess the two most outstanding, specific characteristics of human behavior. They are born of my will, I am completely their author; and they are intelligible to me, I understand what I am doing, and my reason for doing it and what I want to accomplish by doing it.

And now comes the astounding thing. What is the first thing that I do in my friend's house when I enter the room where he and his guests are assembled? What is my initial action, the action that I put before all my other actions, like a first note in the melody of behavior that I am going to execute? Why, something very odd—because I surprisingly find myself performing the following operation: I go up to each of the persons present, take his hand, press it, shake it, and then drop it. This action that I have accomplished is called a "salutation." But was this what I went there to do? To press and shake the hands of all those present, while they press and shake mine? No, this action is not in the list of those that I was going to perform *on my own part*. I had not premeditated it. It does not concern me. I have not the slightest desire to perform it. Sometimes it is even an ordeal. It is not, then, something that proceeds from me, although indubitably I do it, I perform it.

What, then, may the salutation be? It concerns me so little that, in general, I do not even refer it individually to the particular proprietor of the hand that I am squeezing, nor does he to me. What I have said—and this is why I said it—enables us to recognize with perfect clarity that this act of salutation is not an inter-individual or inter-human relation, although in fact we are two men, two individuals, who shake hands. Someone or some X, which we neither of us are yet which envelops us both and is, as it were, above us, is the creating and responsible subject of our salutation. There can be nothing individual in it beyond some very slight variation or detail that I add to the general line of the salutation, something, then, that is not properly salutation, that I slip into it in secret as it were and that does not appear: for example, a greater or less pressure, the way I draw the hand toward me, the rhythm in which I shake it, hold it, let it go. And in fact we do not exert exactly the same pressure on any two hands. But this slight component of emotional, secret, individual gesture is not part of the salutation. It is a bit of embroidery that I add to the canvas of the salutation on my own account. The salutation is the fixed form, with its always identical, well-known, and habitual schema, which consists in taking the other hand, pressing it—the degree of pressure does not matter—shaking it for a moment, and dropping it.

What I am doing now is trying to make sure that no one tells us what the salutation is, but, on the contrary, that each one of us shall for the moment thoroughly consider what happens to him, and only to him, when he executes a salutation and when his salutation is patent to him, something he experiences, that is, that happens to his living self with full evidence. The thing is to avoid making hypotheses, suppositions, plausible as they may seem, and to devote ourselves to contemplating just what happens to us in so far as it happens to us when we execute a salutation. Only this radical method can save us from error.

With each of us, then, keeping well in view what happens to him when he shakes hands, let us take intellectual possession of the most important characteristics that are clearly manifest in this act of ours. *First*, it is an act that I, a human being, *execute*. But, *second*, although I *execute* it, it did not occur to me, I did not invent it or think it on my own account, I copy or repeat it from others, from everybody else who does it, from "people." It comes to me from outside of myself, it does not originate from me as an individual, but neither does it originate from any particular individual. I see that the same thing that happens to me happens to every other individual, that he gets it from "people," from its "being done." Hence it is an act whose origin is extraindividual, it belongs neither to me nor to you nor to any specific person. But, *third*, not only am I not—nor are you—the creator of this act, not only is it pure repetition in us, I also do not execute it of my own spontaneous will; indeed, I often execute it reluctantly, and I suspect that the same is true of you, of every "you." *Fourth*, from all this it follows that I, a human being, find myself executing an act that lacks two of the indispensable characteristics of every strictly human action—originating intellectually in the subject who performs it and being engendered in his will. Hence it is much less like human behavior than like a mechanical inhuman movement.

But the worst is yet to come. For it turns out that this action of mine of taking people's hands and giving them my own, an action that I did not premeditate performing when I went to the gathering, not only did not occur to me nor proceeds from my wish, but despite its being so elementary, utterly simple, frequent, and habitual, *I do not even understand it*. For in fact I do not know why the first thing I have to do when I meet men with whom I am acquainted is precisely to execute this strange operation of shaking their hands. It will be said, a little precipitately, that this is not true, that I know why I do it because I know that *if* I do not give my hand to others, if I do not greet them in this fashion, they will think me ill-mannered, disdainful, proud, and so on. This is certainly true, and we shall later see what decisive importance it possesses. But let us not confuse things, because the whole question lies here. What I know, what I understand, is *that I have to do this*, but I do not know, I do not understand this that I have to do. It is intelligible, it makes sense, when the doctor takes a sick man's hand to feel his temperature and count his pulse. It is intelligible, it makes sense, if I grasp the hand that holds a dagger aimed at my heart. But giving and taking hands in salutation—in that I can see no purpose or meaning whatever. And I find my view confirmed by the fact that, if I go to Tibet, my Tibetan neighbor, under the same circumstances, instead of giving me his hand, turns his head to one side, pulls his ear, and sticks out his tongue—a complicated and laborious performance whose purpose and meaning are far from clear to me.

We will not now pause to review the forms of salutation that have made their appearance in history, and many of which are still in use today. What we must do now is, as accurately as possible, to extract from our own act of salutation the characteristics that it exhibits as an action that we, we human beings, execute. We have already discovered two of them: first, that it is not an inspiration or invention of the individual that each of us is, but comes to us from outside, already invented by we know not whom, that is, it is not born in some other particular individual, but all the individuals who are alive today meet with it exactly as I do and you do. Hence it is an action that is performed by us but that is not ours—it has an anonymous, extra-individual origin. Secondly, in addition to its being extra-individual, our performance of it is not voluntary. We consent to it, but not because we want or spontaneously desire to do it. To these two characteristics, we now add the third and last, which has just revealed itself to us—namely, that what we do when we shake hands is something that we do not understand; it is as meaningless and mysterious to us as the most impenetrable secret of nature could be. Hence, it is irrational.

And now we can reverse the order of these three characteristics and say: if we do not understand the act of salutation, is could hardly have occurred to us, but moreover, if it has no meaning for us, we can hardly want to do it. For us to want to do something, it must be intelligible to us. Hence it is clear that we not only greet each other without knowing what we are doing when we shake hands in salutation—hence, that we do it inhumanly—but that, in consequence, we do it without wanting to, against our will, wish or pleasure. Hence, in addition to being unintelligible, it is an action that is involuntary, sometimes countervoluntary—a further inhuman characteristic.

But what is not done willingly is done unwillingly, and what is done unwillingly is done perforce or under compulsion. And in fact shaking hands is something that we do perforce, very much as the man who falls from a third-story window performs his fall perforce, that is, perforce of the force of gravity. We shall see that the ready and apparently obvious objections to these last words of mine are much less founded than may at first be thought.

I know very well that the lover delights in saluting his beloved; I remember that the whole of the *Vita Nuova*, and, as it says there, Dante's whole life, revolves around his longing for a salutation; I know very well that the lover takes fraudulent advantage of the occasion of the handshake to thrill with delight by causing the skin of his hand to feel the warmth from the skin of another hand. But this pleasure is not a pleasure of the salutation—which is no pleasure at all—but on the contrary is a fraud that we perpetrate on it, an abuse of that usage, the salutation. I do not know how it happens that love always displays a most fertile inspiration in fraud and behaves like a clever smuggler who never lets an opportunity slip. But the same lover is perfectly well aware that the salutation is no delight, since usually the delight of touching the beloved hand is purchased at the cost of having to squeeze several or many other hands, some of them annoyingly sweaty. For him, too, salutation is an operation that is performed perforce.

Very well—but who forces us? There is no doubt about the answer. It is usage. Very well—but who is this usage who has the force to force us? Who is this mighty athlete, usage?

We cannot avoid facing and coming to terms with this new problem. We must find out what usage is. And, in obedience to our method of procedure, we shall do so from the ground up—for, unlikely as it may seem, no one has yet taken this task upon himself. Even we, in taking our inventory of the realities that make up our environment and our world, were on the verge of not perceiving this new reality. And the fact is that no other reality is so abundant and omnipresent all around us. For usage is not only the State's usage of not letting us cross the street and the countless other types of behavior that the State forces upon us; it is not only the norms in apparel that are imposed upon us by our environment; usage thrusts itself into the most purely inter-individual relation —between mother and child, for example, or between lover and sweetheart. For if they are to understand each other they have no recourse but to use a language, and a language is nothing but a vast system of verbal usages, a gigantic repertory of worn-out words and stereotyped syntactic forms. From the time we are born, language is imposed on us and taught us by our hearing people talking, saying things—which, for the present, is language. But since words and syntactic forms always carry meanings, ideas, opinions, "what people say" is at the same time a system of opinions that people hold, of "public opinions," is the immense body of public opinion that penetrates us and is instilled into us, that almost fills us within and incessantly presses on us from without.

It follows that, from the time we see the light, we live submerged in an ocean of usages, that they are the first and strongest reality that we encounter; they are, *sensu stricto,* our environment or social world, they are the society in which we live. It is through this social world or world of usages that we see the world of men and things, see the Universe.

It is, then, worth the effort to try to make it fully clear to ourselves what usage is, how it is formed, what happens to it when it falls into disuse, and what constitutes that violation of usage that is one meaning of the word "abuse."

But if this investigation is to result in making usage manifest and patent to us, we must undertake it by analyzing a concrete usage. And, as I said, none seems to me more suitable for the purpose than the salutation.

# 10

## Reflections on the Salutation. Etymological Man. What Is a Usage?

In our environment there were not only minerals, plants, animals, and men. In addition, and in a certain sense before all these things, there were those other realities, usages. From the moment of our birth they envelop and hem us in on every side; they oppress and compress us; they instill themselves into us; they penetrate us and fill us almost to the brim; we are their prisoners and slaves for life. Well, what is usage?

In ordinary parlance we hear the word "usage" making a pair with "customs." "Usages and customs" trot side by side. But if we take this "and"—which would seem to say that the two things are different—seriously, we see that we cannot distinguish them or that the distinction is arbitrary. That the pair continues to flourish in the language like a happily married couple is because the concept "custom" seems significant and helps to define what people have in mind when they say "usage." Usage would be custom, and custom is a certain mode of behavior, a type of action which has become customary, that is, habitual. Usage, then, would be a social habit. Habit is conduct that, by being frequently repeated, becomes automatic in the individual, and is produced or functions mechanically. When this conduct is not only frequent in an individual, but is frequently repeated by many individuals, we should have a customary usage. This is what has been said, in different words, by the only sociologist who has been willing to put a modicum of effort into analyzing the elementary phenomena of society. The frequency of a behavior in various individuals would, then, be the substance of usage; so that usage would be an individual reality, and only the mere and more or less fortuitous coincidence of many individuals in this frequent behavior would give it the character of a social fact. No less than Max Weber holds this view, and no less than Bergson thinks the same, for eleven years after Weber, he will continue, after not a little beating around the bush, to talk of usage as of a custom and of custom as of *"une habitude,"* "a habit"—in other words, as of an extremely frequent conduct, which, because of its frequency, has become automatic and stereotyped in individuals.

But the fact is that we perform many movements, acts, and actions with the greatest frequency which obviously are not usages. One of the things that man does with considerable frequency is to breathe; yet no one will say that breathing is a usage and that man has become accustomed to breathing. But this—you will violently object—is a mere organic reflex. Right you are—and I brought it up as a point of departure and a point of reference. But to make one's way, to walk, to move one's feet along streets and sidewalks—this is not a reflex act, it is a voluntary act, nothing could be more frequent; and obviously it is not a usage either. On the other hand, there are usages that are infrequent because of their very nature. Some great peoples have the usage of celebrating a ceremonial festival every century. A venerable example was Rome with its *ludi saeculares,* its religious games when the *saeculum* ended. No one can say that, for the individual Roman, celebrating the secular festival was something frequent. It was so little frequent that the heralds called the citizens to come *ad ludos*, to the games, *quos nec spectasset quis-quam nec spectaturus esset*, as Suetonius tells us in his Life of Claudius: "Come to the festival that you have never attended, that you will never attend again." Nothing could more forcefully declare the absolute infrequency of a usage. In passing, we may note something that we see only out of the corner of an eye. It is that this usage is manifested as a custom that is not that of an individual, but is essentially trans-individual; it was a custom not of "the Roman"—this, that, and the other Roman—but— of Rome. Rome is not a man, it is a people, it is a society. To judge from what appears here, usages are not of the individual but of society. Perhaps society is the usual and the user. The basic infrequency of the secular festival would, if possible, appear even more clearly if I could now fully expound the *saeculum* to you, one of the most humanly moving of ideas, one of the most directly vital, that is, lived, ideas, drawn purely from the experience of human destiny. Because it is clear that the century, the *saeculum*, is not the long unit of time defined in the metrico-decimal clumsiness of 100 years, with its two stupid zeros, a duration that clocks can measure with their impertinent and indifferent exactness. The *saeculum* is a unit of time which, like everything that is life, is essentially imprecise; it is a very ancient idea, so ancient that it is not even Roman; it and the word itself are pre-Roman, they are Etruscan; and like everything Etruscan, are touching, mysterious, and confounding.

If we start from today and from all the inhabitants of Madrid who are alive today, and think of a duration of Madrid existence which would extend to the death of the last of those who are alive today, particularly those who were born today—that is the *saeculum*. It is, then, the duration of the continuous human happening that he who attains to see most—that is, to live most—can see or live.

It will be 90 or 100 or 110 or 120 years—the limit is variable like that of life. What is involved, then, is the idea of the generation; we have a human generation prolonged to its maximum of longevity—the most natural and concrete unit, in which time is measured by a human happening (the longest life of a man) and not by geometry and arithmetic.

To see in the formidable reality of usage a simple precipitate of frequency is unworthy of an analytical mind. Let us not confuse things. That many, but by no means all usages can become established as such only on condition that many individuals do the same thing many times, and hence this thing appears frequently, is one fact. We must not confuse it with the other fact that usage, once it is established and is really usage, itself exerts an action through its frequency. Otherwise we might wind up with the opposite proposition, that something is not usage *because* it is frequent; whereas in fact we do it frequently because it is usage.

To escape from this maze there is nothing for it but to inquire of our own behavior what it is that we do when we greet each other, and we immediately see that we do not shake hands because it is frequently done. If this were the case, whenever anyone happened not to feel like doing it, he would simply suppress the operation and then an infrequent conduct of his would contrast with a frequent conduct of others, but nothing in particular would happen to him. The thing is obvious and perfectly simple. We go on from good-day to good-day. But we know that if one day we fail to greet an acquaintance when we pass him in the street, or those whom we find at a gathering, they will be annoyed with us, and that this annoyance carries certain penalties for us—first and at least that they will consider us badly brought up; but sometimes the penalties are serious. *Now* there is no question of frequency or infrequency, no question of habit and occasionally varying from a habit; here we have something really grave, that is, everybody else—that vague entity "everybody else," which is another aspect of "people" —"everybody else" obliges us to greet them, violently imposes it on us, with a force or violence that is moral for the time being. But sooner or later—and it is important to note this—sooner or later, but in the last analysis always —there is the eventuality of a physical violence.

In Europe not so many years ago, when anyone refused a salutation, he would automatically receive a slap in the face, and the next day he had to fight with sword, saber, or pistol. That is why I say that here we do indeed have "something really grave."

Usage, then, makes its appearance to me as the threat in my mind of an eventual violence, coercion, or sanction that other people are going to exercise against me. But the curious fact is that the same thing happens to them, because each of them too finds usage there before him as a threat from "everybody else," from the rest. Only now, for him, among the "rest," there am I, changed without my knowledge into one of them!

Here, then, we have the third attribute of the social fact: the violence or threat of violence that does not proceed from any particular subject—which, rather, every particular subject finds there before him under the aspect of actual or presumable violence by the rest toward him.

This is the first characteristic with which the "social" presents itself in our life. Our will perceives it before our intellect does. We want to do or not do something, and we discover that we cannot; that we cannot, because before us rises a power stronger than ours, which forces and subjects our desire. And this power, which generally manifests itself with euphemisms of moral coercion and pressure, of causing us moral damage, but which in the end always threatens with the eventuality of a physical violence—this power, which, then, is physical, brutal, which—as we shall see—also functions brutally, this power that belongs to no one, that is not human, that, in this sense, is something like an elemental power of nature, like the thunderbolt or the gale, like the storm or the earthquake, like gravity that propels the lifeless mass of the star in its course—this power is the "social power." And "social power" functions in the coercion that is "usage."

It is almost certain that when I said for the first time that saluting by shaking hands was an act without meaning, someone thought: No—shaking hands has a meaning because that was how men assured each other that they were not carrying weapons in their hands. But, I answer, it is obvious that when today we go to a social occasion or an academic meeting we are not afraid that other men, our friends and acquaintances, will be carrying lances, javelins, daggers, arrows, boomerangs in their hands. Of course not, the imaginary objector will say, this fear is not present but past. There was a time, in the dim past, when men did have this fear and so they decided to approach one another in this way, which *had meaning for them,* just as for me it would have meaning to restrain a murderer's hand. But even if we admit that this observation is ingenious, what it proves is that shaking hands *had* a meaning, not that it has one for us today. However, the observation has its use, for it shows us something very important, namely, that at least some social facts, such as the salutation—we shall later see if the same cannot be said in various degrees of all social facts—that at least some social facts are characterized not only by being meaningless but by something sadder still—that they once had a meaning and have lost it. If this proves to be true, it will follow that it is of the essence of usages to have

lost their meaning, hence to have once been inter-individual and intelligible human actions, actions with a soul,
which were then drained of meaning, became mechanized,
automatized, and as it were mineralized, in short, soulless.
They were genuine human experiences (*vivencias*) which,
so it seems, became survivals (*supervivencias*), human
petrifactions. I believe that here for the first time the
word "survival" acquires a new meaning that is, at the
same time, its full meaning. Because survival is not lived
experience, but only its slough, residuum, corpse, skeleton,
or fossil.

My imaginary objector confused what actually happens
to us when we shake hands in salutation, which is something meaningless, with a theory that he holds about the
origin of this fact and which, as is the case with every
theory, he worked out in order to discover in it this
meaning which has so little weight when he is simply
shaking hands and not theorizing.

More significant is the fact that no correctly formulated theory of the salutation exists. This is symptomatic
of the state of sociological studies, for it happens that
there is not a single book in any language on the salutation,
and very few in which there is even a short chapter devoted to it; there is not a single article in a journal, so far
as I know, in which the subject is investigated with any
application, except for one three pages in length and of
no value whatever, published in England some seventy
years ago under the title "On Salutations."

All that is so far to be found on the subject is a chapter
in Spencer's *Principles of Sociology*, a few pages in Jher-
ing's book *Purpose in Law*, an article in the *Encyclopaedia
Britannica*, consisting of a few paragraphs, and one in the
*American Encyclopedia of Social Sciences*—and innumerable vague and inept generalities a few lines long in the

countless treatises on sociology that have wearied the presses.

Now, out of all this, the only intelligent thing that has been said on the subject and which, with a slight change in the method of proof, could be accepted as true, is what Spencer rather cavalierly tells us. So far as I am aware, it has for some unknown reason been entirely overlooked.

Spencer, who employs the methods and viewpoint of a biologist, considers the handshake that is our salutation to be a relic or rudiment of an older ceremonial action. In biology, "rudiment" means the fragment or part of an organ that has not yet been completely transformed or, vice versa, having become useless, has remained atrophied and reduced to that part. Our rudiment of a third eyelid is an example. Whether in its incipient or in its residual form, the characteristic of the rudiment is that, for lack of development, it does not perform the function that the organ of which it is the residuum will perform or has performed.

With this idea in mind, Spencer arranges the forms of salutation—at least, a large group of its forms—in a series, carefully putting each form between the two others that are closest to it. In this way there is a fairly continuous progression from one form to another that differs from it scarcely at all, whereas the difference between the first and last in the series is immense. This method of the almost continuous series has been normal in biological research since the days of positivism.

Spencer derives our handshake as follows:

For Spencer, the salutation is a gesture of submission on the part of an inferior to a superior. Primitive man, when he conquered an enemy, killed him. Before the victor lay the body of the vanquished, a wretched victim awaiting the hour of cannibalism. But the primitive grows more refined, and instead of killing his enemy makes him his slave. The slave recognizes his situation of inferiority, of conquered and forgiven enemy, by feigning death—that is, by lying on the ground before the victor. According to this, the primordial salutation would be imitating a corpse. Subsequent progress consists in the progressive uprightness of the slave in saluting: first he goes down on all fours, later he kneels, placing his joined hands in his master's in token of submission, of putting himself in his hands.

Spencer, of course, does not mention, but I add, that this putting oneself in the master's hands is the *in manu esse* of the Romans; is the *manus dare* that signifies "to deliver oneself over, to surrender"; it is the *manu capio;* it is the *mancipium* or "slave." When he who has been commanded [*mandato*], grasped, or taken in hand [*en mano*] has become used to it, used to this submission, the Roman said that he is *mansuetus,* "used to the hand," "domesticated," "tame" [*manso*]. Command [*mando*] domesticates man, and makes the wild beast that he was *mansuete.*

But let us return to Spencer. After this, the salutation ceases to be the gesture of conquered to conqueror and becomes the general gesture of inferior to superior. The inferior, now the man on foot, takes his superior's hand and kisses it. This is the "hand-kiss." But times become democratic, and the superior, in pretence or sincerity, resists this sign of recognized inferiority. What the devil! We are all equal! And then what happens? I, the inferior, take my superior's hand and raise it toward my lips to kiss it, but he resists and withdraws it; I thereupon insist again, and he again withdraws it, and the struggle, which suggests Buster Keaton in a moving picture, elegantly

results in the handshake, which for Spencer is the residue
or rudiment of the whole history of the salutation.

You will admit that the explanation is ingenious. But,
what is more, it is very close to the truth. What is de-
ficient in it could be made good if, instead of having been
constructed hypothetically, each form being taken from
no matter what people and time, the series of proximate
forms had been studied historically, that is, if it were
shown that a given form not only is very close to another
but is also in fact its historical forerunner, that the second
really derived from the first.

But what cannot be doubted is that our handshake is a
survival, a surviving rudiment—and even as a concrete
act and just as it exists, without the significance of a useful and completely meaningful action. This is easier to
understand if we consider that our form of salutation in
the street—taking off our hats—becomes, when the person
we are greeting is well known to us, reduced to touching
the brim of the hat with our finger tips. From this residue,
which will soon vanish too, to the complicated curves in
the air executed in the Versailles of Louis XIV with
the immense baroque *chapeaux* plentifully laden with
feathers, the way is as long as the way to Tipperary. Indubitably, from that period to today, and perhaps
throughout history, a law has operated which I call the
law of "diminishing ceremoniousness." We shall soon see
the reason for it.

But now our concern is to extract from all this something far more important, an incalculable advance for
the sciences of Man.

We have seen that it is our custom to press or shake our
acquaintance's hand, and that this serves to keep us from
incurring his displeasure, but just why this action serves
that end for us, we saw that we do not know. At least

in this case, the useful act is unintelligible to us who perform it. However, if we reconstruct the history of the
act and look at the series of its earlier forms, we come to
certain forms that had a complete and rational meaning
for those who used them and have it even for us if, by an
effort of imagination, we transport ourselves into very
ancient human situations. Once we have found the earlier
form that we can understand, all the subsequent forms,
down to our residual one, automatically acquire meaning
for us.

On the other hand, on discovering the form—antiquated for us, but still in use among many peoples—by
which the inferior puts his hands between his superior's
hands, I pointed out that superiority, ownership, lordship
was expressed in Latin by *in manu esse* and *manus dare*—
whence our word "command." Now, when we say "command," the saying of it serves for the ends which, at
that moment in our conversation, discourse, or composition, we have in view. But, except for philologists, nobody
knows why the reality "command" is expressed by the
word "command." In order for this word not only to
serve us when we repeat it without understanding it but
also to be understood by us, we had to do exactly what we
did in the case of the salutation—reconstruct its previous
linguistic forms until we came to one that was really intelligible in itself, that we understood. *Manus* in Latin is
the hand, but in so far as it exerts force and is power.
Command, as we shall see, every kind of command, is
being able to command, that is, having the power or
strength to command. This ancient form of the word
has disclosed to us the meaning that, in residual, atrophied,
mummified form, lay dozing in our ordinary and unintelligible word, "command." This operation which, by
virtue of certain operations of the sciences of phonetics
and semantics, resuscitates in the dead soulless word of

today the experienced, vibrant, forceful meaning that it once possessed—this operation is what we call discovering its etymology.

But now we begin to descry something whose bearing is very great—namely, that having an etymology is not a thing peculiar to or even especially characteristic of words, but that all human acts have an etymology because in all of them, to one degree or another, usages intervene, and the "usual" act, being a human action transformed into a mechanical imposition of the collectivity on the individual, goes on existing by inertia and as it were adrift, so that no one can rationally ascertain just how long it will endure. As it continues to lose meaning through its very usualness, through the wear [*usura*] of all use, it also keeps changing its form until it reaches the absolutely unintelligible aspects that we call residual. Words do not have etymologies because they are words but because they are usages. But this obliges us to recognize and declare that man is constitutively, by his inexorable destiny, as member of a society—*the etymological animal.* Accordingly, history would be only a vast etymology, the grandiose system of etymologies. That is why history exists and why man needs it; it is the only discipline that can discover the meaning of what man does and hence of what he is.

You observe how, as we have pursued our small and unpretentious study of the salutation, a window has unexpectedly opened for us through which we suddenly descry a most extensive panorama of humanities, which until today has never appeared under this aspect—universal history as a gigantic etymology. "Etymology" is the concrete name for what is usually and abstractly called "historical reason." But now let us turn from this vast theme to our small one. What I have just said in expounding and at the same time completing Spencer's

ideas about the origin of our handshake is to be taken
only as a schematic model of what its real and formal
explication could be. Spencer oversimplified the matter.
To begin with, his theory assumes that all salutations
originally proceed from an homage rendered by an inferior to a superior. But the complicated salutation of the
Tuareg in the vast solitude of the desert, which goes on
for three quarters of an hour, or that of the American
Indian who, meeting a member of another tribe, begins
by smoking the same pipe with him, the "peace-pipe"—
these do not imply differences in rank. There are, then,
salutations that are originally equalitarian. In our own
form of salutation, which does seem to derive from a behavior between non-equals, there is a component of
simple equalitarian effusiveness that does not fail to show
itself, even though the mechanization and automatism of
our practice of it have expelled all effusion that is sincere.

We should note too that the salutation is not addressed
only to persons but also to things, to symbolical objects,
to the flag, to the Cross, to the corpse on its funeral journey to the graveyard. In a certain sense every salutation
includes a dimension of homage, it is an "attention," a
display of "regard," and its omission arouses displeasure
because it implies "disregard." Let us say, then, that it is
at once homage and effusion. For we must not forget the
words that sometimes accompany gestures of salutation.
The Basutos salute their chief by saying, *Tama sevaba*—
"Hail, wild beast!" It is the most gratifying thing they
can say. Every people, we shall see, has its preferences,
and the Basutos prefer wild beasts. The Arab will say
*salaam aleikun*—"peace be with thee"—which is the He-
brew *sehalom* and which passes to the Christian ritual
with the kiss and the *pax vobiscum*. The Romans said
*salve*—"may you have health" (whence the word
"salute"); the Greeks said *khaire*—"I wish thee joy." For

our part we wish our neighbor good day, good evening, good night—an expression that originally had a magical meaning. In India on the other hand, the morning greeting used to be, "Did you have many mosquitoes last night?"

But all these contents of gesture and word employed by the salutation and whatever is expressed in them—surrender, submission, homage, effusion—can be manifested, and in fact are manifested, at any moment in human intercourse, so that the most characteristic feature of the salutation does not lie in them. Its substance appears in something purely formal—namely, that the salutation is the first thing we do in connection with people we meet, before we do whatever it may be that we have in mind to do in connection with them. It is, then, an inaugural, initial, or inchoative act; rather than an action, it is the prelude to any actual action in respect to our neighbor.

Is it not extremely mysterious that before we do anything with other people, we have first to perform this action, which by itself has no meaning or apparent use of its own, which, then, would seem to be purely ornamental?

To solve the mystery of the salutation, instead of concentrating on its general form, on the way it is employed in our society, let us observe the slight quantitative variations in our employment of it. That is, whom do we greet the most formally, carrying out the complete act with the utmost care, or, conversely, when do we feel, though without deliberate intent, that we can reduce the salutation to the minimum and even suppress it?

Let us exclude the cases in which, because we are to greet persons who deserve our highest respect and admiration, we really make our salutation a pretext for our homage—hence something that is not purely and properly a salutation. Apart from this, we give less of a salutation to those who are closest to us, to our friends, those who

to us are most fully the particular individuals that they
are. Contrariwise, we salute with increasingly formal and
authentic salutations in proportion as the persons involved
are more remote from us, are less particularized individuals
for us, are, in short, only the abstraction of individuals
or abstract individuals, or, to put it differently, individuals
who have only the generic mold of the individual because,
for us, who scarcely know them, they are void of their
particular individuality.

What all this means, then, is that when we know a man
well and hence, even if there were no usages, can foresee
his behavior toward us, we feel that we do not need to
salute him, and that salutation becomes obligatory in proportion as our neighbor becomes less and less a particular
individual for us, less *such and such a man*, and instead
becomes for us more *any* man, more *people*. Now we see
how the word "people" signifies the abstract individual,
that is, the individual emptied of his unique and unmistakable individuality, the anybody, the de-individualized
individual—in short, "a quasi-individual."

Now, since we do not know what the quasi-individual
whom we encounter is like, we cannot foresee his behavior toward us, nor he ours, since I too am for him a
quasi-individual; and since we cannot foresee his behavior,
before doing anything positive with him we have to
make it clear to each other that we will accept the rules
of conduct, the system of behavior that is in accord with
the usages that prevail or are in binding observance in
that particular part of the planet. This puts at our disposal a whole series of established points of reference, of
quiet and safe channels for our action and intercourse.
In short, in shaking hands, we proclaim our mutual will
for peace and sociality with the other; we accept a social
relation with him. In the American Indian salutation—the
thing is obvious and well known—the salutation consisted

in both smoking the same pipe, called the "peace pipe"; but at the bottom of all salutations we should find the same thing.

In other epochs, when no established repertory of usages had spread through a wide area, the unpredictability of the conduct of others—for example, the conduct of the quasi-individual whom a Tuareg encountered in the desert—included endless possibilities, even robbery and murder; hence the Tuareg's salutations are extremely complicated.

Man—let us never forget—was once a wild beast, and, potentially, he continues to be one to a greater or lesser degree. Hence the approach of man to man was always a possible tragedy. What today seems to us such a simple and easy thing—one man approaching another—was until quite recently a dangerous and difficult operation. So it was necessary to invent a technique of approach, which evolves all through the course of human history. This technique, this mechanism of approach, is the salutation.

And it is curious that at the same time the salutation grew progressively simpler. Whereas the Tuareg's salutation began a hundred yards from his neighbor, was a most complicated ceremonial, and lasted half an hour, our handshake is almost like the final abbreviation of a ceremony, is, as it were, the salutation in shorthand. And now we have deciphered the hieroglyph and the riddle that the handshake was to us, now we see that it means nothing in itself; it is not a particular act that claims to have any concrete value in itself, it is simply the declaration that we intend to submit to these common usages and the inaugural act of our relation with "people," in which we mutually declare ourselves ready to accept all the other usages in binding observance in the social group. Hence it is not itself a positive act, it is not a usage with a useful content of its own, it is the usage that symbolizes all others, it is the usage of usages, the password or sign of the tribe. Which is all the more reason for our having chosen it as example of all the social. But if this is so, how can we explain the fact that in various and vast societies, that in various nations, shaking hands was in these last years suddenly abandoned, and instead people raise their fists threateningly or stretch out one arm, palm forward, in accordance with the legionary usage of the Roman *milites?* For it is obvious that these salutations did not, like the handshake, signify a proposal of peace, a proposal to unite, socialize, and solidarize with others, but were precisely the contrary—a provocation to battle.

Does such a fact contravene all this doctrine that we have built up so laboriously? But before we rush to the defense of our doctrine, we must make another supposition, though a more imaginary one—one that we can fortunately deal with in a few sentences, for I have reduced it to its essentials—a supposition that, even though imaginary, will at one stroke illuminate a number of things for us.

Let us imagine that all the persons who make up a gathering believe, each on his own account, that shaking hands is unintelligent—for example, that it is unhygienic —and hence that men should not greet one another in this manner. Now, in spite of this, the usage would remain intact; despite his so thinking, each would go on shaking hands; the usage would continue to exert its impersonal, its brutal and mechanical pressure. For this to cease, the individuals would have to communicate their opinion to one another; that is, each in turn would have to learn that all the others were opposed to this form of salutation. But is not this another way of saying that a new usage had been constituted in place of the first? In the new situation, anyone who greeted by shaking hands would be disobeying the usage now in observance (*not* shaking hands), and the only difference would be this—the new usage would seem to make better sense than the old.

Quite informally, but, in compensation, with the flesh-less and transparent purity that are proper to the sche-matic, what I have just said shows us an abstract model of the way any usage is born, how it comes into disuse, and how it is replaced by another. In addition we now see more clearly than ever before the strange power of usage, which does not live or exist except in individuals and by virtue of individuals, and which nevertheless hangs over them like a mechanical, impersonal power, like a physical reality that manipulates them, moves them this way and that as if they were inert bodies. The suppression of a usage is not in the hands of the individual will—be it mine, yours, or his. To do away with it takes a great deal of work, as it takes a great deal of work to level a hill or to build a pyramid. We have to win over individual after individual, we have to win over everybody else, that vague entity, "everybody else."

For simplicity's sake, I admitted two inexactitudes into my supposition which it is now necessary to correct. One of them is this: I said that, in order to do away with the salutation in this gathering, all must agree. But the fact is that usages are not in fact constituted in this gathering, in this small gathering, but at most are initiated in it. In the last analysis, usages are constituted in the great and more or less multitudinous gathering that is always so-ciety; and for a usage to be constituted, not all individuals need be in agreement. Indeed, never have all the indi-viduals in a society agreed to constitute a usage. More-over, it is not a question of agreement. The error of the eighteenth century was to believe the contrary: that so-ciety and its constitutive functions—usages—are formed by virtue of agreement, contract, and so on. It is enough if—consciously or not, deliberately or not—those who constitute a certain number are in agreement. What number? The majority? This is the majoritarian error. Sometimes it is the majority; but at other times—and nearly always—it is precisely a minority, perhaps a comparatively large one, which, by adopting a particular behavior, succeeds, with a strange automatism impossible to describe briefly, in making that behavior—until then individual, private, practiced only by a few—become that terrible and inexorable social force, a usage.

So it is not a question of figures. Sometimes one man, a single man, does more by his approval to further the constitution of a usage than if it were adopted by a million. The world is full of overcoats because one day about 1840 or 1850 the Count d'Orsay, a French dandy living in London, was returning from the races mounted on his fine dapple-gray mare. It began to rain and he asked a passing workman to lend him the sleeved smock that was then worn by the English populace. Such was the invention of the overcoat. For d'Orsay was the most elegant man in London, and "elegant" is a word that comes from the word *eligere*, "to choose"; he who knows how to choose is "elegant." The following week overcoats began to sprout all through the British Isles, and today the world is full of them.

It is not a question of figures, but of a surprising phenomenon—the most important phenomenon in sociology and, through sociology, in history—the phenomenon that I call "binding observance." *

It is now time to make the second correction in our imaginary supposition. I said that, when each member of the gathering knew that not only he but all the others were opposed to handshaking, that usage fell into disuse and was replaced by another that excluded shaking hands.

* [*Vigencia*. This term, here first formally introduced, is explained below, pp. 268–269.—*Translator*.]

The general characteristics of usage—at least, its being extra-individual and mechanically coercive and persistent —continue through the change. The only difference—I said—is this: the new usage seems to have more meaning than the old one, which had lost its meaning completely— which was why it was abandoned.

Does this mean that the new usage possesses much or even a sufficient meaning? Since the social groups in which usages are constituted are composed of a very large number of individuals and since, if the usage is to become established, a large proportion of them must be won over to it and the rest must at least come to know it and obey it—all this means that the formation of a usage is slow.

From the moment when an individual had the creative idea (only individuals create), the creative idea of the new usage, to the time when it actually becomes an observed usage, an institution (every usage is an institution), a long time must necessarily pass. And during the course of this long period that it takes for a usage to become constituted, the creative idea, which when newborn was completely meaningful, by the time it becomes usual, by the time it becomes a social mode, in short, a usage, has already begun to be antiquated, to lose what meaning it had, to be unintelligible. All of which—I draw your particular attention to this fact—in the meantime does no damage to the usage; because what we do because it is usage we do not do because it seems like a good thing to us, because we consider it reasonable, but mechanically; we do it because it is done, and, more or less, because we have no alternative.

Usage is slow in becoming established and slow in disappearing. Hence all usage—including new usage—is in essence old, viewed from the chronology of our individual life.

Observe that the person is usually all the quicker to

act the more genuinely he is a person. In an instant he
is convinced, makes up his mind for *yes* or for *no*. But
society consists in usages—which are slow in coming to
birth and slow to die; society is tardigrade, slothful, it
drags sluggishly along and advances through history with
the deliberate pace of the cow, which sometimes drives us
to despair by its dilatoriness. And history being primarily
history of collectivities, history of societies, hence history
of usages, we see the origin of its characteristic of extreme
and dilatory slowness, of the *tempo lento* at which universal history moves, needing hundreds and hundreds
of years to accomplish any really substantial advance. It
is as a proverb already ancient in his time that Homer
quotes "The mills of the Gods grind slowly." The mills
of the Gods are historical destiny.

In turn, usage consists of a form of life that the highly
personal man always feels to be archaic, outmoded, antiquated, and already meaningless. Usage is the human
petrifaction, the fossilized behavior or idea. And here we
see the mechanism by reason of which the social is always,
to a greater or lesser degree, the bygone, stuffed and
mounted past, mummy, or, as I have said most seriously
and formally, that the social is essentially anachronism.

Perhaps it is one of society's missions to store up, ac-
cumulate, preserve, keep bygone and ended human life.
Hence the whole of the social is a machine mechanically
preserving and fossilizing personal human life—which in
itself, as human and personal, dies as it is being born, and,
with the magnificent richness and liberality that are characteristic of life, always consumes itself in its own exercise. To keep it, it has to be mechanized, dehumanized,
depersonalized.

We can now hasten back to the defense of our doctrine of the salutation, which was the doctrine of the
peaceful salutation, staggering from the pushing-around

that it has received from these new bellicose salutations.

Unquestionably the person who raises his fist or stretches out his arm means: "By this gesture I announce my enlistment in a party. I am above all a partisan; hence I am against the other parts of society that are not mine. I am a combatant, and what I seek with others is not peace but open battle. To him who opposes me, to him who is not of my party even though he does not oppose me, I offer neither coexistence nor pact; what I offer is first to fight him and vanquish him, then to treat him as vanquished."

There is no doubt about it—this fact represents the greatest contradiction, the most killing blow to my doctrine. We are lost. But just a moment! For if we compare —and that is what we are going to do, again in a very few words, which I shall try to reduce to the essential—if we compare the collective phenomenon of the peaceful salutation with this bellicose salutation, we shall immediately discover three most important and decisive differences. *First,* the peaceful salutation, like every usage (as I have maintained), is slow to become established and will be slow to die out; whereas these bellicose salutations have ousted the other instantaneously, and have imposed themselves at one stroke as soon as a certain party took over power. *Second:* We are not invited to the peaceful salutation by anyone in particular; the suggestion comes to us from that enveloping and as it were atmospheric figure, "everybody else"; the bellicose salutation, on the contrary, is decreed by a man who even signs his name to the order imposing it. And similarly, whereas in the case of the peaceful salutation the coercion, the violence, and the sanction come to us from nobody in particular, no one person feels specifically charged with exercising them (Smith and Jones did not claim to exercise any particular personal office, they did not feel that they had a

right to exercise this coercion)—in the case of the bellicose salutation it is especially designated individuals who
perform the coercive acts, sometimes they even wear
uniforms that distinguish them externally, they have various appellations . . . but let that pass, there is no occasion to cite these titles. What we have here, then, is not
a diffuse social power but one that is precise and organized, that has created special organs to perform its function.

*Third:* In the case of the peaceful salutation, the coercion against the person who offends against the usage
is almost always lax; I mean, that it does not operate directly against the offending act but rather against the person who committed it, in the form of unfavorable judg-
ments on such proceedings, which will produce troublesome consequences for him only in the long run. Observe
that this coercion shows no definite determination to
abolish the offense itself by making it impossible; he who
does not shake hands today can perfectly well not shake
hands tomorrow or on other days. But in the case of the
bellicose salutation, the feeling of coercion is very distinct; he who does not salute with fist or palm is immediately subjected to violence, censured—we see, then, that
this coercion operates directly against the act, does not
tolerate it, is determined that it shall not be repeated.
Whence it follows that this social fact of the bellicose
salutation is not diffuse, vague, weak, and lax; and the
same is true of the inspirer of the act, the social power
that coerces, and the coercion itself.

If the philosophers of law want to do me a favor, let
them review all the most important definitions that have
been given of law, the attempts to differentiate it from
other social phenomena—such as customs, conventions,
morality, and so on—and let them compare what is said
there with the remark I have just made.

If we leave the difference in tempo in the establishment of usages—which in the peaceful usage is a *tempo ritardando* and in the bellicose a *prestissimo*—for discussion in another lecture, and concentrate on all the rest of what I have just said, you will observe that it reveals to us the existence of two classes of usages—those that I call "weak and diffuse usages" and those that I call "strong and rigid usages." An example of the "weak and diffuse usages" is what has always been vaguely called "customs and usages" in dress, food, common social intercourse. But another and equally valid example of them is the usages in speech and thought that constitute "what people say," the two forms of which are the language itself and commonplaces, these latter being what is vaguely called "public opinion."

For a genuine personal idea, which was evident when an individual thought it, to become "public opinion," it must first undergo the dramatic operation that consists in having become a commonplace and hence having lost its evidence, its genuineness, and even its timeliness; every commonplace, since it is a usage, is old, like all usages.

Examples of the "strong and rigid usages" are—aside from economic usages—law and the State, within which appears that terrible but inexorable and indispensable thing, politics.

But now we must observe that the bellicose salutation is not properly a salutation—as we should clearly have seen—because this *salu*tation does not promise *salus*, health, to him whom it salutes. It is not a salutation; it is an order, a command, a law, and even a law emanating from an extreme jurisprudence that springs from an extreme State—I mean, from a State that is a State in the superlative degree. It has, then, nothing to do with the peaceful salutation, unless in the negative sense that it has prohibited peaceful salutations. Therefore our theory is saved and indeed, confirmed.

As for the poor little handshake that has led us into this lengthy discourse, what can we say as a last word about it? For a last word has yet to be said.

For reasons that are so radical and decisive in the reality of human life that I have not even been able to refer to them in these lectures—they belong precisely to the most definitive base of my philosophical thought— I am convinced that everything human—not only the person but his actions, what he constructs, what he fabricates—always has an age. That is, every human reality that presents itself to us is either in its infancy, or its youth, or its maturity, or its decline and decadence. With a little perspicacity—it does not take very much— one can pretty well see what its age is, as we can see the age of a horse by forcing open its lips and looking at its teeth. Now in this sense, I believe for a considerable number of reasons that the form of salutation that we have in the handshake is in its decrepitude, is on its deathbed, and that we shall soon see it disappear, not under the blows of the bellicose salutations and sur- rendering to them but because it is a usage that has reached its last hours, that is in disuse. I will go even further: I have never yet visited England, I know nothing of what has been happening in this respect in England during the last ten years; but *a priori* I make bold to affirm that, some ten or twelve years ago, more or less, the phenomenon of the disappearance of the salutation, of the handshake, and its replacement by something still simpler—a slight bow of the head, or an inaugural smile—*must* have begun in England.

Why particularly in England? The reason is one of the ideas that has interested me intensely for years, which seems to me absolutely obvious, of tremendous impor- tance, and which I have never seen noticed even by the English themselves. It is that when we study the history of any mode of Western life, with the rarest exceptions—which would only prove the rule—we find that before this particular mode of life makes its full and brilliant appearance on the Continent, it always had a precursor in England. In other words, in view of the many facts that confirm it, nothing could be plainer than what I call "England's priority in respect to the Continent." This priority is evident in almost every mode of life—and not only from the time that England became a world power, but from the beginning of the Middle Ages.

It is almost shameful to have to say and remind you that the English taught us—the rest of Europe—to speak Latin, good Latin, when they sent Alcuin and some others to the Continent in the days of Charlemagne.

Well—the English too have failed to see this. But I could point to occasional statements by those English thinkers who have meditated most deeply on their people, in which I divine that they divined something of the sort without succeeding in seeing it.

As you see, there is such an abundance of themes that they rush me from one to another. When the man who devotes himself to thinking reaches a certain time of life, there is almost nothing for him to do but to fall silent. Because there are so many things that ought to be expressed, that fight and come to blows in his throat and strangle his speech. This is why I have been silent for almost ten years. And yet you have seen that in these lectures I have behaved quite correctly, following straight after my theme, and even the episodes that at the time might seem to be the contrary have later proved to be substantial advances. That is, I have held ascetically to my path, restraining myself from taking shots at the magnificent problems that have flown up on either hand like pheasants.

In an earlier lecture we had occasion to make it thoroughly clear to ourselves that the other man is always dangerous, though sometimes, in the case of our neighbors and intimates, his dangerousness is so slight that we disregard it. The fact that the usage of the salutation exists is a proof that men are vividly conscious that they are dangerous to one another. When we approach our neighbor, even at this period of history and so-called civilization, something like a try-out, like a buffer or cushion to deaden the element of shock in the approach, is imperative.

For we have seen that the form of the act in which the salutation consists has atrophied in exact proportion to the diminishing degree of danger. If a residue of the act subsists today it is because there is still a residue of danger. In other words, through all its changes, and even in its present form of extreme survival, this usage of salutation continues to be useful, an instrument and apparatus that renders genuine service. Imagine for a moment that the salutation should, by some magic, be abolished tonight and that tomorrow when we met our acquaintances we should have to begin positive dealings with them at once, without the previous ornamental contact of the salutation. Should we not find this kind of a beginning difficult, harsh, impertinent, except when the persons involved live together in the most continuous and extreme intimacy? But when this is the case there is, properly speaking, no meeting; for example, we do not "meet" someone who lives in our own house—parents, brothers, children, close relatives. On the contrary, the unusual thing is not finding him at our side. On the other hand, if we consider closely, we shall see that in two meetings with another person we scarcely ever feel that we are on the same level of human proximity, in the same frame of mind toward each other. Involuntarily we find ourselves as it were calculating how our neighbor

confronts us, and we carry about a sort of thermometer
of sociability or friendship that registers his contact as
colder or warmer on each occasion. The salutation commonly serves to make the first thing that we shall say
to our acquaintance successful. Probably only the angels
do not need to greet one another because they are mutually transparent. But it is so congenital to men to be
more or less arcane, mysterious, and, for that reason
alone, more or less dangerous to one another, that this
defect and constant miniature drama has developed into
something that lends savor and attraction to our living
together—to the point that if we should suddenly become
translucent to one another, should interpenetrate one another, we should undergo an immense disillusionment and
should not know what to do with an ethereal life that
did not constantly come into collision with our neighbors. It is necessary—nay, it is perhaps the most important of all things, given the state of vital experience that
the West has reached and the inevitability of establishing
a new culture, new in its deepest roots, since our traditional culture (and I refer to the most opposed traditions)
has run out like an exhausted quarry—I say, it is our
most important task to learn to see that, the human
condition being at every moment limited, finite, and hence
ultimately made up of negatives, it is on these negatives
that we must depend, since they are what we substantially
are, and that we must therefore see them as positives.
Anything else would result not in bettering life, but on
the contrary in emptying it of that limited and finite
content which it does after all possess. Thus, instead of
seeking, with the utopianists, some magic by which man
will cease to be dangerous to man, we should recognize
the fact, emphasize it, depend on it, as the bird depends
on the negative resistance of the air to fly, and exert our
ingenuity to make use of this destiny of ours and render

it attractive and fertile. Instead of crying over our limitations, we should use them for our benefit, as we use waterfalls. Culture has always consisted in taking advantage of obstacles.

But to return to our subject: I shall be told that, even if the present-day salutation has a certain, if evanescent usefulness, the fact is that it is practiced only among acquaintances, whereas we do not practice it with the strangers whom we meet as we pass through the city streets. Would it not be of more use to us with the latter class than with the former? Why do we salute those who have been introduced to us, and not those whom we do not know at all, when in the desert or the forest the practice is more or less the opposite, the longest and most meticulous compliment being paid to the nameless man who suddenly appears on the horizon? The reason why these things are as they are is plain. Precisely because the city is a place in which people who do not know one another live continually together, their meetings and their living together could not be adequately regulated by such a usage as the salutation—which, after all, is merely ornamental and of very slight efficacy. The salutation remains restricted to circles where the coefficient of danger is lower, to the already well-defined and domestic living together of groups composed of people who are acquainted. When someone introduces two people to each other, he plays the role of guarantor of their mutual peacefulness and good will. To regulate the friction between strangers in the city, and particularly in the great city, a more peremptory, forceful, and precise usage had to be created in society; this usage is, in plain terms, the police. But we cannot discuss this last usage until we have confronted another and more extensive one, which is its foundation—public power or the State. And this, in turn, can be clearly understood only when we know what the system of intellectual usages that we call "public opinion" is, which in turn owes its existence to that system of verbal usages, the language. As you see, usages are interconnected and rest one upon another, forming a gigantic architecture. This gigantic architecture of usages is, precisely, society.

# 11

# What People Say: Language.
# Toward a New Linguistics

---

THERE is no more superlatively human relation than that
between mother and child, between the man and woman
who love each other. A completely individual being, *this*
mother, lives toward another completely individual being,
*this* child. *This* man is in love with *this* irreplaceable,
incomparable, unique woman. What the one does in respect to the other is a maximum example of inter-individual
action. Now, what the two lovers do most is to talk to
each other. Yes, I know that between them there is also
the caress. But let us leave that aside for the present; perhaps we shall find that the caress in love is—I do not say
it is only, but that, more than anything else, it is like—
going on conversing in a new form. What form? Let us
leave that aside too. What appears to be beyond doubt
is that the love of lovers, which lives in looks, which
lives in caresses, more than in all this lives in conversation,
in an endless dialogue. Love is talkative, warbling; love
is eloquent, and if anyone is silent in love, it is because
he cannot help it, because he is abnormally taciturn.

So then, this intensely individual inter-action, loving
each other, in which both participants act from their most
personal depths, which is therefore a ceaseless original
creation, must be realized through speech. But to speak
is to use a particular language, and that language is not the
creation of either of the two lovers. The language in
which they converse was there, confronting them and

outside of them, in their social environment. From their childhood it has been instilled into them by their hearing people talking, saying things. Because language, which is always and finally one's mother-tongue, is not learned in grammars and dictionaries, but in what people say.

They, the lovers, want to say things to each other, many things, but all those things are one thing—the proper being, the most individual being, of each of them. At the very beginning of this study, when I pointed out that human life in its ultimate truth is radical solitude, I added that love is the attempt to exchange two solitudes, to mingle two secret inwardnesses—an attempt that, if it succeeded, would be like two streams mingling their waters, or two flames fusing into one. This is why lovers say "my love," or use some other similar expression. We must distinguish between what they want to say to each other by this expression, and the expression itself by which they say it. What they want to say by it is their feeling toward the other, a genuine feeling that invades them, that springs from the roots of their person, that they feel and understand perfectly. The expression "my love," on the contrary, which is to convey the declaration or manifestation of this feeling from one to the other, comes to them both from outside and they do not understand it. We find ourselves in the same situation as in the case of the salutation: I understand that I must shake hands, but I absolutely do not understand why what I have to do with others is to shake hands with them. Lovers understand that in order to communicate their feeling to each other they have to speak these words or others of the same tenor. But they do not understand why their feeling is called "love," is spoken or expressed by "love" and not by any other sound. Between their personal intention to speak out their feeling and the act of enunciating and producing a certain sound, there is no intelligible connection. If lovers perform this act of enunciation, it is because they have heard that it is done when two people love each other, but not for any reason that they find in the word "love."

Language is a social usage that interposes itself between them, between their two inwardnesses, and whose exercise or use by individuals is predominantly irrational. The most scandalous and almost comic proof of this is that we apply the words "rational" and "logical" to our most intelligent behavior—when these words come from *ratio* and *logos,* which in Latin and Greek originally meant "speech," a performance that is irrational, at least on one of its constitutive sides and frequently on all of them.

I repeat: We understand, more or less, the ideas that we want to express by what we say, but we do not understand what *what* we say says, what is meant by *what* we say, in itself—that is, by our words. The parallel with the salutation is perfect. And just as, in its case, we can only understand the act of shaking hands when we stop doing it and fall to theorizing on the origin of the salutation and discover the etymology of our usage, even so it is with speech. Sometimes we fail, and the word remains unintelligible. This is the case with the word *amor* ["love"]. We Spaniards received it from the Romans; but it is not a Roman word, it is Etruscan. Who knows from what experiences of their own or from what other people it came to the Etruscans! It is most unfortunate, but we do not know why such an important thing in our lives as love is called *"amor."* Similarly, we say "fear entered me." For us, this expression has no meaning in itself. We do not understand how fear, an emotion that is produced in ourselves and that has nothing to do with space, can be outside and "enter us." But this time the etymology illuminates the meaning for us. It tells us that Greek and other Indo-European languages have an identical expression, which shows us that the primitive Indo-European people believed that passions, like sicknesses, are cosmic forces that are outside, in space, and from time to time invade us.

But the other attribute of usage is that we feel coerced to practice it, to obey it. Where is the coercion in talking? Who gets angry or threatens me with reprisals if I do not use the words of any particular language but sounds of my own invention?

In discussing coercion in the case of the salutation, I confined myself to stating the kind of reprisals that neglecting it provoked. But we shall see that in each type of usage the coercion takes a different form. These differences are of the utmost importance; better than anything else, they reveal what function each type of usage performs in society. The maximum coercion is physical coercion, and society employs it when there is contravention of a certain very characteristic type of usages called "law." We shall see why this is so. For the present it suffices to say that, if we compare this coercion with the coercion that threatens us if we do not greet someone, we see that the latter is much weaker, more diffuse, and slower to function than the former. If somebody steals a watch and is "caught in the act," a policeman immediately grabs him and he is taken to the police station by force. In this case, then, society's response to a contravention of usage is physical, of maximum intensity, and instantaneous. This shows us once again that usages can be classified as "weak and strong." These two degrees of force in usage are measured by the force manifested in the accompanying coercion. Salutations and everything that we commonly call "customs" are weak usages; law, on the other hand, is a strong usage. I hope to be able to show that, precisely because it is a strong usage, its most frequent aspect and *prima facies* have a different profile from other usages—that is, from those that have always more or less been regarded as usages; and that this has been the reason why jurists and philosophers of law have failed to see in it what it is and cannot help being —a usage among other usages. But it is not yet time to speak of what law is. I have said that our environment, in so far as it is social environment, manifests itself as permanent and universal coercion. But now it is time very briefly to correct the current and erroneous idea of social or collective coercion. For this is held to consist only in particular acts, positive or negative, that the other members of the collectivity practice on us. Such is not the case. This is only one form of coercion, of which we have already seen two different kinds: the displeasure of others if we do not greet them, which is merely withdrawal of their friendship, their esteem, and possibly of their company; and the forceful intervention of the police if somebody steals a watch or forges a will. But it seems to me perfectly natural to use the expression "coercion on my behavior" to designate any unpleasant consequence, of whatever nature, produced by the fact of my not doing what is done in my social environment.

For example: the lover wants to say something to his sweetheart but refuses to use any particular language. Obviously, the police will not intervene on this account, but what happens is that his sweetheart does not understand him and he is left not having said what he wanted to say to her. Without any to-do or apparent violence, the usage that is language imposes itself on us in the simplest but most automatic and inexorable way possible, preventing us from being fully understood and hence basically paralyzing any fertile and normal living with our neighbor. Here is a coercion that does not consist in either positive acts or negative acts—that is, omissions—on the part of anybody, for I assume that no one will call "not understanding" an act, when it is simply something that one undergoes. So let us say, formally, that there is coercion whenever we cannot choose a behavior different from that which is practiced in the collectivity and and not suffer punishment for it. The punishment or correction can be of the most various sorts and degrees; it can, for example, simply mean that not to do what is done in our milieu costs us more effort than to do it. To cite only a trivial case, but one that its very triviality makes significant: if we decide to make our breakfast something different from the ordinary repertory of breakfasts, we shall find ourselves in difficulties, we shall very quickly learn what effort we have to put into such a trivial and everyday matter—for example, when we are traveling or changing our place of residence. Society, on the other hand, saves us even the effort of thinking up a breakfast by handing us the usual bill of fare. With no melodramatic figure of speech, this very simple thing is the decisive reason why society exists; I mean, why it persists. Because at one time or another almost all men have felt longings to flee from society. But the vivid image of the effort implied by a solitary life, in which one would have to do everything for oneself, is enough to suppress this impulse to flee. Man is said to be a naturally sociable animal. This is a confused idea, which I have not now time to reduce to order. But in the end I should admit it, provided that I were allowed to add to it, inseparably, that man is also and at the same time naturally unsociable, that in him there is always, more or less somnolent or awake, an urge to flee from society. Periodically, it appears on a scale that is visible in history. All over the world during these last years—earlier in some countries, later in others—there has been an epidemic of wanting to get away; to get away from the society in which one lives, and if possible from all society. For example, there is no reckoning the number of Europeans who in these last years have dreamed of a desert island.

When Napoleon invaded Germany and approached Weimar, Goethe said: "One would like to be out of it!" But there is no "out of it." During the first centuries of the Roman Empire, many men, disillusioned with everything collective and public, fled to the desert to live immersed in their own desperate solitude. The Christian monks were far from being the first to go into isolation. They were only imitating those who, in Syria and Egypt, had for two centuries been becoming "desert-dwellers" —*eremitas*—in order to practice *mone*—solitude. Hence they were called *monachoi*—monks. This kind of life gave them immense prestige and started a sort of epidemic. The deserts were peopled by thousands of "solitaries," who thereby ceased to be "solitary" and became a "community"—*cenobium*—from *koinos*, "common." But individuals more determined to isolate themselves, finding it impossible to do so horizontally, hit upon the idea of fleeing from their fellows vertically by building a tall column or pillar, on top of which they lived. They were called *stylites*. But they too failed; and even the Emperor sent his ministers to consult St. Simeon on matters of state, shouting up to him from the ground.

Less simple as a phenomenon than the salutation, language is the fact in which the characters of social reality are given most clearly and purely, and hence the being of a society is manifested in it with incalculable precision. Basically, society is the continuous, stabilized living together of men in a collective unit, that is, a separate living together, separated from other co-livings and collectivities. As soon as a group of men separates from the collectivity in which they formerly lived, automatically, without any individual willing it, the language that they formerly spoke begins to change and, if the separation lasts, a new language begins to be created. If by some dramatic chance we who are here in this hall should remain separated from all other Spaniards for several years and then rejoin our compatriots, we should observe with surprise that, without our having been aware of it, our Spanish would be markedly different from that spoken by the others, different in the pronunciation of many words, in the meaning of others, in syntactic forms, in locutions or idioms. What in our case is imaginary has actually occurred countless times in history. Vice versa, this oft-repeated occurrence demonstrates that for *a* society to exist there must be a pre-existing *separation*. This can have been brought about by all sorts of different causes. The most obvious is the geographical disturbances that isolate a human group. If I had more time, I should say something about a people recently discovered and studied in New Guinea, whom a geological catastrophe isolated centuries ago in some valleys from which its members had no egress. But the cause of the isolation can be *solely* political, or can stem from more complicated causes to which I cannot give a single simple name if I am to be understood.

If sociological studies had been properly conducted, sociologists would have thoroughly studied, both in the past and the present, this influence of separation on collective life in automatically producing "society" with all its attributes or a part of them. If the subject had been pursued, both in the past and the present, we should today have an ample and reasonably clear collection of "case-histories," which could be of greater use to us than we may at first suspect. For example: Present-day means of communication have had the result that, for the first time, it is normal for large numbers of people to travel with the greatest frequency from their own to other countries, including the most distant. This phenomenon, which began to appear some years ago, will in all probability only increase in the years ahead. Together with corporeal transfer, there is the action exercised by the constant presence in the press of whatever occurs in other countries. Now, what effects will all this have on the life of each society? Because we cannot take it for granted that these effects will necessarily be beneficial, or at least that the speed with which this process is advancing will not bring about serious consequences, even if only temporarily.

That sociologists and ethnologists have not accorded due importance to the subject is abundantly clear when we observe that facts such as the following are not regarded as problems worthy of study:

In Nigeria, numerous tribes differing completely in race, language, usages, and so on, live in such close proximity to others that it would be no exaggeration to say that they live mingled together. Nevertheless the individuals of each tribe remain attached to their particular society and are completely conscious of the others as absolutely foreign. Since for primitives the sacred drums symbolize all the usages of their tribe and hence *their* society, when they see someone belonging to another tribe they say, "That man dances to another drum"; that is, "that man" has other beliefs, another language, other taboos, and so on. How can we explain it that in this quasi-living-together differences are not wiped out and that the identity of taboos and so on maintains such a full social cohesion within each tribe and, amid the most active living together, suffices to isolate? The identity of taboos produces the social cohesion and, in the midst of the most active living together, isolates.

But the reaction of language to the characteristics of society is so subtle that not only do the languages of two societies differ, but in the same society the language is modified in accordance with the social group. One of the most ancient of historical documents—earlier than the year 3,000 B.C.—informs us that in the Sumero-Accadian cities two languages were spoken; one was the language of men, *eme-ku*, the other the language of women, *eme-sal* —which also means the language of the wary. Can it be that men and women so early began not to understand each other? The fact was maintained by none less than E. Meyer. A few years ago, Hrozny, the decipherer of the Hittite cuneiform script and of the hieroglyphics of the other Hittite people, contested it. But it is hard to understand his reluctance to admit it, since today there are still many peoples among whom a masculine and a feminine language coexist. C. A. Bernouilli calls attention to this feminine idiom that no man can understand and that is the only language employed in the strictly female mysteries, as among the Swahili. Flora Kraus has studied the character and dissemination of this language.

Our Spanish language, in the form of it which—with something of idealism or utopianism, but, when all is said and done, with sufficient reason—we can call normal, is the result, or perhaps better the mechanical resultant, of collaboration between the different classes of society. For in fact each of them has its own language. And this is not due to haphazard differences, but to a fundamental reason that makes these various classes independent organs, each with its role in the existence of our normal language. For the situation is that the so-called lower class, the middle class, and the upper class use the language with radically different attitudes. As Lerch points out, the way of speaking, that is, of using the language, differs in three distinct social groups: there are those who speak without thinking of how they speak, in pure freedom and just as they happen to; this is the lower-class group. There are those who reflect on their own speech, but reflect erroneously, which gives rise to comic deformations, such as that of the lady who, to show how "refined" she is, says that her husband is suffering from "p-neumonia." Finally, there is the upper group, which reflects and reflects correctly.

Let us leave out the middle group, which rarely has any influence on normal language. We are left with the people and the cultivated aristocracies. Their attitude in language is only a special manifestation of their general attitude toward life. For there are two ways of being in life. One is to abandon oneself, letting one's acts come out as they will. The other is to restrain our first movements and try to make our behavior conform to norms. Lerch shows how the "cultivated man," who usually belongs to the upper classes, speaks *from* a linguistic "norm," from an ideal of his language and of language in general. The people, on the other hand, speak as the good God puts it into their heads to speak. Hence Lerch maintains, in opposition to the romantic thesis, that the elect, the aristocracies, by being faithful to the norm, fix and preserve the idiom, and thus prevent it from reaching the final degeneracy at which it would arrive under the phonetic laws that completely govern popular speech. The loss of consonants at which French had arrived when the upper classes began their vigil is immense: of *pediculum* nothing remains but "pou," of *parabolare* "parler," of *cathedra*, "chaire" or "chaise," of *oculus* "oeil," of *augurium* "heur." Hence the numerous convergences that have loaded French with ambiguous sounds: "sen" comes from Latin words as different as *centum, sanguem, sine, se inde* ("s'en"), *ecce hoc inde* ("c'en"); whence the expression that is today stupidly written "sens dessus dessous," and earlier—in Vaugelas, in Madame de Sévigné—"c'en dessus dessous." Shortening words accented on the antepenultimate—*tepidus*, "tiède"

—leaves only paroxytones and oxytones—from *portum*, "port," from *porta*, "porte." But this -e is mute, and without the intervention of the educated, the final -t would disappear by confusion with "port" and then both would be reduced to *port*. Thanks to the educated there are abstract words and many devices of the utmost usefulness, for example, certain conjunctions.[1]

In the sixteenth century French was still at the mercy of individual caprice. The first years of the seventeenth saw the beginning of pressure from a norm emanating from the upper classes. And the figure chosen for the norm is—not that of the scholar or pedant who speaks from himself—but that of court speech, in which the dominant point of view is that of the person who hears and is to answer, because the courtier speaks not as a solitary writer but explicitly as a conversationalist. The norm adopted, then, is one that arises from the most essential characteristic of idiom: sociability. It is man in so far as he is social who will be the legislator. But within this concept of the sociable man, the preference goes to the sociable man in whom talking—conversing—is formally an occupation; the man who talks for talking's sake—the courtier, the "man of society" and *l'honnête homme, l'homme de bonne compagnie*. It is right that in this spoken discourse in which the decisive consideration is to be heard with pleasure, this type of man decides upon the form of discourse, inasmuch as he says *how* something is to be said. On the other hand, in written discourse, in which the decisive consideration is that *what* is to be said gets said, the writer should decide.

Complete abandonment to the functioning of phonetic laws would lead to a language of ambiguous monosyllables, many of them identical, as we have just seen,

[1] E. Lerch, "Über das sprachliche Verhältnis von Ober- und Unterschichten," *Jahrbuch für Philologie*, I (1925), p. 91.

although originating from very different words. This has happened in English and in Chinese. Hence that unhappy state of the English language which frequently forces those whose mother-tongue it is to spell out some word they have just uttered in conversation. We might sometimes suspect that, if one Englishman understands another, it is because, since conversation among them normally consists of pure commonplaces, he knows beforehand what the other is going to say. In Chinese the problem has been solved by complicating enunciation through different pitches of tone, which makes it an unmusical music and baffles any attempt to transcribe it into Latin characters or any other nonideographic script.

My love! No one will say that this is not a good beginning for a paragraph! Luckily, no one can possibly surmise or suspect to whom this verbal sigh is addressed! From a pure indiscretion, uttering this endearment before an audience of over a thousand people makes it discretion itself, indeed something more than discreet. For discretion consists in keeping silent what should be kept silent, but on the supposition that what is kept silent could actually be said because it has a meaning. But these two words, despite their having the appearance of words and having a vague meaning, something resembling a meaning, are not discourse, they do not say anything. Why not—if their sound is intact and correctly pronounced? They say nothing, because they do not carry an address to a consignee; they have a sender, myself, but they lack a receiver; hence, once they are in the air, like the pigeon that has lost its course and flutters indecisively not knowing which way to go, they accomplish no journey, they arrive nowhere, they do not speak. The words "my love," that is, are now in the air, they have remained in the air exactly as they are in the dictionary. In the dictionary, words are *possible* meanings, but they say nothing. They are curious things, those obese books that we call dictionaries, lexicons. All the words in a language are in them, yet their author is the only man who when he writes those words does not *say* them. When he conscientiously sets down the words "fool" or "blockhead" he says them neither *of* anyone nor *to* anyone. Which brings us face to face with the most unexpected paradox: namely, that language, that is, the lexicon or dictionary, is the very opposite of language and that words are not words except when they are said by someone to someone. Only then, functioning as concrete action, as living action of one human being on another human being, do they possess verbal reality. And since the men between whom the words are interchanged are human lives, and every human life is at every instant in a particular circumstance or situation, it is clear that the reality "word" is inseparable from the person who says it, from the person to whom it is said, and from the situation in which this takes place. Anything other than taking the word in this way is simply to turn it into an abstraction, is to empty it of its virtue, to amputate it and leave only a lifeless fragment of it.

Thus in the case of my uttering the words "my love" —not being said to anyone, they would not be "saying," discourse, and not being that, they would not be a genuine verbal action. They would be only sound—what linguistic scientists call a "phoneme." Nevertheless, this sound would have a meaning. What meaning? No—we are not going to embark on the perilous undertaking of defining the reality that is love. At most our task would be only to define what this expression "my love" signifies, to delimit the meaning that, as soon as these words were uttered, we found in our minds. But if we should attempt it, we should find that what happens is this: various real

or imaginary, more or less definite, but always concrete
situations in which those words are actually said by
someone to someone arise before us, and then the meaning differs in accordance with the situation and the persons involved in it. It is, for example, a mother saying
"my love" to her child, or it is a lover saying it to his
sweetheart. Mother love is not the same as the love of
lovers. But this is too obvious to be of concern to us.
Rather, let us compare either one of these two meanings
that the word "love" has when it is actually spoken and
is a living moment in a life, with the meaning that it
seemed to have when I first uttered it. In the case of the
mother and in that of the lover, the word "love" states
and speaks out an actual, real, complete feeling, with all
its components and appurtenances. I have expressed myself badly—it is not one real feeling that the word designates or represents in the two cases, but two very different feelings. Hence, one and the same word is used to
name two very different realities. This must not be confused with the fact that there are ambiguous words,
affected by what linguistic scientists call "polysemia" or
multiplicity of meanings. Thus, the same vocable *león*
means the African carnivore [lion], the Spanish city
[León], a number of Popes [Leo], and the two statues
that guard the stairway of our parliamentary building.
In this example the fact that the same phoneme—*león*
—signifies all these things is pure chance, and in each
case the coincidence is due to a particular and different
cause. The name for the animal simply comes from the
Latin root *leon*—of *leo, leonis*—but the name of the city
of León comes, by phonetic changes, from *legion*, because
the military and administrative headquarters of a Roman
army corps was located there; so that *león*, the name of
an animal, and León, the name of a city, are not one word
with two meanings but two words that have nothing to

do with each other and that the successive changes in the pronunciation of two phonetic series that begin in *leo* and *legio* have finally happened to make identical, producing a genuine homonym. In order that we may draw profit from all this, but also with an eye to what I said before, I will add that this example shows us how, if language were abandoned to the phonetic changes of vocables, it would end by being full of paronomasias and we could not possibly understand one another because conversation would be perpetual punning. In the case of the Congressional lions, what has happened is that the meaning has been changed by becoming metaphorical, so that from an animal of flesh and blood the word comes to mean a piece of bronze or marble having a somewhat similar shape.

But in the "my love" of the mother and the "my love" of the lover there is, the grammarians tell us, no homonymy. Here we have one and the same word with one and the same meaning. On the other hand, there is no question but that in these two cases it names feelings that are extremely different, so that "love," all by itself, ought to mean *either* mother love *or* the love of the lover, but we cannot see how it can at the same time mean both. We can only understand this if we observe that the word "love," standing alone, removed from any living situation in which it is actually said, means neither this, that, nor any other real, concrete love, hence a complete and actual love, but only certain attributes that must be present in any love at all—be it love of a person, of God, of one's country, of science—but which by themselves do not suffice to make a love exist. The same thing happens if I say "triangle." With the meanings that this word seems to offer on the face of it, no one can draw a triangle on the blackboard. To do that, we must on our own account add certain further attributes that are not contained in this meaning—such as a specific length of the sides of the figure and a specific aperture of its angles. Only with these additions is a triangle a triangle. "Love," "triangle," do not, strictly, possess a meaning but only an embryo of meaning, a schema of meaning, something like the algebraic formula, which is not itself a calculation but only a schema for possible calculations, a schema that requires to be completed by the substitution of specific figures for its letters.

I do not know whether with all this I have succeeded in showing you the strange condition that adheres to words and hence to language. For it turns out that if we take the word by itself and simply as a word—"love," "triangle"—it does not properly have a meaning since it has only a fragment of a meaning. And if instead of taking the word by itself, in its pure and strict verbality, we say it —then it becomes charged with actual and complete meaning. But from whence does the word, does language, receive what it lacks and needs in order to fulfill the function commonly attributed to it—namely, to mean, to have meaning? For it does not receive it from other words, it does not receive it from anything that has to this day been called language and which is what appears in mummified form in dictionaries and grammars. No— it receives it from outside itself, from the human beings who use it, who say it in a particular situation. Here, then, in this particular situation, talking with the precise inflexion of voice with which they enunciate, with the expression that they assume while they are doing it, with the concomitant gestures, free or restrained—are the human beings who properly "speak," "say." The so-called words are only one component of this complex of reality, and in fact they are only words in so far as they function in this complex, are inseparable from it. The sound "dark" gives rise to several series of possible meanings and hence to no actual meaning. But said by someone in a tavern, the vocable automatically completes itself with non-verbal elements, with the whole setting of the "pub," and, instantly, the word perfectly performs its task, unequivocally releases its meaning, and means: "That man wants dark beer." [2] The thing is immense in its very triviality, for it shows us how all the other ingredients of a circumstance, the non-verbal ingredients, those which are not *sensu stricto* "language," possess a declaratory potentiality and that language therefore consists not only in saying what language says by itself but in actualizing this potentiality of speech and meaning possessed by the environment. The indubitable fact is that it is surprising how the word freely enters as a word—that is, as fulfilling its declaratory function—into sudden coalescence with the beings and things around it which are not verbal. What the word says by itself is very little, but it acts as a percussion cap that sets off the quasi-verbal power of everything else. This is not also the case with the written language—but let us leave that aside, since it is obvious that written language is secondary and subsequent to oral language, or, as Goethe said, that writing is simply an inadequate substitute or stopgap for the spoken word.

We saw earlier that "I, you, here, there" were words that had different meanings in accordance with who is speaking them and the place where the speaker of them happens to be; hence grammarians called them "words of occasional signification." I said at the time that it could be argued with the linguists whether these words, rather than *an* occasional signification, have not countless occasional significations. But now we discern, even from these very brief considerations, that, strictly speaking,

---

[2] [The illustration is substituted from the parallel passage in "Del Imperio Romano" (*Obras completas*, VI, 55) for the untranslatable illustration that makes the same point here.—*Trans.*]

something of the same sort happens to all words, that their genuine meaning is always occasional, that their precise sense depends on the situation or circumstance in which they are spoken. The meaning that the unabridged dictionary attributes to every vocable is only the skeleton of its real significations, which, always more or less different and new, in the never-ceasing, ever-varying flow of talk, clothe the skeleton with the flesh of a concrete meaning. Instead of a skeleton we might perhaps better say that they are the malleable matrix in which words, when they are really such, hence when they are spoken to somebody, for certain reasons and for a particular end, receive a first molding.

Linguistics had to begin by isolating this skeletonic and abstract side of real language. This procedure enabled it to elaborate grammar and vocabulary—which it has done thoroughly and admirably. But scarcely was this achieved before linguists saw that they had only made a beginning, because actual speaking and writing is an almost constant contradiction of what grammar teaches and dictionaries define—and to such a degree that it could nearly be said that speech consists in offending against grammar and outraging the dictionary. At least, and in all formality, what is called being a good writer, that is, a writer with style, is to subject grammar and vocabulary to frequent erosions. Hence such a great linguistic scientist as Vendryès could define a dead language as one in which it was not permissible to commit errors; and this, turned around, is equivalent to saying that a living language lives by committing them. Which brings us to the curious situation in which linguistics finds itself today and which consists in surrounding the grammar and vocabulary that linguistics itself had established in its previous stage by a fringe of constantly narrower investigations that study the how and why of these errors,

errors which, obviously, are now admitted to have a positive value; that is, they are exceptions that are as much a constitutive factor of language as the rules themselves. This fringe that is developing around traditional linguistics is stylistics. To give the crudest and most commonplace example, if somebody shouts "Fire!" he offends against grammar because by shouting it he wants to say, to state something, and grammatical correctness demands that every statement should be a complete sentence (the word by itself, Aristotle had already told us, states nothing)—for example, "in this house fire has produced a conflagration." But the feeling of panic and the vital urgency of the situation make the man renounce this complex statement which, according to the old linguistics, would be the correct one, and condense the sentence into one eruptive word.

As we see, stylistics, in contradistinction to grammar, enlarges the scientific study of language to include such extra-verbal elements as the emotional state and the particular situation in which someone utters the word and precisely part of all that which, as we saw before, is inseparable from the word but which grammar and the dictionary had separated from it. This means that stylistics is not, as people still think, a vague addition to grammar but is neither more nor less than a whole new incipient linguistics which is determined to take hold of language closer to its concrete reality. And I do not believe that it is foolhardy to prophesy that recent stylistics, today a slight fringe softening the severe profile of grammar and lexicology, is destined to swallow them up and to make a clean sweep of all linguistics. For quite a number of years now I have been asking for a linguistics that should have the courage to study language in its integral reality, as it is when it is actual living discourse, and not as a mere fragment amputated from its complete configuration. For example, this new philology—the example, please note, is chosen for its comparative simplicity—will raise to the status of a formal principle of linguistics, the old saw that, as a subsidiary rule, has always oriented the practical interpretation of texts and which runs: *duo si idem dicunt non est idem*, "if two say the same thing—it is not the same thing."

Linguistics—be it phonetics, be it grammar, be it lexicology—has studied an abstraction that it *calls* "language"—which, always assuming that its configuration is susceptible of precise definition, is something that I have described as wonderful and which we should very much like to possess in any of the other humanistic disciplines. But it is obvious that linguistics has not thereby come to know *language* except in a first approximation, because what it calls "language" really has no existence, it is a utopian and artificial image constructed by linguistics itself. In effect, language is never a "fact" for the simple reason that it is never an "accomplished fact" but is always making and unmaking itself, or, to put it in other terms, it is a permanent creation and a ceaseless destruction. Hence precisely the splendid intellectual achievement represented by linguistics as it is constituted today obliges it (*noblesse oblige*) to attain a second and more precise and forceful approximation in its knowledge of the reality, "language." And this it can do only if it studies language not as an accomplished fact, as a thing made and finished, but as in the process of being made, hence *in statu nascendi*, in the very roots that engender it. Linguistics would be wrong if it believed that, to know a language in the making, it need only reconstruct the forms of it that preceded its present form, or, more generally, that preceded the form it exhibits at a particular date. Linguistics has already accomplished this, and it is a most important branch of knowledge. But this so-called "history of language" is really nothing but a series of grammars and dictionaries of the aspect that the language as constituted at each of its previous stages exhibited at that date. The history of a language shows us a series of successive languages, but not their making.

Although obviously a most fruitful undertaking, it is not necessary to go to the past to study the making of a language for, since a language is always being made and unmade, this takes place today just as it did yesterday. Important as the past of a language may be, it would be more important for linguistics to resolve to approach the phenomenon of language on a deeper level, namely, before the word is made, at the roots, in the genetic causes of language.

Very briefly, I would expound my idea of a new linguistics as follows:

To speak is *principally* (the reason for this reservation will appear later) to use a language as constituted and as our social environment imposes it on us. But this implies that the language has been made, and to make it is not simply to speak, it is to invent new modes of the language, and, originally, to invent them absolutely. Obviously new modes of a language are invented because those that exist and that it already possesses do not satisfy, do not suffice to say what needs to be said. Saying—that is, the desire to express, to manifest, to declare—is, then, a function or activity previous to speech and to the existence of a language in the form and manner in which it now exists and is found.

Saying is a deeper stratum than speaking, and it is to this deeper stratum that linguistics should now apply itself. Languages would not exist if man were not constitutively the Sayer; that is, he who *has* things to say. Hence, he postulates a new discipline, which shall be basal to all the others that make up linguistics, and which

I call "Theory of Saying." Why is man a sayer and not silent, or at most a being like others that confine themselves to signaling to their fellows, by cries, howls, and songs, a repertory of practical situations given once and for all? Von Frisch has succeeded in clearly distinguishing a small repertory of different flights that produce different sounds, with each of which the bee signals a particular situation to its fellows. But these signals are not a "saying" on the bee's part, they are automatic reflexes that these different situations release in it.

One of the disadvantages of not starting from "saying" —an earlier human function than speaking—is that language is considered to be the expression of what we want to communicate and manifest, whereas the fact is that a great part of what we want to manifest and communicate remains unexpressed in two dimensions, one above and the other below language. Above, there is all the ineffable. Below, is all that "goes without saying." Now, this situation, this silence, constantly acts on language and is the cause of many of its forms. Humboldt already said: "In the grammar of every language there is a part that is expressly designated or declared and another part that thought adds silently. In Chinese the former part is in infinitely small proportion to the latter. In every language the context of what is said has to come to the aid of grammar. In Chinese it is the basis of comprehension, and the construction can often be derived only from it. The verb itself can be recognized only by virtue of the verbal concept"—that is, of a verbal action suggested by the context (Humboldt, V, 319). It is only in the light of this that we can explain sentences without subjects, such as "Raining," or exclamations, "Fire!" "Thieves!" "Come on!"

But if man is he who "says," it would be of the first importance to determine what it is that he says, or, expressed in another way, what are the primary directions of his saying, what are the things that move him to say and what are those that leave him silent; that is, which he leaves unsaid. It is obvious that this need to say—and not a vague and indeterminate need, but a precise system of things that had to be said—is what led to the invention and subsequent existence of languages. This makes it possible for us to determine whether this instrument invented for saying is adequate and in what measure it is or is not so.

Man, when he sets himself to speak, does so *because* he believes that he will be able to say what he thinks. Now, this is an illusion. Language is not up to that. It says, more or less, a part of what we think, and raises an impenetrable obstacle to the transmission of the rest. It serves quite well for mathematical statements and proofs. In talking about physics it already begins to be ambiguous and inadequate. But in proportion as conversation treats of more important, more human, more "real" subjects than these, its vagueness, clumsiness, and confusion steadily increase. Obedient to the inveterate prejudice that "talking leads to understanding," we speak and listen in such good faith that we end by misunderstanding one another far more than we would if we remained mute and set ourselves to divine each other. Nay, more: since our thought is in large measure dependent upon our language—though I decline to believe that the dependence, as is commonly maintained, is absolute—it follows that thinking is talking with oneself and hence misunderstanding oneself at the imminent risk of getting oneself into a complete quandary.

In 1922 the Philosophical Society of Paris devoted a session to discussing the problem of progress in language. Together with the philosophers of the Seine, the participants included the great masters of the French school of linguistics, which was, in a certain sense, at least as a school, the most distinguished in the world. Reading the abstract of the discussion, I came upon certain remarks by Meillet—Meillet, the supreme master of contemporary linguistics—which left me stupefied: "Every language," he said, "expresses whatever is necessary for the society of which it is the organ. . . . With any phonetics, with any grammar, anything can be expressed." With all due respect to the memory of Meillet, does it not appear that there is obvious exaggeration in these words? How did Meillet ascertain the truth of such an absolute declaration? It could not be as a linguistic scientist. As such, he knows only languages, not what the peoples who speak them think; and his dogma supposes that he has compared the two and found them coincident; furthermore, it is not enough to say that every language can formulate every thought, but whether all languages can do so with the same ease and immediacy. So any particular language not only interposes difficulties to the expression of certain thoughts, but also obstructs the reception of others, paralyzes intelligence in certain directions.

The stupendous reality that is language cannot be understood unless we begin by observing that speech consists above all in silences. A being who could not renounce saying many things would be incapable of speaking. And each language represents a different equation between manifestations and silences. Each people leaves some things unsaid *in order to* be able to say others. Because *everything* would be unsayable. Hence the immense difficulty of translation: translation is a matter of saying in a language precisely what that language tends to pass over in silence. A "theory of saying, of languages," would also have to be a theory of the particular silences observed by different peoples. The Englishman leaves unsaid countless things that Spaniards normally say. And vice versa!

But in an even more radical sense linguistics will have to orient itself toward a "theory of saying." Until now it has studied languages just as they present themselves and are found, that is, as made and finished. But strictly, a language is never finished but is always being made and unmade, like everything human. Linguistics believes that it answers to this strict reality by not stopping with studying the language present today but by investigating its evolution, its history. This is De Saussure's famous distinction between "synchronic linguistics," which considers the phenomena of language which coexist at the present time, and "diachronic linguistics," which traces back the changes that these phenomena have undergone in the history of a language. But this distinction is utopian and inadequate. It is utopian because the body of a language does not remain still even for a moment, strictly speaking there is not synchronism of all its components; but also because all that diachronism accomplishes is to reconstruct other comparative "presents" of the language as they existed in the past. All that it shows us, then, is changes; it enables us to witness one present being replaced by another, the succession of the static figures of the language, as the "film," with its motionless images, engenders the visual fiction of a movement. At best, it offers us a cinematic view of language, but not a *dynamic* understanding of how the changes were, and came to be, *made*. The changes are merely results of the making and unmaking process, they are the externality of language, and there is need for an internal conception of it in which we discover not resultant *forms* but the operating *forces* themselves.

Linguistics has declared the problem of the origin of language tabu, and this is reasonable if we consider the total lack of sufficiently primitive *linguistic data*. But the fact is that language is never only *datum*, linguistic forms finished and ready, but is at the same time continually *originating*. This means that to one degree or another the generative powers of language continue to function to-day; and there seems to be no reason for thinking that it would be impossible to demonstrate these powers in the speech of today. It is not attempting this which makes it impossible to discuss the origin of language with any degree of probability.

Hence theories concerning the origin of language have always oscillated between two extremes. Either they considered that language had been bestowed on man by a divine power, or they sought to derive language from needs that are the normal needs of any animal, such as the cry, the summons, the command (so, latterly, G. Revesz), or the song as in birds (Darwin, Spencer), the exclamation, onomatopoeia, etc. In this case as in all others, the theological explanation is the opposite of an explanation. For to say that God made man a "rational animal" from the beginning, that is, that He bestowed so-called "reason" on him and that reason implies language, hence that He bestowed language on him, is equivalent to saying that neither "reason" nor language requires explanation. The truth is that man was neither rational from the beginning nor has he become rational even yet. Man is a species that appeared a million years ago and took a path in its evolution—that is, in its history—which in future millennia *can* lead to a real rationality. For the present we have to content ourselves with comparatively clumsy intellectual instruments and with the fact that we possess only a small dose of *something resembling* "reason." But it is also an error to try to derive language from the supposition of a being who was an animal in the same sense as other animals. Otherwise it is incomprehensible why other species—since these theories assume that their needs are the same as man's—have not succeeded in elaborating languages for themselves. These need not even have been phonic articulated languages. In principle, a language of cries would do. And many animal species, not only the primates, have in their brains an electronic apparatus more than adequate to retain a system of differential cries sufficiently rich to be called a "language," a "tongue," even if the tongue played only a minor role and the larynx did the bulk of the work.

It is obvious that from the time when he began his "humanity," there must have existed in man a need for communication incomparably greater than that of all other animals, and that so vehement a need could only have originated in the fact that this animal who was to become man "had a great deal, an *abnormally* great deal, to say." There was in him something that was not found in any other animal, namely, a teeming "inner world" that demanded to be manifested, expressed, to get said. The error lies in supposing that this inner world was rational. We need only look a little closely at what so-called "rationality" is in us *today*, and it will plainly show us the symptoms of a mental behavior which has been obtained with great effort all along humanity's journey and which, far from being native to man, is a product of selection, education, and discipline exercised over hundreds of thousands of years. But what must have welled up, in abnormal development and superabundance, in the animal who later came to be "man" was a primigenial function—fantasy. And this function was acted upon by the millenary discipline that has succeeded in making it what we today rather erroneously call "reason." Why this torrent of fantasy, of imaginative hyperfunction, gushed forth in an animal species is a subject to which I alluded in the first lecture and of which I have treated in another work. I cannot go into it here. But what I do wish to point out is that, in opposition to the theological doctrine that makes man a special divine creation and the zoological doctrine that confines him within the normal limits of animality, there is room for a third point of view which sees in man an abnormal animal. His abnormality would have consisted in this superabundance of images, of fantasmagorias, which began to flow in him and in him created an "inner world." Accordingly, man would be —and in various senses of the word—a fantastic animal. This inner wealth, foreign to other animals, gave an entirely new character to the common living and the type of communication that exist between other animals. For it was no longer only a matter of sending and receiving useful signals referring to the situation in their environment, but of manifesting the *intus* that in its exuberance pressed on those beings from within, disturbed them, excited and frightened them, demanding externalization, participation, true companionship; that is, an endeavor toward interpretation. Zoological utilitarianism does not suffice to enable us to represent to ourselves the genesis of language. The sign that is associated with something that exists or is happening outside and which we can perceive is not enough. No—we must suppose in each of those beings an incoercible need to make clear to the other what was secretly seething in its own "inwardness"—the intimate world of fantasy—a lyrical need to confess. But since the things of the inner world cannot be perceived, it is not enough to "signal" them; the simple sign had to become expression, that is, a sign that bears a meaning, a signification within it. Only an animal that "has a great deal to say" about what is not "there," in the environment, will find itself unable to be content with a repertory of signs but will come into collision with the limitation that this repertory represents, and the shock of the collision will lead it to overcome the limitation. It is curious that this collision with an inadequate means of communication, to which it seems that we must attribute the "invention" of language, is what continues in language and continues to act in a ceaseless series of small creations. It is the permanent collision between the individual, the person, who wants to *say* the new thing that has arisen within him and that others *do not see*, and the language as constituted—the fertile collision of expression against *speech*.

This is why I suggested earlier that the origin of language could be partly investigated today. A language, *speech*, is "what people say," it is the vast system of verbal usages established in a collectivity. The individual, the person, is from his birth submitted to the linguistic coercion that these usages represent. Hence the mother tongue is perhaps the most typical and clearest social phenomenon. With it "people" enter us, set up residence in us, making each an example of "people." Our mother tongue socializes our inmost being, and because of this fact every individual belongs, in the strongest sense of the word, to a society. He can flee from the society in which he was born and brought up, but in his flight the society inexorably accompanies him because he carries it within him. This is the true meaning that the statement "man is a social animal" can have (Aristotle, to say "social," used the word "political"). He is social even though, as often happens, he is unsociable. His *sociality* or belonging to a particular society does not depend on his sociability. His mother tongue has stamped him forever. And as each language carries in it its own particular image of its world, it imposes on him, together with certain fortunate potentialities, a whole series of radical limitations. Here we see with the utmost clarity that what we call "man" is very decidedly an abstraction. The most intimate being of each man is formed, shaped by a particular society.

But the reverse is also true. The individual who wants to say something that is very much his own, and hence new, does not find in "what people say," in the language, a verbal usage adequate to express it. Then the individual invents a new expression. If it has the luck to be repeated by enough other people, it may possibly end by becoming established as a verbal usage. All words and expressions were originally individual inventions that later degenerated into mechanized usages and only then began to form part of the language. But the greater part of these inventions do not produce consequences or leave any trace because, being individual creations, they are not understood by others. This conflict between personal expression and collective cliché, individual "saying" and "what people say," is the normal form in which a language exists. The individual, prisoner of his society, frequently aspires to escape from it in order to live by forms of life that are his own. This is sometimes brought off successfully, and the society alters one or another of its usages and adopts the new forms; but what usually happens is that the individual attempt is defeated. Thus we have in language a paradigmatic example of the social.

Ethnologists tell us that among many primitive peoples it frequently happens that when individuals are excited by their situation they utter phonemes that do not exist in the language. These phonemes are created because the physiognomy of their sound adequately expresses what at that moment the individual feels and wants to say. This must have occurred more frequently during the primary stage when languages were originating and were only rough drafts of language.

What seems not to be so clear is whether, in the creation of vocables, the decisive factor, what leads to one sound being produced rather than another, is its phonic physiognomy, as I just said in order to adhere for the present to what linguistic scholars commonly hold. But I have a suspicion that phonetics, too, needs to be built up from a deeper stratum.

The reduction of language to the word *sensu stricto*, that is, to its phonic part, is already an abstraction; hence, something that does not coincide with the concrete reality. This abstraction, prime constituent of the science of linguistics as it has been developed until now, did not impede the completion of a very full and, of its type, exemplarily strict study of the phenomenon, "language." But precisely the triumph achieved by linguistics impels it to increasingly refined investigations, and then the limits that this initial abstraction imposes begin to appear. We have already seen the need for linguistics to include in its analysis of speech a good many things that speech leaves unsaid. But now we must make bold to announce a more radical point of view—namely, that speech does not consist only in words, in sonorities or phonemes. The production of articulate sounds is only one side of speech. The other side is the whole gesticulation of the human body while it is expressing itself. This gesticulation of course includes not only movements of the hands, arms, and legs, but also the slight changes of muscular tension in eyes, cheeks, and so on. All students of linguistics have long been ready to recognize this officially, but they do not take it seriously. Yet it must be taken seriously; we must make up our minds to accept the forceful formula: to speak *is* to gesticulate. And this in a more pointed and concrete sense than is apparent at first hearing.

Some peoples, especially some Western peoples, have for the past two centuries observed a discipline in speaking which has reduced and, in extreme cases, practically abolished macroscopic gesticulation. We may think of the English, who did not talk as quietly in the days of Merry England as they do now. Between Falstaff and Mr.

Eden there has been an immense pruning of gestures. Whether this is good or bad for the speaking function is very much a question. But as we go back to more elementary stages, gesticulation increases to the point where even today not a few African primitives are unable to understand an explorer or a missionary who knows their language, simply because he gesticulates very little. Indeed, there are Central African peoples among whom individuals cannot converse at night, when it is completely dark, because they cannot see each other and not seeing each other leaves their speech gestureless.

But facts of this nature are not the final foundation that gives its meaning to the formula, "To speak is to gesticulate."

When at the beginning of the last century linguistics wanted to enter upon what Kant calls "the sure road of a science," it decided to look at language from the side most accessible to strict investigation and set about making a fundamental study of the oral apparatus when it emits the sounds of a language. It called this study "phonetics," an improper name because the subject of study is not sounds as such but only the articulatory movements that produce them. Hence in classifying the sounds of language it gave them names taken from the functioning of the mouth—labials, dentals, and so on. Nevertheless, there is no doubt that this method achieved exemplary efficacy. But, obviously, concentrating on articulation is a secondary point of view. It is looking at language from the speaker's standpoint and not from the listener's, and the word is not a word in the mouth of him who utters it, but in the ear of him who hears it. Now, he who utters makes an effort of articulation in order to produce a particular sound, a *phoneme* that he has previously heard from others. In a constituted language, then, hearing is primary and language is above all an acoustic phenome-

non. Hence it was an excellent idea of Prince Trou-
betskoi's when, some thirty-five years ago, he began to
study the sounds of language as sounds and to determine
which phonic part of the phoneme it is that in fact makes
each of them differential or discernible and hence effica-
cious for the function of speech. This study—and this
time the name is appropriate—he called "Phonology."

There can be no doubt that this point of view is primary in comparison with the viewpoint that inspires
Phonetics. But we may ask if beyond it there is not still
another and more radical characteristic of language.
Phonology studies the sounds of a language as such. Now
these sounds, fixed in the constituted language, had once
to be articulated for the first time; that is, once again
articulation presents itself as primary, but in a very different sense from that which appears in Phonetics. For
now we have not an articulation that attempts to repro-
duce a pre-existent sound and hence is imitative, but an
articulation that, having before it no phonic pattern or
model to be reproduced, does not consist in adaptive
movements, selected from outside the speaker by the
phonic image of the pre-existent word. And as each language consists in a peculiar system of phonemes, we must
suppose behind these a peculiar system of articulatory
movements that are spontaneous and not voluntary and
imitative. But movements with these attributes are those
which we call *expressive* movements or gestures, in contrast to the movements by which we seek to attain an end.

However surprisingly, this leads us to suspect that the
sounds of language have sprung from the internal gesticulation of the oral apparatus, including the lips. It would
seem that in each people there predominated, and continues to predominate today, an unpremeditated, involuntary preference for certain articulatory movements
that *express* its commonest inner characteristics. And since

intra-oral gesticulation is accompanied by the gestures that the rest of the body emits, it would follow that the phonic system of each language is a projected representation of the "soul" of the corresponding people. Linguistic scientists have already suggested that in learning a foreign language the first thing to do is to assume a particular bodily attitude. To learn English, you must begin by thrusting the jaw forward, almost clenching the teeth, and practically immobilizing the lips. In this way the English produce the series of unpleasant little mews of which their language consists. On the contrary, to learn French, you must project the entire body in the direction of the lips, extend these as if to kiss, and make them slide over each other, a gesture that, it would seem, symbolically expresses the self-satisfaction that the average Frenchman is able to feel. Another variant of self-satisfaction, of entertaining a great idea of oneself, is the strong nasalization to which the Americans have subjected the English language. When we nasalize a sound we draw it upward from the bottom of the mouth, to delight in making it resound in the nasal fossae—which is a way to feel ourselves more strongly, to hear ourselves within. And since linguistic scientists are not lacking in daring, Americans can read how the Englishman Leopold Stein, in his book *The Infancy of Speech and the Speech of Infancy*, attributes the origin of nasalization to Pithecanthropus.

Thus language by its very root, which is articulation, remains a part of man's repertory—it might be better to say system—of gestures. Now, this repertory of gestures that the individual emits is personal only in very small part. Almost all of our gestures emanate from our society, they are movements that we make because people make them. Hence merely from seeing a man gesticulate, we can usually tell to what nation he belongs. Gesticulation is a body of usages like those that we have studied in the preceding lectures, and in its exercise we encounter the same problems. Here too the individual feels pressure on him from what is done in his environment, here too there are binding observances, and if the history of gesticulation had been written it would clearly appear that the use, disuse, and misuse of gestures obey the general laws of usage. In gestures each society lives with its most visible characteristic and each people feels a shock at seeing the peculiar gesticulation of another. This shock frequently consolidates into uncontrollable antipathy and repulsion —whence a thing apparently so trivial as the expressive movements of each human collectivity contributes more than is usually realized to the remoteness and hostility between them.

# 12

LANGUAGE: SOME PRINCIPLES

# What People Say: "Public Opinion," Social "Observances." Public Power

---

THE mother tongue is there. It is there outside of each one of us, in our social environment. And from our earliest infancy, it enters us mechanically and constantly as we hear people talking, saying things, around us. If by "speaking" we strictly mean making use of a particular language, speaking is simply the consequence of our having mechanically received that language from outside. Speaking, then, is an operation that begins in the direction from without inward. Mechanically and irrationally received from outside, it is mechanically and irrationally returned there. "Saying," on the other hand, is an operation that begins in the individual. It is the endeavor to exteriorize, to manifest, to make patent something that is within him. To this conscious and rational end, he tries to employ whatever means lie to hand; one of them is speaking, but it is only one of them. All the fine arts, for example, are ways of saying. Speech is at the individual's disposal in greater or lesser degree in proportion as he has assimilated a language, several languages, more or less well. Speech is like a series of phonograph records that he plays in accordance with what he wants to say. This contrast enables us to see clearly that whereas saying, or trying to say, is a properly human action, the action of an individual as such, to speak is to practice a usage which, like all usages, is neither born in the person who practices it, nor properly intelligible, nor voluntary, but is imposed on the individual by the collectivity. Hence in speech, which the ancients called nothing less than *ratio* and *logos*, we see once again the strange reality that every social fact is: strange, because it is at once human—for men do it, men practice it with full consciousness that they are practicing it—and at the same time inhuman because what they are practicing, the act of speech, is mechanical. But if we trace back the history of every word in a language, of every syntactic construction, we often arrive at what we can, at least relatively, call their origin, and then we see that in its origin—its etymology—the word or the turn of speech was a creation that had meaning for its inventor and for its immediate recipients; hence, that it was a human action, which, by coming into use in the language, became drained of meaning, became a phonograph record, in short, became dehumanized, soulless. During our Civil War, someone invented the expression "manda-más" ["commands more," i.e., "top boss"]. Doubtless its inventor no more knew why *to command* is expressed by "mandar" than he did why *more* is by "más," but the combination of the two words was an original creation on his part, which for him and his milieu had a meaning, was intelligible, and intelligently explained a fact of public life such as it was in those days; it explained and illuminated it so well that to describe, even approximately, the tragi-comic meaning of the word—I emphasize the two components of "tragi-comic"—would give us the most exact definition of the situation in which public power then found itself. Now that this situation—which, being superlatively anomalous, could not endure and become established—no longer exists, the word is used far less frequently, and probably is destined to disappear after its short life. We here have, then, an example of a usage—that of this word, which enjoyed linguistic currency for some years and which very soon began to fall into disuse. But suppose that for one reason or another it continued to live in popular speech; within a few generations *"manda-más"* would probably have become shortened to *"malmás"* or something of the sort. Then those who continued to use it would not know why, in certain confused situations of authority, "bossing" was called *"malmás."* (I should add, parenthetically, that if the word does persist, this phonetic change is not very probable, as Señor Lapesa informs me, because compounds of syllables in *a* are usually highly resistant to any alteration in sound.)

By being transformed into a pure verbal usage and a part of the common language, the human and meaningful action of the compatriot whose genius invented it would have been dehumanized. This is precisely what happens to us today with the words *mandar* and *más*. This is so much the case that not even the great linguistic scientist Meillet was able to understand the latter rightly. We must dwell on it for a moment, for in addition to furnishing us with another example of the devitalization, the dehumanization that the usage of language is, it anticipates important matters that we shall soon encounter.

*Más* ["more"] comes from the Latin *magis*, whose meaning becomes apparent to us if we say, for example, *magis esse*. From the same root comes *magnus*. Meillet adds two remarks, as it were in the margin, which apparently suggest nothing to him for he draws nothing from them. He observes that there were two other words in Latin for saying "more"—*grandis*, which refers to spatial dimensions, and *plus*, which indicates numeral, quantitative abundance. On the other hand, he adds, *magnus*, and hence *magis*, often have an accessory idea of force, of power, which is not found in *grandis* or *plus*. Meillet gives nothing more, but what he says suffices for us to draw an important meaning from this root *mag* or *mai*. From *magis esse*—from "to be more"—comes *magister*, strictly *magistero*—whence *magisteratus, magistratus*. But in Rome, the magistrate is the governor, he who rules or commands. He is, then, more than other citizens, because he is "he who commands," and we saw earlier that *man-dar* ["to command"], from *manu-dare*, is to impose oneself because one can, because one has greater power, because one is powerful. Meillet's mistake, here as in many cases, lies in his stopping short when he has the thing named by the word before him as if the thing existed by virtue of pure magic; I mean, he fails to see that everything that is before us is mere result, the decantation or precipitate of a force that has caused it and "maintains it in being," as Plato said. The magistrate is he who *is more*—but this "being more" is "being more able." This puts us on the track of what was originally meant by the root *mag* of *magnus* and *magis*, which also appears in nothing less than *majesty*. For if we turn to the Germanic languages, we find that this same root does not mean merely "to be more" but, cynically and clearly, "power"—*Macht;* in High German, *magan* is "to be able." In Old French we find *amaier*—"amaze, cause terror," *es-moi*—whence in modern French *émoi*. English has *may* [originally: to be able]; and the noun *might*. In contemporary German, *mögen* is "to be able, to be capable of"—*möglich* is "possibility," that which has power to be, which can be. But in Greek we have the same: *megale* is not only "great in size or quantity" but is "ability to do something"—*mechane*, mechanism, mechanics, and machine.

All this shows us that at one stage of Indo-European evolution *mag–mas* meant "power," "strength." And as every man possesses some strength and power, it obviously signified from the first a greater power or potency than those of others—hence prepotency, to be more able [*poder más*]—and since to command is "to be able," it follows that "magistrate" properly means "commands-more" [*manda-más*]. The different shade of meaning borne by our recent word *manda-más* will become clear to us presently. No one today in saying "magistrate" thinks of all this, but that only shows to what a degree words are the corpses of old meanings. For if we reflect, not on the word but on the reality "magistrate," even with the value that the office holds today, we shall at once realize that the magistrate is a magistrate because he causes the police powers to function. To say nothing of Rome, where the magistrate, the Consul, was at the same time commander-in-chief of the army.

Etymology is no empty game, for it almost always lays bare to us crude realities of human life which later centuries, more inclined to hypocrisy and euphemistic forms, gloss over. I have paused for a moment to elucidate one more etymology because—in addition to emphasizing again that words, when they cease to be individual inventions and enter into the system of verbal usages that is language, lose their intelligibility, their soul, and remain lifeless, mere mechanical counters—this particular etymology anticipates something extremely important, which is not a matter of linguistics and which we shall very soon encounter.

But with these mechanical counters, words that have lost their proper meaning, we say—more or less, now better, now worse—what we think. For the fact is that our social environment, people, by instilling into us from our childhood the language used and re-used in our society, at the same time breathes into us the ideas that it expresses with and through these mechanical counters. This is something far more serious. Ideas about what things are, what other men and ourselves are, in short, about what life is—this

is what most fundamentally constitutes us and, it could
be said, is what we are. Life is a drama and, as such, always
has a plot. And the plot varies largely in accordance with
our ideas about the world and man. Clearly, there is a
great difference in plot between the life of the man who
believes that there is a God and the man who believes
that there is only matter. Now, the greater part of the
ideas by which and from which we live, we have never
thought for ourselves, on our own responsibility, nor even
rethought. We use them mechanically, on the authority
of the collectivity in which we live and from which they
waylaid us, penetrated us under pressure like oil in the
automobile. If it were possible—which it is not—it would
be interesting to obtain statistics on how many people
in a society, for example in our whole country, have ever
thought, really in the true sense of the word thought, that
two and two make four or if the sun is going to rise tomorrow. From which it follows that the overwhelming
majority of our ideas, despite being ideas and acting in us
as convictions, are nothing rational but are usages like
our language or the handshake; in sum, no less mechanical,
unintelligible, and imposed on us than these are. Let me
make this clear: We are aware of what in a rough and
primary sense a sentence repeated around us countless
times signifies; we distinguish two from three, and this
enables us to form a vague idea of the idea that the sentence states. But observe that the sentence "two and two
make four" represents an idea because it declares an opinion about these numbers, hence something that claims to
be a truth. Ideas are ideas of or about something, and are
therefore opinions—true or false. Hence they are ideas
only when, in addition to their strict sense, we have also
made ourselves clearly aware of the reasons that substan-
tiate their truth or demonstrate their falsity. Only then,
by virtue of their reasons, are they rational. Now, none

of this takes place in the constant emission of ideas in which we indulge. We keep saying things about every subject in the universe on the authority of what people say, as if we were forever drawing on a bank whose balance sheet we have never read. Man commonly lives intellectually on the credit of the society in which he lives, a credit that has never been questioned. Only occasionally, in regard to one point or another, does anyone take the trouble to go over the account, to submit the accepted idea to criticism and reject it or readmit it, but this time because he has himself rethought it and examined its foundations.

Our social environment, which is full of words, of things said, is *eo ipso* full of opinions.

If we contemplate the countless ideas or opinions that forever hover and buzz around us, swarming from what people say, we shall observe that they can be divided into two great classes. Some of them are said as something that is self-evident and in saying which the speaker is confident from the outset that they will be accepted by what is called "everybody." Other ideas or opinions, on the contrary, are uttered with the more or less definite suggestion that they are not accepted opinions, or sometimes as completely and confessedly opposed to commonly accepted opinions. In referring to the first case, we shall speak of "prevailing opinions"; in referring to the second, of "private opinions." If we turn our attention to the different physiognomy that the utterance of these two classes assumes, we shall observe that private opinions are emitted boisterously, as if to make them emphatically clear, or, on the contrary, timidly, in fear of displeasing, but in either case almost always with a certain inner vehemence that seeks to be persuasive and contagious, and to that end almost always sets forth, if only in briefest summary, the arguments in their favor. In any case, it is clearly apparent that the person emitting such an opinion is fully conscious that if this private opinion of his is to have any public existence, he or a whole group of like-minded people must affirm it, declare, maintain, support, and propagate it. All this becomes even more obvious if we compare it with the expression of opinions that we know or suppose to be accepted by everybody. No one thinks of uttering them as a discovery of his own or as something needing our support. Instead of saying them forcefully and persuasively, it is enough for us to appeal to them, perhaps as a mere allusion, and instead of assuming the attitude of maintaining them, we rather do the opposite—we mention them to find support in them, as a resort to a higher authority, as if they were an ordinance, a rule, or a law. And this is because these opinions are in fact established usages, and "established" means that they do not need support and backing from particular individuals or groups, but that, on the contrary, they impose themselves on everyone, exert their constraint on everyone. It is this that leads me to call them "binding observances" [*vigencias*]. The binding force exercised by these observances is clearly and often unpleasantly perceived by anyone who tries to oppose it. At every normal moment of collective existence an immense repertory of these established opinions is in obligatory observance; they are what we call "commonplaces." Society, the collectivity, does not contain any ideas that are properly such—that is, ideas clearly thought out on sound evidence. It contains only commonplaces and exists on the basis of these commonplaces. By this I do not mean to say that they are untrue ideas—they may be magnificent ideas; what I do say is that inasmuch as they are observances or established opinions or commonplaces, their possible excellent qualities remain inactive. What acts is simply their mechanical pressure on all individuals, their soulless coercion. It is not without interest that in the most ordinary speech they are called "prevailing opinions." * Their mode of being in society is extremely like that of the Government—they prevail, they rule, reign. They are what is called "public opinion," of which Pascal said that it is queen of the world, and which is not a modern notion. Protagoras already used the very expression in the fifth century B.C.—*dogma poleon* (I quote it because it is little known); and Demosthenes, in the fourth century, says in his eighteenth oration that there is "a public voice of the country." It prevails or reigns as the salutation and other similar customs reign; it reigns as language reigns. Everything that is truly social is, in its action on individuals, prevalence, pressure, coercion, and therefore "reign."

There is, then, a radical difference between the private opinion of a group—however energetic, aggressive, and proselytizing—and public opinion, that is, opinion actually established and in observance. For the latter to assert itself, no one has to bother to maintain it; of itself, and without any need for defenders, *so long as it is in observance*, it predominates and rules, whereas private opinion has no existence except strictly in the measure to which one person or several or many people take it upon themselves to maintain it.

Almost always in books, studies, and more especially in the "polls" conducted by certain Institutes dedicated to the office of investigating public opinion in the English-speaking countries, public opinion is confused with a private opinion maintained by a greater or smaller number of individuals. But *the fundamental sociological phenomenon of binding observance*, which is found not only in opinion but in every usage, which therefore is the most essential character of the social fact and of society as a

* [The Spanish idiom is "reigning opinions."—*Translator*.]

body of social facts, does not consist in individual adherence however great or small numerically. The entire ac-
complishment of a sociology rests on seeing this clearly.
When something is usage, it does not depend on the adherence of individuals; on the contrary, it is usage precisely because it imposes itself on them. Because of this the
social in its entirety is a different reality from the individual. In connection with the salutation, an example of
usage that served us as paradigmatic, I already pointed out
that even if all the individuals who make up a gathering
are in their hearts opposed to shaking hands, the usage
continues to make its weight felt on them so long as they
do not openly agree to annul it among them. But since
usage is not constituted in this small gathering but in the
great and multitudinously populous spaces of a whole
society, is it necessary, if a usage is to cease to be in binding observance—or, vice versa (which is what now concerns us), if a behavior, for example an opinion, is to succeed in becoming a usage, that is, to demand observance,
is it necessary that all the individuals of a society agree on
it; what proportion of the total number of individuals is
required? At that time I indicated that the inauguration
or establishment of a usage is not necessarily, nor is it
usually, the result of coincidence among a majority of individuals. In this regard we are suffering from an optical
error that we inherit precisely from its having been an
opinion in observance, a reigning commonplace, for almost a century—the majority principle which our great-
great-grandfathers and great-grandfathers stupidly believed must ineluctably follow from the democratic idea.

As we see, determining the conditions by virtue of
which something—be it an opinion or any other usage—
acquires this peculiar character of binding social observance is a question that in itself provides material for most
alluring investigations. Unfortunately it is a subject that

we must leave untouched. But what I do wish to make clear is that, important as the subject is, it is far more important that we thoroughly understand the idea of binding observance itself, which is the alpha and omega of all sociology, but which is not easy to see and even when once seen tends to escape from our intellection. I emphasize the fact that its two most marked characteristics are these: (1) that the binding social observance, whatever be its origin, does not present itself to us as something that depends upon our individual adherence but, on the contrary, is indifferent to our adherence, it *is there*, we are obliged to *reckon with it* and hence it exercises its coercion on us, since the simple fact that we have to reckon with it whether we want to or not is already coercion; (2) contrariwise, at any moment we can resort to it as to an authority, a power to which we can look for support.

The term "binding observance" [*vigencia*] comes from legal terminology in reference to laws that are in force [*vigente*] in contrast to those that have been repealed. The law in force or observance is that which, when the individual needs it and resorts to it, automatically goes into action like a mechanical power apparatus. But observe that not only the term "observance" but also the two characteristics that we attribute to it coincide with those that are traditionally attributed to Law and the action of the State. This in itself shows that it has been an error on the part of philosophers of law to hold that its functioning being independent of our adherence, and its serving us as collective authority to which we resort or can resort, are attributes peculiar to law. For we found them clearly perceptible in the first usage that we analyzed, even though it was a weak, merely ceremonial usage—the salutation. We are, then, in the presence of constitutive attributes of every social fact. On the one hand, society, a body of

usages, imposes itself on us; on the other, we feel it as an
authority to which we can resort and which will protect
us. Both these things—being an imposition and being a
recourse—imply that society is, in essence, power, an in-
superable power facing the individual. Public opinion,
"reigning" opinion, has this power behind it and makes it
function in the various forms that correspond to the various dimensions of collective existence. This power of the
collectivity is public power.

But a creeping intellectual vice that has never been
wholly cured impedes seeing social phenomena clearly.
It consists in not being able to perceive a social function
if there is not a specialized social organ to serve it. In this
way, until quite recently, ethnologists, studying the most
primitive societies in which there are no judicial magis-
tracies nor a body or individual that legislates, supposed
that Law—that is, the juridical function and the function
of the State—did not exist among them.

The same thing happens in regard to public power. It
is seen only when, in a very advanced stage of social evolution, it takes the form of a special armed body, with its
regulations and its commanders at the orders of those who
govern. But the truth is that public power has constantly
acted on the individuals who make up the collectivity
from the time that a human group has existed; and that in
our own, it operates unceasingly quite apart from the in-
terventions of the police and the army. What happens is
that, because it is so constant and ubiquitous, we do not
perceive it as such, just as we do not perceive the pressure
of the atmosphere or the hardness of the ground on which
our feet find support. But its efficacy is constantly manifest in our behavior, which is regulated in us by it; but as
soon as, whether voluntarily, carelessly, or by chance, we
depart from the channel marked out by customs, we find

ourselves assailed by the menacing protest of our environment, which rises into a storm against our contravention
of usage.

Among primitive peoples there is obviously no accred-
ited police with powers of surveillance and inspection.
Does this mean that the social body does not exercise this
function? The truth is the contrary—it exercises it, and
with a minuteness and continuity far greater than those
of our police.

Speiser, in his contribution to *The Depopulation of
Melanesia*, points out that in the New Hebrides the men
spend the whole day together apart from the women and
vice versa. A man's absence is always noticed and therefore has to be justified. We will say nothing of a man's
presence among the women!

Under these conditions, customs are bound to be what
is usually called—I know not with what justification—
"good." Without any premeditation, the collectivity exercises surveillance during every minute of the individual's life. What need is there for a special "body" of
police? When the Europeans arrived and broke down the
native society by attracting men into industrial and agri-
cultural work, the spontaneous surveillance of the collective body disappeared and was replaced by real police-
men. Now, at the very same moment the customs of the
islanders began to be "bad."

I could cite many facts of the same sort, but I think the
one I have given will suffice, for the present, to train our
vision in the perception of the functions that every society exercises without appearing to do so.

Public power, then, is only the active, energetic emana-
tion of public opinion, in which all the other usages or
binding observances that draw their nourishment from it
are afloat. And the form that public power takes, that is,